Can Neighbourhoods Save the City?

For decades, neighbourhoods have been pivotal sites of social, economic and political exclusion processes, and civil society initiatives, attempting bottom-up strategies of redevelopment and regeneration. In many cases these efforts resulted in the creation of socially innovative organisations, seeking to satisfy the basic human needs of deprived population groups, to increase their political capabilities and to improve social interaction both internally and between the local communities, the wider urban society and the political world.

SINGOCOM – Social INnovation GOvernance and COMmunity building – is the acronym of the EU-funded project on which this book is based. Sixteen case studies of socially innovative initiatives at the neighbourhood level were carried out in nine European cities, of which ten are analysed in depth and presented here. The book compares these efforts and their results, and shows how grass-roots initiatives, alternative local movements and self-organising urban collectives are reshaping the urban scene in dynamic, creative, innovative and empowering ways. It argues that such grass-roots initiatives are vital for generating a socially cohesive urban condition that exists alongside the official state-organised forms of urban governance.

The book is thus a major contribution to socio-political literature, as it seeks to overcome the duality between community-development studies and strategies, and the solidarity-based making of a diverse society based upon the recognising and maintaining of citizenship rights. It will be of particular interest to both students and researchers in the fields of urban studies, social geography and political science.

Frank Moulaert is Professor of Spatial Planning at the University of Leuven, Belgium, and Visiting Professor at Newcastle University (Planning Department) and MESHS (CNRS, Lille, France).

Flavia Martinelli is Professor of Analysis of Territorial Systems at the Mediterranean University of Reggio Calabria, Italy. She works on the dynamics of socioeconomic development and disparities – at the local, regional, international scale – and on actions to govern territorial transformations and support the development of depressed areas.

Erik Swyngedouw is Professor of Geography at Manchester University. He has published extensively on urban political economy and urban political ecology, urban governance, and socio-spatial theory.

Sara González is Lecturer in Human Critical Geography at the School of Geography, University of Leeds and the Spanish editor of ACME. Her research focuses on issues around urban political economy, territorial governance and uneven development particularly in European cities.

Regions and Cities

Series editors: Ron Martin, University of Cambridge, UK; Gernot Grabher, University of Bonn, Germany; Maryann Feldman, University of Georgia, USA; Gillian Bristow, University of Cardiff, UK.

Regions and Cities is an international, interdisciplinary series that provides authoritative analyses of the new significance of regions and cities for economic, social and cultural development, and public policy experimentation. The series seeks to combine theoretical and empirical insights with constructive policy debate and critically engages with formative processes and policies in regional and urban studies.

Can Neighbourhoods Save the City?

Community development and social innovation

Edited by
**Frank Moulaert, Flavia Martinelli,
Erik Swyngedouw and
Sara González**

LONDON AND NEW YORK

First published 2010
by Routledge
2 Park Square, Milton Park, Abingdon, Oxon OX14 4RN

Simultaneously published in the USA and Canada
by Routledge
270 Madison Avenue, New York, NY 10016

Routledge is an imprint of the Taylor & Francis Group, an informa business

© 2010 selection and editorial matter:
Frank Moulaert; individual chapters: the contributors

Typeset in Bembo by
Florence Production Ltd, Stoodleigh, Devon
Printed and bound in Great Britain by
CPI Antony Rowe, Chippenham, Wiltshire

British Library Cataloguing in Publication Data
A catalogue record for this book is available from the British Library

Library of Congress Cataloging in Publication Data
Can neighbourhoods save the city?: community development and
social innovation/edited by Frank Moulaert ... [et al.].
     p. cm.
   Includes bibliographical references and index.
   1. Community development, Urban.   2. Neighborhoods –
Social aspects.   3. Urban renewal.   I. Moulaert, Frank.
HN49.C6C358 2010
307.3'3626 – dc22   2009052097

ISBN: 978-0-415-48588-3 (hbk)
ISBN: 978-0-203-84913-2 (ebk)

This book is dedicated to all who suffer
and found the courage to fight back collectively.

Contents

Illustrations

Figures

Tables

Boxes

Contributors

Oana Ailenei (Suceava, Romania, 1972) Ph.D. in Economics at the University of Lille 1 (France) on the role of social economy in economic development and social inclusion. She has published articles on social economy and social innovation.

Lucia Cavola (Naples, Italy, 1956) Founder and general executive manager of the socio-economic research limited liability company ITER in Naples. As a project manager she coordinates studies, research and project monitoring for either private or public institutions (including the European Union). Over a period of thirty years, she has coordinated and participated in socio-economic research on labour markets, quality of work, employment policy, individual learning account programmes and local development policy.

Etienne Christiaens (Deinze, Belgium, 1952) Attaché at the Federal Government Agency for Urban Policy in Brussels, Belgium. Architect-engineer and town planner. As consultant, he realised projects and studies on neighbourhood and town planning, mobility, environment and socio-economic development on behalf of the European institutions, Belgian local and regional authorities and private organisations.

Jon Coaffee (London, England, 1972) Professor of Spatial Planning at the University of Birmingham, UK; Ph.D. in Urban Studies, Oxford Brookes University, England. He has published books and articles on urban policy, regeneration practice and the social and economic futures of cities and is the editor of the *Journal of Urban Regeneration and Renewal*. Personal website www.curs.bham.ac.uk/staff/coaffee_j.shtml.

Liz Court (1951) Head of Operations, Community Development Foundation, Wales. Originally trained as a teacher, working for ten years in schools in England. Since 1987 has worked in the community development sector in Wales with a two-year part-time post as a Research Assistant for Cardiff University.

Sophie Donaldson (Bristol, UK, 1979) Senior Strategic Planner in a London Borough Planning Authority; Ph.D. City and Regional Planning, Cardiff University. Her research outputs relate to regeneration funding, management and governance, and she has an ongoing professional interest in community development, regeneration, spatial planning and sustainable urban development.

Sara González (Barakaldo, Basque, 1974) Lecturer in Critical Human Geography, University of Leeds. Ph.D. in Sociology and Political Science at the University of the Basque Country, Spain. She has published on neoliberal urbanism, urban and regional policy, and social innovation in European cities. She is the Spanish editor of *ACME* an *International e-Journal of Critical Geographies*. Personal website: www.geog.leeds.ac.uk/people/s.gonzalez/.

Elisabeth Hammer (Vienna, Austria, 1977) Lecturer at the Department for Social Work, University for Applied Sciences in Vienna. She has done research on social innovation as well as on transformations in social policy, social assistance and social work.

Bénédicte Lefebvre (Roubaix, France, 1947) has been working as a researcher in sociology at CNRS in the Lille Sociology and Economics Research laboratory (CLERSE, UMR) at the University of Lille since 1980. Prior to working at the CNRS, she worked at the Centre for Analysis of Development where she specialised in urban research and focused on housing for miners. Her research specialises in household trajectories and housing renovation in old neighbourhoods, public space, neighbourhoods' relations, utopias of new towns and lately, urban imaginary in a post-industrial mining district.

Bernhard Leubolt (Klosterneuburg, Austria, 1979) Ph.D. candidate, Global Social Policies and Governance programme at Kassel University; scientific assistant, Vienna University of Economics and Business. MBA, Vienna University of Economics and Business, MA in Latin American Studies, Lateinamerika-Institut Vienna. He has published books and articles on participatory governance and regional development. Personal website: www.social-globalization.uni-kassel.de/kollegin.php?ko_id=13.

Flavia Martinelli (Trieste, Italy, 1952) Full Professor of Analysis of Spatial Systems at the School of Architecture of the Università Mediterranea di Reggio Calabria, Italy. She has a Ph.D. in City and Regional Planning, obtained at the University of California, Berkeley, US. She works in the area of and has published on regional development and policy, with a particular focus on services, industrial models and the Mezzogiorno of Italy. Personal webpage: www.architettura.unirc.it/scheda_persona.php?id=310.

Paola di Martino (Napoli, Italy, 1963) Graduate in Economics, Post-graduate master on the tertiary sector. Consultant in socio-economic research methodology. Since 1989 has worked on research and training projects, mainly in collaboration with ITER srl, but also with universities and public/private institutions dealing with, among others, local development and social exclusion/inclusion dynamics.

Andrea Membretti (Milan, Italy, 1971) Assistant Professor of Sociology at the University of Pavia, Italy. Ph.D. in Sociology at the University 'Statale' of Milan, Italy. He has published books and articles on urban social movements, quality of life and youth studies. Personal website: www.sociability.it.

Frank Moulaert (Bruges, Belgium, 1951) Professor of Spatial Planning at the Katholieke Universiteit Leuven, Belgium; Ph.D. in Regional Science, University of Pennsylvania, Philadelphia. He has published books and articles on social innovation and spatial development. Personal website: http://users. skynet.be/frank.moulaert/frank/.

Johan Moyersoen is a co-founder of the *City Mine(d)* initiative, a production house for social–artistic projects in (semi-)public places in the city. This organisation is especially active in Brussels, London and Barcelona. He recently also set up i-propeller, a 'broker's office' for social city renovation. His interests include conflict management, social and economic innovation, and urbanism.

Pasquale de Muro (Naples, Italy, 1960) Professor of Human Development Economics at the Università degli Studi Roma Tre, Italy. Ph.D. in Agricultural Economics, Università degli Studi di Napoli, Italy. He has published works on human development in rural and urban areas.

Andreas Novy (Vienna, Austria, 1962) Assistant Professor for Urban and Regional Development at the Vienna University of Economics and Business. He has published books and articles on development studies, urban and regional planning and development, social movements and governance dynamics, and on transdisciplinary research.

Erik Swyngedouw (Sint-Truiden, Belgium, 1956) Professor of Human Geography at the University of Manchester, UK. He was previously professor of Geography at Oxford University. He holds a Ph.D. in Geography and Environmental Engineering, The Johns Hopkins University, Baltimore, MD. He has published books and articles on geographical political economy, political ecology, urbanisation and radical politics.

Geoff Vigar (Trowbridge, United Kingdom, 1969) Director, Global Urban Research Unit at Newcastle University, UK. Ph.D. in Politics of Paradigmatic Policy Change and the Greening of UK Transport Planning, University of Newcastle upon Tyne, UK. Geoff's research majors in the analysis of spatial planning and transport policy. He is the author of three books in this area and a range of associated articles.

Tommaso Vitale (Milan, Italy, 1973) Assistant Professor of Sociology at the State University of Milan-Bicocca, Italy, where he also teaches Political Science; Ph.D. in Sociology, State University of Milan, Italy. He has published books and articles on conflicts and urban change, on Roma and Sinti policies and on the local governance of industrial restructuring.

Preface

This book is a new step in a never-ending story about how people in big cities and their neighbourhoods continue to struggle for empowerment and to stand up for their basic rights, which are constantly challenged by economic restructuring, global finance, one-sided public policies, etc.

In the cities where the case studies presented in this book are located, socio-economic change and policy reorientations are part of daily life. Sustaining continuity is not easy for any of the initiatives, although amazingly most have managed to survive or transform themselves. As many of our interlocutors would argue, there is an urgent need for clear urban policy guidelines, coordinated at the EU level, that would guarantee institutional stability and access to the resources needed to give neighbourhood development and urban cohesion a chance. As long as this condition is not met, social innovation initiatives in European cities only survive thanks to the extreme political courage and solidarity of grass-roots activists, community workers, committed inhabitants, diehard intellectuals and devoted artists – to name just a few typical agents – who just don't give up.

This is all the more reason for academic researchers working on urban development to maintain links with these people and help progress the debate on sustainable multilevel urban governance.

We wish to thank all those who took the time to talk to us both during and after the research. Their names are mentioned in many case study chapters in this book. We also wish to thank Margaret Macharia and Prathiwi Putri for their editorial assistance and Bernadette Williams for her language editing of the manuscript.

October 2009
The Editors

Introduction

This book presents the main findings – theoretical and empirical – of a three-year multinational research project named *SINGOCOM – Social INnovation GOvernance and COMmunity building*, funded by the European Commission within the Fifth Framework Programme.[1]

The aim of the project was to formulate an alternative model of local innovative development and governance (ALMOLIN). This model has been built up by combining discussions of existing theories of social innovation and spatial development on the one hand, and the analysis of lived experiences of primarily neighbourhood-based community development on the other (for further details see the SINGOCOM website and the Report published by the EC[2]).

Sixteen case studies of local innovative initiatives were carried out in nine European cities,[3] of which ten are presented here. The other experiences examined in the SINGOCOM project, although not included here, significantly concurred with the general findings of the research, or showed interesting unique features, and are occasionally mentioned in the transversal analyses presented in the last two chapters of the book.

The book is subdivided into fifteen chapters. The first chapter puts forward the theoretical underpinnings and the building blocks of our notion of *social innovation*, as well as the reasons why we contend that socially innovative processes and initiatives occur first and foremost at the *local* level. Indeed, over the past decades neighbourhoods have been pivotal sites of social, economic and political exclusion processes, as well as of civil society initiatives, attempting strategies of redevelopment and regeneration. In many cases these efforts resulted in the creation of socially innovative organisations, seeking to meet the unsatisfied human needs of deprived population groups or to improve the quality of communication and social interaction not only within neighbourhoods and local communities, but also between these neighbourhoods and the wider urban society and political world.

The second chapter takes a historical perspective and reviews the social philosophies and socially innovative experiments that have characterised social change movements in Western society since the eighteenthth century. Not only do the 'old' philosophies and approaches to social change still matter today, but many of their aims, actions and organisational forms are still part of the contemporary 'repertoires of action'. The chapter, thus, stresses the existence of a common European heritage in the deployment of social movements, although these are articulated in different national and regional trajectories, and makes the bridge between social mobilisation and social innovation.

The third chapter puts forward the analytical methodology applied to the case study investigation. Here we also explain fully our focus on the local scale as an empirical entry point and present our heuristic model for the analysis of local innovation, *ALMOLIN – ALternative MOdel of Local INnovation*. This model explains social innovation as essentially a dialectical process between exclusion conditions on the one hand, and collective processes and practices deployed to overcome them – mostly at the local scale, but also interacting with other spatial scales of governance – on the other. ALMOLIN accounts for a diversity of actors and agency, social relations and governance processes, and can be considered as an attempt to build a post-disciplinary research model.

Chapters 4 to 13 provide detailed accounts of the selected case studies. The ten cases are presented stressing the main dimensions of the social innovation pursued and/or achieved, and the associated historical roots, organisations and network, governance dynamics and strategies.

Chapter 14 summarises and compares the dimensions and features of social innovation across the ten case studies, as well as the strengths and weaknesses of the different initiatives. It especially focuses on the local community dynamics. In which way have the social innovation initiatives been a collective strategy against exclusion and alienation? What have been their historical roots and the socio–political context in which they emerged and developed? What have been their conditions for success and which constraints undermined their future? Particular attention is given to the role of human resources, public funding, governance relations and organisational modalities and how they contribute to the sustainability of the initiatives. Finally, this comparative perspective allows conclusions about 'good practices' to be drawn that could inspire new social innovation initiatives elsewhere.

Chapter 15 considers the governance dynamics and potentials for change in urban policy emerging from the different local experiences. Particular attention is given to the wider political context in which our socially innovative initiatives developed, their ambivalent relationship with both the state and the market, and their institutional embeddedness. Suggestions for policy – at a variety of geographical scales – that might enhance and strengthen the proliferation of such initiatives are also put forward. The chapter concludes with general recommendations for social policies and governance that might respond successfully to the dynamics of urban fragmentation and social exclusion, stressing the transformative capacity of socially innovative projects in urban development.

The Editors

Notes

1   The SINGOCOM project was financed within the Key Action Improving the Socio-economic Knowledge Base, Contract nr. HPSE-CT2001–00070, Project nr. SERD-2000-0028. The project was coordinated by Frank Moulaert, IFRESI-CNRS, Lille, France and GURU/APL, University of Newcastle upon Tyne, UK. The Research Partners included: Oxford University, UK; Humboldt Universität Berlin, Germany; Università degli Studi di Pavia, Italy; ITER, Napoli, Italy; Wirtschaftsuniversität Wien, Austria; University of Cardiff, UK. The project started on 1 September 2001 and lasted forty months. Updates of all case studies were made for this publication.
2   http://users.skynet.be/bk368453/singocom/index2.html. To obtain a pdf copy of the final report please Google SINGOCOM = CORDIS.
3   Kommunales Forum Wedding, Berlin, Germany; QuartiersAgentur Marzahn NordWest, Berlin, Germany; Butetown History and Arts Centre, Cardiff, UK; *Arts Factory*, Rhondda Cynon Taff, South Wales, UK; *Association Alentour*, L'Epeule, Roubaix, France; *BOM*-Neighbourhood Development Corporation, Antwerp, Belgium; *Olinda*, Milano, Italy; *Centro Sociale Leoncavallo*, Milan, Italy; *Associazione Quartieri Spagnoli*, Naples, Italy; Piazziamoci, Scampia, Naples, Italy; New Deal for Communities, Newcastle, UK; *Ouseburn Trust*, Newcastle, UK; Local Agenda 21, Vienna, Austria; *Grätzelmanagement*, Vienna, Austria; *City Mine(d)*, Brussels, Belgium; LimiteLimite, Brabant Neighbourhood, Brussels, Belgium. The cases not presented here can be found in the final report to the EU and in Moulaert *et al.* (2005, 2007).

1 Social innovation and community development

Concepts, theories and challenges

Frank Moulaert

Social innovation: thirty years later, at the local level

This book is about specific local communities in cities; communities that have been exposed to often pervasive dynamics of social exclusion over the past decades. It is also a book about how these communities fought back in socially innovative ways.

More than a quarter of a century ago, Jean-Louis Chambon, Alix David and Jean-Marie Devevey (1982) published their *Les Innovations Sociales* (Social Innovations) in the famous 'Que sais-je?' series of the Presses Universitaires de France. In this little book, they provided a synthetic overview of the debate on social innovation as it had (re-)emerged after May 1968 and the revolutionary 1970s. The focus was mainly on French initiatives, but they also extensively referred to experiences and policy measures in Great Britain and to debates in other parts of Europe. In their overview of the world of social innovation, they raise themes which contemporary researchers on social innovation have 'discovered' recently: the diversity of daily experiences (*la diversité du quotidien*), the role of local communities, social innovation as a means to fight social exclusion and to improve the quality of life, the importance of institutional support and embedding for local innovation initiatives, the role of the state, the call for a Social New Deal, etc.

Chambon *et al.* (1982) also examine the relationship between social innovation and the pressures caused by societal change, showing, in particular, how the mechanisms of crisis and recovery both provoke and accelerate social innovation. In their view, social innovation signifies satisfaction of specific needs thanks to collective initiative. The latter is not synonymous with state intervention. In fact, for them, the state can act as a barrier to social innovation, as a facilitator of public debate and as a regulator of social innovation initiatives by civil society or by state agencies, and all this is especially relevant at the local level. Finally, the authors stress that social innovation can occur in different communities and at various spatial scales, but is conditional on processes of consciousness raising, mobilisation and learning.

These reflections on social innovation are a useful entry to situating the idea that 'Neighbourhoods [can] Save the City'. The initiatives we cover in this book are almost exclusively neighbourhood- or small community-rooted. Most of them have been initiated in reaction to conditions of social exclusion or the absence of existential quality of life. All of them had, from the beginning, to face up to challenges of good organisation and governance, finding resources, networking with peers and other supportive partners. And all of them discovered early on that it would not work if their network did not include partners from 'elsewhere', connected to agents and institutions active at higher spatial scales than the local. And virtually none of them could be sustained without at least some form of partnership with the state, or some other formal institutional system, that enabled the creation and sustained the operation of socially innovative initiatives.

This book contends that urban neighbourhoods as heterogeneous, yet decidedly localised, assemblages are pivotal sites for initiating and implementing social change that may ripple through the city. They offer these experimental innovative sites from which new and emancipatory initiatives emerge. The main argument running through this book and documented in the case studies is that locally based initiatives, often much more so than official state-led programmes, can galvanise a range of publics to engage in activities that have city-wide (if not greater) impacts on the dynamics of urban cohesion and social development. What we wish to explore further in this book are the conditions, prerequisites and neighbourhood dynamics that may lift local initiatives to the scale of the city and beyond.

In the next section of this chapter we explain the meaning of community dynamics and social innovation. We argue that a deeper understanding of the dynamics and agencies of community development and social innovation require an approach valorising the diversity of disciplinary insights within a joint approach *(inter-disciplinarity)* and the interaction with, as well as the active involvement of, 'practitioners' in the research *(trans-disciplinarity)*. Such an approach is often called *post-disciplinary* (Jessop and Sum, 2001).

Concepts of community development and social innovation: potential for post-disciplinary research and action

What do we mean today by social innovation and socially innovative initiatives within or led by, communities? Is there any added value in using this relatively new term, seldom used before the 1960s, in contrast to, or to clarify for example, social economy, third sector, solidarity economy, etc.? And why use the controversial term 'community' to refer to socio-political dynamics at the local level that hamper or foster social innovation? Let us start with the second question.

Community and social innovation

An interesting paradox has emerged of late. While 'globalisation' – which of course stands for the increasing liberalisation of markets and spiralling capital flows accompanied by state policies that externalised many of the state functions and management capacities it had acquired throughout the twentieth century – began to shake national spaces as the privileged scale of intervention; other scales (the local, regional or urban) became more conducive, both in generating a sense of identity and belonging, and as privileged spaces for social, economic or political action. According to many analysts (Sennett, 1977), the rising tide of market fundamentalism and the consolidation of the neoliberal state has indeed reduced the governance of public space to the management of the exchange and control of property and property rights, reducing places to objects managed according to strict market logics. This means that great parts of public space have not only been privatised, but depoliticised too (in the sense of closed to contestation, dispute and differential claims) (Swyngedouw, 2009). Governance became hollowed-out, foreclosing public debate about the uses of spaces or collective action around their possible re-socialisation (Mitchell, 2003). Many domains of public life have become commodified: welfare rights are considered as personal compensation for negative externalities of the market, social relations increasingly materialise by way of market transactions and through the search for protection against insecurity. This insecurity grows as the sense of a common societal project or the belonging to shared and common state-space declines, and rights to become part of society are established through the acquisition of property and membership to privileged groups (Beck, 1999).

Public life, which was so typical of the first wave in modernity, has eroded in what is often called 'the second modernity' (Raes, 1997), because of the growing dominance of the 'labour society' (Arendt, 1958), as well as the fragmentation and individualisation of public space (Sennett, 1977). Progressives and conservatives alike actively look for alternatives in the restoration of public space. However, there are marked differences between them on how to achieve this. Conservatives put forward the 'community of equal interests' as the new protractor of public space and the cornerstone of social life. This view of community building can lead to a fragmented society made up of subgroups, structured around identitarian politics (religious, ideological, professional, ethnic, etc.), a process that often erodes inter-group solidarity and cohesion. This view of the reproduction of public life has been severely criticised by several progressive authors (Raes, 1997).

'An alternative notion is emerging, especially from those active in local communities and neighbourhoods, who consider communities as the enablers of citizenship rights in social life.' This conception of community (Silverman *et al.*, 2004) advocates a broadening of the notion of citizenship and the inclusion of further rights (political, social, or even entitlement to a job and housing), while at the same time recognising the responsibilities of citizens. Communities are considered as the concrete life-experience settings, where citizenship rights are fought for, where mobilisations against social exclusion are initiated and staged, and where new political rights are defined. However, while such initiatives operate at a certain 'distance from the state', they recognise the pivotal role of a well-functioning state-regulated political system that defines these rights through a democratic process of decision-making. Communities are therefore the nexus between the search for a democratic state guaranteeing basic rights on the one hand and the continuous reinvention of social life on the other; they are, in other words, the loci and drivers of social innovation, and this is also the way we have encountered them in our case studies in the SINGOCOM project.

In our empirical investigation we did not start from 'socially' defined communities in the sense of shared values, knowledge and experiences as structured through ethnic, class or other socio-cultural axes, but decided instead to focus on 'spatialised' urban communities, i.e. neighbourhoods. While often expressing distinct characteristics with respect to each other, they rarely, if ever, are socio-culturally homogeneous. In fact, in addition to showing strong features of ethnic and socio-economic identity, they often bring together a diverse set of people from a range of backgrounds. Yet, despite (and perhaps thanks to) this diversity, many such neighbourhoods have expressed an extraordinary capacity to generate socially innovative and politically progressive initiatives. And it is these we shall focus on in this collection.

But what is the relevance of social innovation with regard to these community dynamics? Is it just a new label for old practices? Or a significant new concept? The answer is: both. Many of the experiences we have encountered and analysed in our cross-European research are the legacy of a socially creative past, with types of initiatives that were either known already or very similar to those in a near or remote past: co-operatives, mutualities, artistic communities. The literature on the history of social movements and experiments is abundant, as the survey in Chapter 2 will show. At the same time, social innovation 'today' (or over the past twenty years) has responded to new challenges and is also based on new ideas, new ways of organising co-operation, new dynamics for society building, making better use of academic research, etc. But most of all social innovation today (i) has been refocused as a concept, linking concrete, down-to-earth, bottom-up initiatives to necessary transformations in governance; (ii) is a concept that has both a strong academic and an ideological meaning, therefore playing an active role in both the social science and politico-ideological debates (see Nussbaumer and Moulaert, 2007: 73–78).

In this perspective, community has a powerful, often area-based, political and analytical meaning as the real-life setting where needs resulting from exclusion can be satisfied, where initiatives grow and are established and which serves as a springboard for multiparty, multi-governance dynamics. In other words, in its academic scope, the concept grasps the full dialectics of the problem of the reproduction of society in the 'new' modernity, with conse-quences also for the theoretical approach that research on social innovation is to follow (see below). This socio-spatially embedded community concept may therefore offer a worthwhile development of Sen's 'spaces of capabilities' (Sen, 2005). As Dean (2009) points out, Sen's spaces do not account for the complex interdependency of human relations and, most importantly, for the relations of power 'within which [the individual's] identity and [her] life chances must be constituted' (ibid. 2009: 267). Sen's theory offers a one-sided, voluntarist view of community empowerment (compare with Friedmann, 1992, for example). His capability concept, thus, is powerful to normatively guide personal emancipation within *negotiated* community dynamics, but it can't possibly cope with the socio-political complexity of community–society dialectics. In this sense, it offers design principles for a bottom-up, people-centred micro-governance, but remains inadequate for the collective action, social movements and political forces needed for a sustainable (at least) two-tier governance dynamics.

Theorising social innovation

Having taken positions on the meaning of community and its relevance to social innovation for our analytical and public action perspectives, let us return to the contemporary literature on social innovation. Debates on social innovation go further back in the histories of thought and practice than we are able to present in this introductory chapter (see e.g. Chambon *et al.*, 1982; Klein and Harrisson, 2007; Moulaert, 2009). For our purpose we have singled out four main fields that use the concept of social innovation today. As social innovation is evolving increasingly into a multi- and even interdisciplinary concept, these fields do not always overlap neatly with a particular academic discipline.

The first field is that of *management science and economics*. For instance, within the social science literature, some authors (Lee, 2006) emphasise opportunities for improving social capital, which allow economic organisations either to function better or to change, thereby producing positive effects on social innovation in both the profit and non-profit sectors. This re-reading of social capital, which has also been adopted in management science, permits – among other things – a reinterpretation of economic aspects of human development, facilitating the integration of broader economic agendas, such as those which advocate strong ethical norms (fair business practices, respect for workers' rights) or values (justice, solidarity, co-operation . . .) within the very core of the various entrepreneurial communities (Moulaert, 2009, p. 14). Other examples of fruitful sharing of concepts and approaches between management science and economics, on the one hand, and other social sciences, on the other, are the analysis of and proposals for social innovation through micro-credit communities, social economy networks, sustainable entrepreneurship, organisation of work processes and stakeholder involvement in corporate decision-making.

The second field is that of *arts and creativity*, where the role of social innovation in creativity (André *et al.*, 2009), but also artistic creativity as instrumental to social change, are addressed. In effect, the arts reinvent themselves as sociology, as in the 'Sociologist as an Artist' approach (Du Bois and Wright,

2001). Michael Mumford already wrote extensively about social innovation in the sphere of arts and creativity. He covered different types of innovation from the 'macro-innovations' symbolised by Martin Luther King, Henry Ford or Karl Marx to 'micro-innovations' such as new procedures to promote co-operative working practices, the introduction of new core social practices within a group or the development of new business practices (Mumford, 2002: 253). He presented his own view of social innovation referring to three main 'lines of work': the life history of emblematic individuals whose contributions are primarily in the social or political arena; the identification of skills that leaders must possess to solve organisational problems; the development, introduction and adaptation of innovations in industrial organisations with both an interest in process and in technological innovation (ibid., 2002: 254).

The third field in which social innovation is stirring the frontier of the debate is *political science and public administration*. Criticisms of the hierarchical character of political and bureaucratic decision-making systems are well known and have pioneered new proposals concerned with change in the political system and, above all, in the system of public administration. Several modes of (re)organisation have been proposed: territorial decentralisation (regionalisation of administration and devolution of power and competences to localities) in order to promote citizen access to governance and government; greater transparency – hence accountability – of public administration; democratisation of administrative systems by promoting horizontal communication; simplification of data-management systems through a reduction of the number of codes and a flexibilisation of access for the diversity of its users; diminution of the number of hierarchical layers and decision-making units within bureaucracies. All are designed to give more control and influence to both users and other 'stakeholders', but also to simplify procedures and save time for more creative activities than filing data (Swyngedouw, 2005; Novy and Leubolt, 2005). Most innovative in this field, however, and probably closest to the community approach we are proposing in this book, is the 'bottom-linked' approach to social innovation which recognises the centrality of initiatives taken by those immediately concerned, but stresses the necessity of institutions that would enable, gear or sustain such initiatives through sound, regulated and lasting practices and clearer citizen rights guaranteed by a democratic state-functioning (Garcia, 2006).

The fourth field concerns social innovation in *territorial development*. Social innovation analysis and practice have indeed a strong territorial dimension, and both scholars and activists devote particular attention to the 'local' space. It is probably this micro-spatial scale, with its particular focus on community dynamics that deals best with the diversity of agents and agencies relevant to social innovation, thus leading to innovative trans-disciplinary and inter-disciplinary research methodologies.

For this reason, before fully addressing the territorial dimension of social innovation it is useful to dwell on the trans- and interdisciplinarity of social innovation research.

Post-disciplinary enabling of social innovation

The above short overview already suggests the overlaps and permeability of the boundaries between academic disciplines (especially in social science and the humanities) for social innovation research. Most of the new directions identified above straddle at least two disciplines, and are therefore multidisciplinary, or even work beyond the limits of the methodology of single disciplines toward a joint methodology, which is then usually called interdisciplinary (Moulaert and Nussbaumer, 2008). Significant examples of interdisciplinarity are contemporary social innovation works on the social economy in relation to local development. The former falls within the first field we cited above, while the latter will be covered in the next section. Social economy studies focus, among other ideas, on the co-operative firm and make use of contributions from e.g. labour sociology, corporate governance theory and political analysis of social movements (e.g. co-operative movements) (Klein and Harrisson, 2007; Nyssens, 2006). But they also make connections to sustainability studies (Moulaert and Nussbaumer, 2008). Still, for 'proper' social innovation research, interdisciplinarity is not sufficient. Social innovation, as this book will show in greater detail in the case study chapters, is about the satisfaction of basic needs and changes in social relations within empowering social processes; it is about people and organisations who are affected by deprivation or lack of quality in daily life and services, who are disempowered by lack of rights or authoritative decision-making, and who are involved in agencies and movements favouring social innovation.

Therefore, research about social innovation must be trans-disciplinary (Novy *et al.* 2009), that is, moving from research to practice, and thus giving an explicit place to 'practitioners' in two ways: by making them a core theme within the mobilised analytical frameworks and by considering them as real partners in the research activity itself. Making them a core theme means analysing their role by distinguishing several types of agents within theories of social innovation. This has been the case in the already cited social economy literature, for example, by scrutinising the relationships between stockholders and stakeholders in decision-making processes about corporate strategies, or in area-based human development strategies where the roles of neighbourhood committees, social workers, charismatic leaders, local authorities, are analysed, mobilising network and community development theories (Silverman, 2004). Making stakeholders partners in the research activity is another aspect of trans-disciplinarity that has been explicitly pursued in action-research (Autonomous Geographies Collective, 2009; Andersen, 2010).

The combination of trans-disciplinary and interdisciplinary concerns in social innovation research has thus turned this field into a multiform domain of experimentation in social science methodology (Godemann, 2006). *Social Polis*, the first social platform funded by the EC's Framework Programme Social Science and Humanities is a good example of how this can be done. By bringing academics and practitioners together for research agenda setting, methodology development (e.g. fine-tuning of action research methods) and debating the relationships between research and public action in social innovation, trans-disciplinary research in this field has made a significant leap forward (www. socialpolis.eu). Shared reflections on local and community development initiatives, in particular, have been key factors in facilitating this leap.[1]

It is important to stress, however, that in our approach the word 'local' refers to an *articulated spatiality*, in which the local is the site of existence of a proactive community, but also a node in a complex geography of community life, with many a community transcending the confines of the local. In other words, our approach is certainly not localist (see Chapter 3 for more on this issue).

The territorial dimension: social innovation in local communities

In Western Europe, but also in other 'post-industrial' world regions such as North America and Latin America, urban neighbourhoods have been the privileged spatial foci of territorial development strategies based on social inno-vation.[2] There are many explanations for this affinity between social innovation and urban neighbourhoods. *First*, the *tangibility* of decline and restructuring at the urban neighbourhood level is high: economic restructuring is visible in closed-down plants, brownfields and reduced activity which erodes the local job market; average low income is expressed in substandard consumption patterns; social interaction moves away from the formal economy, and lived experience of the consequences of physical and socio-economic decline is mani-fested in community life, and so on. But, *second*, and *in contrast*, it is the very *spatial concentration* of exclusion factors and people reacting to them that works as a catalyst for seeking alternatives, even if their potential impact is small; urban neighbourhoods also spatially showcase the 'cracks of hope' in the system (to paraphrase *City Mine(d)*, which uses the term KRAX, see Chapter 11) or urban ruptures or crack lines, to indicate the emergence of spaces that permit innovation of, and rupture with, established conditions and practices.

The ambiguous – ambivalent – potential of local territories as breeding grounds for socially innovative development is well known in the literature. Very often many of these territories have lived through long histories of 'disintegration', marked by the absence of enabling economic circuits, frag-mentation of local social capital, breakdowns of traditional and often beneficial professional relations, loss of quality of collective action and policy delivery systems, etc. Moulaert and Leontidou (1995) have called such areas 'disinte-grated areas' (see also Moulaert, 2000). However, many of these areas have dynamic populations and have experienced inflows of creative migrants. These are often instrumental in (partly) revalorising social, institutional, artistic and professional assets from the past, discovering new opportunities and synergising these into experiments in search of a better future. This leads us to an artificial opposition within the local community-based development literature between the more traditional 'deprived needs satisfaction', 'problem solving', approach on the one hand, and the more diversity-based, future-oriented community development approach on the other. The latter focuses, in particular, on the identification of hopes, strengths and assets of communities and their potential to move towards a future of hope (Gibson-Graham and Roelvink, 2009; Kretzmann and McKnight, 1993; Kunnen, 2010).

In reality, however, these two approaches cannot be separated, neither for the purpose of analysing local socio-economic development trajectories of the past, nor for the construction of alternatives for the present and future. The philosophy of the Integrated Area Development (IAD) approach (Moulaert, 2000) – which is the starting point for our model *ALMOLIN – ALternative MOdel of Local INnovation*, developed in Chapter 3 – was based on the satisfaction of basic needs in ways that reflect not only the alienation and deprivation of the past, but also the aspirations for a new future. IAD was socially innovative in at least two senses. First of all, from a sociological perspective, IAD involved innovation in the relations between individuals, as well as within and among groups. This can be reformulated in terms of the dialectics between community- and society-building. In other words, solidarity-based community-building is not possible without guaranteeing generalised citizen rights, for example through the working of a state-for-all within an inclusive society (see first section above). Therefore, governance relations at intertwined spatial scales are a part of the social relations of Integrated Area Development; without the transformation of institutions and practices of governance through a redefinition of state–civil society relations, it becomes more or less impossible to overcome the fractures caused by different disintegration factors within communities and their local territories (Garcia, 2006; LeGalès, 2002). This observation can also be reformulated in 'social capital' terminology: social capital has been recognised for its instrumentality in local economic development, but only when defined in network and social relations terms (rather than in a 'culturalist' way) and if connected to the political (Triglia, 2001). The second meaning of social innovation within IAD reinforces the first: it evokes the 'social' of the social economy and social work (Amin *et al.*, 1999). The challenge here is to meet the fundamental needs of groups of deprived citizens.

The combination of these two readings of social innovation highlights the importance of creating 'bottom-linked' institutions for participation and decision-making, as well as for the production and allocation of goods and services (Garcia, 2006). But, again, we must be wary of overly localist interpretations of community development initiatives, which consider local culture and communitarian interests as predominant, if not exclusive, levers of local development, at the expense of trans-local processes and configurations.

Experiences of alternative territorial development, inspired and/or steered by socially innovative agencies and processes, unveil different aspects of the double meaning of social innovation at the level of cities and urban neighbourhoods. Satisfaction of human needs is attempted through professional training that targets the reintegration of the unemployed into the regular labour market, but also into new production initiatives in the construction sector, the consumption goods sector, ecological production activities, etc. (Community Development Foundation, 1992). In many localities, new networks for production, training and neighbourhood governance are being explicitly constructed (Jacquier, 1991; OECD-OCDE, 1998; Favreau and Lévesque, 1999; Fontan *et al.*, 2004; Drewe *et al.*, 2008). But to achieve human needs satisfaction, bottom-linked institutions for participation and decision-making, embedded in wider movements and governance structures, are essential. The empowerment of the local population is a precondition for democratic governance and the building of connections between sections of the local system (Novy and Leubolt, 2005). It is, in the first place, implemented by jointly designed procedures of consultation and shared decision-making about the needs to be revealed and met, and about the assets that could be mobilised to this end.

And, thus, the linking of the different dimensions of social innovation through community dynamics leads us back to post-disciplinary research in social innovation and community dynamics. As we illustrated in this brief survey, many of the studies cited implicitly or explicitly use an organised mix of disciplinary perspectives (interdisciplinarity). For example, the connection of governance with the transformation of social relations, and of decision-making processes with needs-revealing procedures, calls for contributions from political science, social economy, public administration and urban sociology. At the same time, the recognition of the diversities within local development agendas, the multiplicity of actors and ambitions that characterise social innovation strategies and networks, also indicate the other major feature of post-disciplinarity, that is, trans-disciplinarity or the active involvement, in various roles, of different actors–practitioners (Moulaert and Nussbaumer, 2008).

This involvement implies theorising and placing the agency of a multiplicity of actors, together with their social relations and ambitions, within the interdisciplinary theoretical framework that we have used to build our research methodology. The ALMOLIN case study methodology presented in Chapter 3 has indeed come a long way to take into account these different features of post-disciplinary research.

Notes

1 The current interest in trans- and interdisciplinary research could also be considered as a contemporary upsurge of pragmatic scientific practice, which in the first quarter of the twentieth century was built on dialogue between scientists, public action agents and policy-makers leading to regular refinement of theoretical frameworks, research methods and policy analyses in social science research (compare e.g. with Ramstadt, 1986).

2 For a more detailed account of this literature, see Moulaert (2009).

References

Amin, A., Cameron, A. and Hudson, R. (1999) 'Welfare as work? The potential of the UK social economy', *Environment and Planning A*, 31(11): 2033–51.

Andersen, J. (2011) 'Action research and social innovation – knowledge and collective action for change', in F. Moulaert, D. MacCallum, A. Hamdouch and A. Mehmood (eds) *Social Innovation: Collective Action, Social Learning and Transdisciplinary Research* (forthcoming).

André, Isabel., Enriques, Brito and Malheiros, Jorge (2009) 'Inclusive places, arts and socially creative milieux', in D. MacCallum, F. Moulaert, J. Hillier and S. Vicari (eds) *Social Innovation and Territorial Development*, Aldershot: Ashgate, pp. 149–66.

Arendt, H. (1958) *The Human Condition*, Chicago, IL and London: University of Chicago Press.

Autonomous Geographies Collective (2009) 'Beyond scholar activism: making strategic interventions inside and outside the neoliberal university', *ACME*, 9(2): 245–75.

Beck, U. (1999) *World Risk Society*, Cambridge: Polity Press.

Chambon, J.-L., David, A. and Devevey, J-M. (1982) *Les innovations sociales*, Paris: Presses Universitaires de France.

Community Development Foundation (1992) *Out of the Shadows: Local Community Action and the European Community*, Dublin: European Foundation for the Improvement of Living and Working Conditions.

Dean, H. (2009) 'Critiquing capabilities: the distractions of a beguiling concept', *Critical Social Policy*, 29(2): 261–78.

Drewe, P., Klein, J.-L. and Hulsbergen, E. (eds) (2008) *The Challenge of Social Innovation In Urban Revitalization*, Amsterdam: Techne Press.

Du Bois, W. and Wright, R. (2001) *Applying Sociology: Making a Better World*, Boston, MA: Allyn and Bacon.

Favreau, L. and Lévesque, B. (1999) *Développement Economique Communautaire. Economie Sociale et Intervention*, Sainte-Foye: Presses Universitaires du Québec.

Fontan, J-M., Klein, J-L and Tremblay, D-G. (2004) 'Collective action in local development: the case of Angus Technopole in Montreal', *Canadian Journal of Urban Research*, 13(2): 317–36.

Friedmann, J. (1992) *Empowerment: The Politics of Alternative Development*, Cambridge, MA and Oxford: Blackwell.

García, M. (2006) 'Citizenship practices and urban governance in european cities', *Urban Studies* 43(4): 745–65.

Gibson-Graham, J.K. and Roelvink, G. (2009) 'Social innovation for community economies', in D. MacCallum, F. Moulaert, J. Hillier and S. Vicari (eds) *Social Innovation and Territorial Development*, Aldershot: Ashgate, pp. 25–37.

Godemann, J. (2006) 'Promotion of interdisciplinary competence as a challenge for higher education', *Journal of Social Science Education*, 5(2): 51–61.

Jacquier, C. (1991) *Voyage dans dix quartiers européens en crise*, Paris: L'Harmattan.

Jessop, B. and Sum, N.L. (2001) 'Pre-disciplinary and post-disciplinary perspectives', *New Political Economy*, 6(1): 89–101.

Klein, J-L. and Harrisson, D. (eds) (2007) *L'innovation sociale: émergence et effets sur la transformation des sociétés*, Montréal: Presses de l'Université du Québec.

KRAX Journadas 2.0 (n.d.) Autonomia (conference website) http://krax-jornadas.citymined.org/index-eng.html

Kretzmann, P. and McKnight, J.L. (1993) *Building Communities from the Inside Out: A Path Toward Finding and Mobilizing a Community's Assets*, Evanston, IL: Institute for Policy Research.

Kunnen, N. (2011) 'Research strategies for Asset-Based Community Development', in F. Moulaert, D. MacCallum, A. Hamdouch and A. Mehmood (eds) *Social Innovation: Collective Action, Social Learning and Transdisciplinary Research* (forthcoming).

Lee, Ming-Dong (2006) 'The effects of institutions and social movements on corporate social behaviour. An open system approach' (unpublished text).

LeGalès, P. (2002) *European Cities: Social Conflicts And Governance*, Oxford: Oxford University Press.

MacCallum, D., Moulaert, F., Hillier, J. and Vicari, S. (eds) (2009) *Social Innovation and Territorial Development*, Aldershot: Ashgate.

Mayer, M. (forthcoming) *Urban Social Movements*, Oxford: Basil Blackwell.

Mitchell, D. (2003) *The Right to the City*, New York: Guilford Press.

Moulaert, F. (2000) *Globalization and Integrated Area Development in European Cities*, Oxford: Oxford University Press.

—— (2009) 'Social innovation: institutionally embedded, territorially (re)produced', in MacCallum *et al.* (eds) *Social Innovation and Territorial Development*, Aldershot: Ashgate, pp. 11–24.

—— and Leontidou, L. (1995) 'Localités désintégrées et stratégies de lutte contre la pauvreté', *Espaces et Sociétés*, 78: 35–53.

—— and Nussbaumer, J. (2008) *La logique spatiale du développement territorial*, Sainte-Foye, Qc: Presses de l'Université du Québec.

Mumford, M.D. (2002) 'Social Innovation: Ten Cases from Benjamin Franklin', *Creativity Research Journal* 14(2): 253–66.

Novy, A. and Leubolt, B. (2005) 'Participatory budgeting in Porto Alegre: the dialectics of state and non-state forms of social innovation', *Urban Studies*, 42(11): 2023–36.

—— and Leubolt, B. (2009) 'Social innovation and governance of scale in Austria', in J. Hillier, F. Moulaert, S. Vicari-Haddock and D. MacCallum (eds) *Social Innovation and Territorial Development*, Aldershot: Ashgate, pp. 131–48.

Nussbaumer, J. and Moulaert, F. (2007) 'L'innovation sociale au cœur des débats publics et scientifiques', in J.-L. Klein and D. Harrisson (eds) *L'innovation sociale*, Sainte-Foye, Qc : Presses de l'Université du Québec, pp. 71–88.

Nyssens, M. (2000) 'Les approches économiques du tiers secteur', *Sociologie du travail* 42: 551–65.

—— (ed.) (2006) *Social Enterprise – At the Crossroads of Market, Public Policies and Civil Society*, London and New York: Routledge.

OECD-OCDE (1998) *Intégrer les quartiers en difficulté*, Paris: OCDE, Développement Territorial.

Raes, K. (1997) *Het moeilijke ontmoeten. Verhalen van alledaagse zedelijkheid*, Brussels: VUB Press.

Ramstadt, Y. (1986) 'A pragmatist's quest for holistic knowledge: the scientific methodology of John R. Commons', *Journal of Economic Issues*, 20(4): 1067–105.

Sen, A. (2005) 'Human rights and capabilities', *Journal of Human Development*, 6(2): 151–66.

Sennett, R. (1977) *The Fall of Public Man*, New York: Knopf.

Silverman, M. (ed.) (2004) *Community-based Organizations. The Intersection of Social Capital and Local Context in Contemporary Urban Society*, Detroit, MI: Wayne State University Press.

SINGOCOM (n.d.) project website: http://users.skynet.be/bk368453/singocom/index2.html

Swyngedouw, E. (2005) 'Governance innovation and the citizen: the Janus face of governance-beyond-the-state', *Urban Studies*, 42(11): 1991–2006.

—— (2009) 'The antinomies of the post-political city. In search of a democratic politics of environmental production', *International Journal of Urban and Regional Research*, 33(3): 601–20.

Triglia, C. (2001) 'Social capital and local development', *European Journal of Social Theory*, 4(4): 427–42.

2 Historical roots of social change

Philosophies and movements

Flavia Martinelli

Introduction

In this chapter we trace the historical roots of contemporary socially innovative initiatives in Europe – especially as we have observed them in the SINGOCOM case studies – by reviewing the cultural matrixes of movements and experiments in the eighteenth and nineteenth centuries and their legacies in the twentieth-century social movements.

In the first section of the chapter we sketch the basic features and dynamics of social movements. In the second section we review European social philosophies, experiments and movements, from the nineteenth century to date, highlighting national trajectories and differentiations. In the last section we make the bridge between historical and contemporary social movements, as well as between social movements and social innovation, stressing their highly contextual character in time and space.

Social movements: main features and dynamics

There is by now a very wide literature on the history and comparative analysis of social movements (see, among others, McCarthy and Zald, 1977; Tilly, 1978, 1995, 2004; Klandermans *et al.*, 1988; McAdam *et al.*, 1996; Tarrow, 1998; Mayer, 1997, 2009; Zald, 2000; Snow, 2004; Staggenborg, 2008). Despite significant differences in focus and interpretation there is convergence in defining social movements as 'forms of sustained collective action or challenges, based on common purposes and social solidarities, against or interacting with, authorities, opponents or elites' (adapted from Tarrow, 1998: 4[1]). What differentiates them from other forms of organised action (e.g. market relations, lobbying, representative politics) is that they mainly involve ordinary people in some form of organised contention. In social movements claims are elaborated and put forward, constituencies are rallied and resources mobilised, ideologies are (re)elaborated, collective identities are created, organisations are formed, and actions are implemented, outside established agency structures.

Main features, properties and dimensions of social movements

This said, social movements are characterised and specified by a number of interconnected features: purpose, identity, ideological 'frames', scope, types of actions ('repertoires'), organisational forms ('mobilising structures'), relationships with the system. It is worthwhile to explore briefly these features, as they are the basis for assessing and classifying social movements, past and present.

Purpose: A first distinctive feature of social movements is their collective purpose, which is generally a challenge to the established order, to existing authority, to other groups or to dominant cultural codes and value systems (Tilly, 1995; Tarrow, 1998; Snow, 2004). In our own language (see Chapter 3) we talk about this in terms of 'in reaction to what?'. Purpose is then articulated in a number of concrete claims, ranging from the satisfaction of material needs to civil and political rights to the defence of specific resources or communities.

Identity: A corollary of the collective purpose is the existence or the formation of a collective identity, which in turn involves social solidarity among members of the movement. Collective identity is a crucial step in the formation of social movements, as it is the basis for social aggregation, provides visibility and 'marks' members from outsiders ('us' and 'them'). Collective identity may be based on natural or structural variables – such as class, trade, gender, ethnicity, age, religion, locality – and may be created by opposition to other groups or determined by specific conjunctural issues.[2]

Scope: The collective purpose may address a single issue or claim (such as cheap housing, no redevelopment, or better services), that benefits the challenging group alone, or may be oriented to broader or even structural changes that encompass society as a whole (such as civil rights, health insurance for all or environmental quality). This in turn involves a geographical dimension: many social movements have a local, community-oriented scope, but others have a national and even international reach. The two are not mutually exclusive, as many movements that started at the local level subsequently 'jumped scale' and evolved into broader waves of social contention.

Frames: Zald (2000) defines social movements as ideologically structured action. But what motivates social movements is not just ideology. Several authors use the term *frame* to indicate the set of ideologies, symbols, values, visions, cognitive approaches, and discourses that 'frame', that is, provide a shared 'meaning' – and identity – to social movements (Klandermans *et al.*, 1988). 'The transformation of social issues into "collective action frames" (…) is a process in which social actors, media and members of a society jointly interpret, define and redefine states of affairs' (Klandermans, 1997: 44). Frames are the way social movements construct meaning for their action.[3] Thus, the notion of frame involves the cultural dimension of social movements. They are the result of the interaction between inherited or borrowed ideas, traditions, philosophies, utopias and symbols, on the one hand, and conjunctural or structural issues and grievances, on the other, as mediated by local or national culture.

Forms of action ('repertoire'): What characterises social movements – as opposed to other forms of political claim and bargaining – is their *direct*, generally disruptive, forms of action, whether violent or peaceful.[4] Actions may be destructive (such as the burning of property), but may also be demonstrative (alternative, experimental ways of living or producing), or reformist (petitions, protests, or strikes to obtain legislative change). Tilly (1995) proposes the notion of 'repertoire of contention', as the set of actions – later routines – that people invent, learn, select, adapt, combine, share and apply to express their grievances and claims. The 'repertoire' is at once a structural and a cultural concept and as such it evolves over time (Tarrow, 1998).[5] But, as stressed by Tilly (1995) and Tarrow (1998), most contemporary forms of contentious action draw on a repertoire inherited from the past, albeit with important adaptations, permutations and innovations, as a result of interaction with authorities and opponents, as well as of technological and cultural changes. In fact, as we will see in our case studies, many contemporary forms of action are in direct continuity with older repertoires,[6] often enlivened and renovated, such as in the ludic and colourful youth actions or the provocative artistic creations of the last quarter of the twentieth century.

Resources and organisation ('mobilising structures'): As stressed by McCarthy and Zald (1977), grievances can always be found. What transforms them into social movements is the mobilisation of resources and the formation of some sort of organisation. Resources are tangible (funding) and intangible (commitment). They may come from the beneficiary constituency (the people who directly benefit from the success of the movement), but also from 'conscience constituents' (people who do not directly benefit) (McCarthy and Zald, 1977). More importantly, resources are mobilised and structured in more or less formalised organisations or 'mobilising structures'. There is a wide spectrum of possible organisational models,[7] with varying degrees of institutionalisation, ranging from highly formalised, often hierarchically structured organisations of regional, national or even international scope (such as workers' unions), to highly autonomous, ad hoc informal and localised forms of action. In fact, as we shall see in the course of the book, there is a constant tension between hierarchy and spontaneity, formalisation and disruption, institutionalisation and innovation.[8] The development of new information and communication technology, though, has opened new organisational opportunities in allowing more fluid forms of coordination among different independent movements (such as e.g. in the Social Forum).

Relationship with the system:[9] Although their roots can be traced far back in history, 'modern' social movements are generally associated with the emergence of liberal notions of 'human rights' as put forward by the Enlightment in the eighteenth century and 'political rights' as claimed throughout the nineteenth century, parallel to the development of the institutions of capitalism (Facchi, 2007). But, as stressed by Tilly (1975, 1978) and Tarrow (1998) they are also an accompaniment to the rise of the modern state. All social movements challenge such institutions, but they also operate within the conditions set by market mechanisms and state intervention. Some movements attempt to change the existing order through reforms of established formal institutions (e.g. new legislation, public programmes); others seek to implement alternative institutions, outside the market or the state, with a demonstrative or self-contained purpose; yet others seek revolutionary change through the overthrow of existing institutions.

The life cycle of social movements

Once the main features of social movements have been reviewed, we can address them in dynamic terms, that is, analyse their evolution. This is important also in understanding and assessing their social innovation potential.

In a dynamic analysis of social movements, life cycles can be identified, typically made up of three phases: a) the rise of social movements or mobilising phase; b) the broadening and diffusion phase; c) the demobilising phase.

Emergence: To explain the rise of social movements in particular historical moments, Tilly (1978) introduced the notion of political opportunities and constraints – changes in the socio-political context that create new spaces or threats to challengers. Among these we must also include structural changes, that is, in the accumulation regime. These new conditions – whether for example increased political access or exclusion, famine or greater prosperity, war or peace – provide incentives or disincentives for collective action, but also affect people's expectations of success or failure.

Growth and diffusion: In order to actually become a social movement, any contentious collective action needs to grow, spread and be sustained over time (Tarrow, 1998). This occurs when consensus and mobilisation around specific issues broadens, interaction between challengers and opponents intensifies, and widely shared new or transformed collective action frames are established and consolidated. When collective mobilisation encompasses several issues, groups or places across a social system, Tarrow (1998) speaks of 'waves' or 'cycles' of contention.[10]

Demise: Social movements do not last forever and inevitably subside. This happens for a variety of reasons, both internal (waning or factionalisation of interests, loss of leadership or motivation) and external (repression, institution-alisation or co-optation[11] of contentious action), and is strongly linked to the actual *outcome* of social movements. Outcomes can be positive (achievement of claims, institutionalisation of actions) or negative (repression, exhaustion, disillusionment) and they affect access and opportunities, institutions and policies, culture and values (Rochon and Mazmamian, 1993; Giugni, 1998). Gamson (1990) proposed a fourfold typology of outcomes: full response, co-optation, pre-emption, and defeat. As we shall see, the outcome of social movements is actually a major variable in our definition and assessment of social innovation.

In assessing the life cycle of social movements, the *context* is crucial (Tilly, 1984; Kriesi, 1996; Rucht, 1996). Not only do social movements arise because of changes in economic, social, political and/or cultural conditions, but they in turn influence economic and social relations, political opportunities and constraints, as well as beliefs and values. In this dialectical process, the state – in its double role of target and mediator of contention – is a central actor, since opportunities and threats, as well as outcomes, are conditioned by the permissive or repressive stance of local and national authorities (Tilly, 1978).[12] Thus, their interaction with both the socio-economic structure and state strategies explain to a great extent the different national – and local – trajectories of social movements, as we shall see in the next section.

Philosophical roots and historical trajectories of social movements

Once the main analytical elements have been set out to assess social movements and their evolution, we can address the historical roots of contemporary social movements, in order to unveil their legacies in our case studies.

The historical roots of social philosophies

In the historical review of European social movements carried out in the SINGOCOM research project (Martinelli *et al.*, 2003), starting in the nineteenth century, four main philosophical traditions were identified: a) liberal-bourgeois philanthropy and reformism; b) church-initiated charity initiatives; c) utopian, mutual aid and co-operative experiences; d) workers' movements (see Table 2.1). The initiatives belonging to the first two philosophical models were generally characterised by a top-down approach, that is, were engineered from above the actual beneficiaries; the others, in contrast, had a more bottom-up, self-initiated and self-organised character, with a trade, community or class base.

Differences among these early social philosophies are not clear-cut. Trajectories overlapped and contaminated each other, merged and split into diverse sub-streams, often with strong national and regional specificities, giving rise to interesting hybrids and variants. Many actions initiated by the church or a bourgeois patron eventually evolved into self-organised associations and, vice versa, many bottom-up initiatives turned into quite authoritarian structures. In general, however, workers-initiated movements expressed stronger claims

Table 2.1 Historical roots of social philosophies and movements (eighteenth and nineteenth centuries)

	Bourgeois philanthropy and reformism	Church-initiated movements	Mutual aid, self-help, cooperatives	Workers movements		Socialism/Communism	Social democracy
				Anarchism			
Philosophies ('frames') and charismatic figures	Liberalism cum philanthropy (Saint Simon, Fourier, Godin)	Social Christianism (de Lammenais, von Keteler, Pope Leo XIII)	Utopian socialism; mutualism (Babeuf, Owen, Raiffeisen, Schulze-Delitzsch, Lassalle)	(Proudhon, Bakunin)		Scientific socialism (Marx, Engels)	Reformism
Aims/purpose	Charitable, moralising and social control aims; but also genuine social reform intent.	Moralisation and Christian charity (satisfaction of basic human needs; human dignity.	Improvement of human (workers') living and working conditions; a more balanced distribution of wealth; political rights	Revolutionary change through proliferation of alternative experiments or violent shocks.		Revolutionary change through class struggle, the seizing of power and the implementation of a new social organisation	Reform of existing system: political rights, reduction of exploitation, mass education, redistributive measures.
Actions ('repertoires')	Legislation reforms. Poverty relief initiatives (food, housing, education). Some experimental communities.	Wide range of poverty relief initiatives (food, housing, education, work, health).	Generally single issue-oriented initiatives (services, insurance, credit, exchange, or housing).	From alternative libertarian and 'niche' experiments, to violent and subversive initiatives.		Militant political action through structured collective organisations (party, unions) and initiatives (demonstrations, petitions, general strikes).	Democratic struggle through the state: legislation reforms, regulation of capitalist accumulation, public services.
Recipients (beneficiaries)	The poor; factory workers.	The poor; the parish or community.	Members; the community	People; the exploited		The working class; society as a whole	The least represented groups; society as a whole

	Bourgeois philanthropy and reformism	Church-initiated movements	Mutual aid, self-help, cooperatives	Workers movements		Social democracy
				Anarchism	Socialism/Communism	
Organisations ('mobilising structures')	Foundations, charity and voluntary work associations; social (company) communities.	Foundations, religious orders, voluntary work (parish, community); also self-help and cooperative initiatives.	Self-help and mutual aid associations. Cooperative organisations. Structured experimental communities.	Fragmented, informal initiatives; non-hierarchical, loose federation of 'free' organisations.	Strong (hierarchical) organisations: the party, the unions.	Formal organisations: parties, unions, the parliament.
Approach	Authoritarian and paternalistic reformism. Mostly top-down.	Authoritarian and paternalistic; top-down, but also self-help and some empowerment.	Originally paternalistic (top-down utopian experiments); later truly self-organised, bottom-up.	Bottom-up, collective, but in small groups; from demonstrative to subversive.	In principle bottom-up; in fact hierarchical, increasingly bureaucratic.	Top-down with bottom-up inputs.
Relationship with 'the system'	Did not challenge the system. Worked partially through the state (legislation); but mostly outside the state and the market.	Did not challenge the system. Explicitly geared to act as 'third' party between the state and the individual.	Strongly critical of the system but no attempt to overturn existing order: change through example and single-leverage self-help initiatives.	Totally critical. Outside and against the system. Seeks to destroy the state and any form of institutionalised authority.	Totally critical. Overthrowing of capitalist system through the dictatorship of the proletariat and the control of the state.	Critical but attempts to change the system by (legislative) reforms and regulation through the state.
Scope of action (spatial reach)	Local and national	Local, community	Local, community, regional	Enclosed communities	National, international	National

Source: Author

for social equity than many charity initiatives. This said, these early philosophical models have set the background for subsequent social movements and their legacy resurfaces in twentieth-century movements, not only in terms of vision, purpose, repertoires and organisation, but also in the antagonism among them.

Liberal-bourgeois philanthropy and reformism

The liberal philosophy of the eighteenth century, based on individualism, did not contemplate collective action, especially from the lower classes.[13] However, in the face of the deprivation and urban degradation consequent to the full deployment of the industrial revolution, wealthy people – often the very patrons of industrial factories – occasionally launched initiatives to ease the living and working conditions of the poor. Such actions ranged from reformist pressures for social legislation, to community initiatives, to utopian experiments, with philanthropic, charity and/or 'moralising' aims.

In the 'pure' liberal vision, actions were geared to enable people to act as individuals. In the most enlightened forms, initiatives were aimed at increasing the human rights of the masses, that is, enabling the poor to improve their individual potential within a society of free people (through for example education), or to better their living and working conditions (through legislation or 'model' living communities). Most initiatives had strong paternalistic overtones and in many cases had a straightforward social control function – keeping the poor out of crime, alcohol and prostitution, and away from unions.

Nonetheless, elements of the nineteenth-century bourgeois reformist-utopian analyses and some of their practical attempts to find a solution to the class conflicts that were maturing within industrial society represented a very important precedent and left a lasting trace in the co-operative and mutual aid movement, further elaborated in the second half of the century within the organised socialist workers' movement (see Appendix). Eventually, as we shall see, the legacy of the bourgeois-liberal approach – especially the utopian idea of alternative 'community' organisations – will re-surface in many twentieth-century social movements and experiences.[14]

Although they introduced significant innovative social and organisational principles, the bourgeois-liberal initiatives did not challenge the established order. They merely attempted to improve the system or compensate for its inevitable shortcomings, through legislative reforms, housing schemes or the controlled diffusion of alternative communities, generally tackling one[15] or few social issues (education, housing).

Church-initiated charity initiatives and Christian social reformism

Under this heading we have grouped all those actions initiated by Christian foundations, religious orders, and parish or church voluntary organisations. Quite influential in this area were the Reformist movements and related autonomous religious congregations (e.g. the Methodist and Wesleyan currents

Box 2.1 Liberal-bourgeois national trajectories

It was in England, earlier than anywhere else, that the profound social crisis engendered by the industrial revolution spurred bourgeois-liberal poverty-relief initiatives. Besides the legislative reforms and the many philanthropic initiatives implemented by the Victorian bourgeoisie (González *et al.*, 2003), a major contribution to the utopian approach came from the industrialist and reformer, Robert Owen, in the early nineteenth century, with his model community in New Lanark (see Appendix). Owen's ideas inspired several other experiments of alternative industrial communities, most of which were implemented in the United States of America.[a]

While England was dealing with the social question engendered by the industrial revolution, in France the blocked transition to capitalism was dealt with by means of a 'political' revolution.[b] It thus provided a particularly fertile context for more radical and utopian thinking, giving birth to Babeuf, on the one hand, and Saint Simon and Fourier, the founding fathers of the utopian vision, on the other (see Appendix). Although structurally paternalistic, utopian experiments were genuinely oriented to improving the well-being of workers and promoting their individual capabilities. Of a more authoritarian nature were the industrial patronage experiences that developed later in the most rapidly industrialising regions (Nord-Pas de Calais, Alsace) of the country (Ailenei, 2003). Although 'enlightened', most of the latter initiatives were implemented within a bigoted, paternalistic approach, with the aim of limiting social disorder and better controlling the workers by tightly organising their life (home, work, church). The improvement in workers living conditions and the provision of cheap housing were instrumental in increasing productivity and social control, often with a Christian 'moralisation' hat.

The bourgeois-liberal approach was also strong in Germany, especially in the second half of the nineteenth century, with several civic associations supporting professional training programmes and employment institutions. The family remained the central pillar of society and, as in France, German bourgeois reformism focused on decent housing as a major means of reducing what was stigmatised as social 'depravation' and preventing socialist mobilisation (Gerometta and Hausserman, 2003).

[a] Many of the principles of the utopian workers' 'communities' had an important urban planning dimension, which translated into utopian model 'cities'. This dimension was later rationalised by Ebenezer Howard (1850–1928) in his Garden City 'model', based on integrated low-density housing, factories, farms and public services.
[b] While the British classical political economists laid the basis for industrial liberalism, the French physiocrats still argued about agrarian liberalism (Hofmann, 1971).

Box 2.2 Social Christianism trajectories

In Belgium, social Christianism (see Appendix), although paternalistic and anti-socialist in principle, had quite a critical stance and strong emancipatory and truly democratic connotations. Catholic action, in particular, was aimed at making the church an 'intermediate' institution, between the isolation of the individual, preached by liberalism, and the annihilation of the individual in the state, preached by socialism (Christiaens and Moyersoen, 2003). Christian social reformism was also strong in Germany, where Lammenais and Ketteler were the first to raise the social question in the Catholic doctrine. In the early twentieth century Catholic workers' associations and co-operatives spread in northern Italy as well.

The legacy of church-led initiatives is quite strong today in all the countries examined in this book. The Roman Catholic Church is still very active, especially through its Caritas organisation, with thousands of staff members and hundreds of thousands of volunteers throughout the world, who support numberless communities and social initiatives. In Italy, Caritas is particularly active in the domain of immigration, but many other catholic organisations were, and remain, a pillar in the area of social work. Likewise, in the Anglican and Protestant world, church- or parish-based initiatives are still the engine for many local community actions. In Germany, where Christian social reformism was initiated, both Catholic and Protestant associations still constitute a very large part of the third sector (Gerometta and Haussermann, 2003).

---

in the UK). But such initiatives existed also within the more hierarchical Roman Catholic Church, later sanctioned by Pope Leo XIII in his *Rerum Novarum* encyclical of 1891, to counter the spread of socialism (see Appendix).

Church initiatives were first and foremost informed by Christian charity aims, i.e. providing satisfaction for basic human needs, without challenging the established order. In the most authoritarian forms they also had strong moralising and social control aims – keeping the poor away from sin and perdition, as well as from socialist mobilisation. On the other hand, many church and parish initiatives had quite progressive 'empowering' aims, with a strong community basis. This was particularly evident in their support of the Christian co-operative movement, deployed in the second half of the nineteenth century to counter socialist co-operatives in many European countries.

Mutualism, utopian communism and co-operativism

Under this heading we have grouped diverse movements and initiatives, which differ from the previous two groups because characterised by self-organisation and self-help, that is, they were set up from below to provide benefits to their own members. They include mutual aid associations, utopian communities promoted from below, as well as co-operative organisations.

The pre-capitalist roots of mutual aid associations and networks, whether trade- or community-oriented, can be traced back to the Medieval and Renaissance guilds, brotherhoods and civic associations. But the mutualist tradition was significantly enriched by the utopian philosophies and experiments implemented in the early part of the nineteenth century (see Appendix) and the socialist and communist philosophies of the second part of that century, thereby merging with the workers' movement and triggering the very rich and diversified realm of workers' co-operatives.

Although critical of the system and engineered from below, these initiatives did not directly challenge the established order. They set alternative forms of productive organisation, often on a trade basis, or experimented with alternative forms of communal organisations, with the aim of providing their members with benefits either not available or too expensive – whether services, credit, insurance, cheaper goods or housing. In some instances these organisations were considered as a stage in the progression towards a revolutionary society.

Workers' co-operatives were the most structured and lasting legacy of this particular philosophical trajectory, at the crossroads between mutualism and the socialist doctrine. Born within the mutual aid tradition, they received further political impetus during the 1830–48 revolutionary years, especially in France and in Germany.

The co-operative organisational model actually had a profound political, if not structural, impact in the whole of Europe, throughout the nineteenth and twentieth centuries. Overshadowed by monopoly capital during the Fordist regime they regained centre stage in the post-Fordist restructuring as the backbone of the third sector in many European countries (see Mayer, 2006).

Workers' organisations and socialist movements. The first 'modern cycle' of contention

The workers' movement went through several historical phases, generating powerful unions and eventually splitting into different political trajectories (see Appendix). Initially, workers' associations were scattered and organised on a local or factory basis,[16] mostly with a self-help aim. However, the very nature and conditions of the factory, which bred cohesion and solidarity, enhanced the growth of class-consciousness among workers. Thus, although the first isolated revolts at the factory level were easily repressed, the associative movement diffused rapidly. Between 1830 and 1848 socialism, from a utopian ideal, evolved into a class-based political movement alongside the liberal and the democratic/radical political forces, in all those regions where the industrial revolution had deeply transformed the social structure.[17] After the revolutions of 1848, it found its 'scientific' doctrine in the works of Marx and Engels and grew into national – and international – organisations with clear political

---

Box 2.3 The self-help and co-operative national trajectories

In England both the mutualist and the co-operative traditions were already quite strong in the nineteenth century. The Friendly societies were community or workers' associations that pooled resources to provide relief to their members and their families in case of sickness or death (González *et al.*, 2003).[a] In the co-operative domain, the Pioneers of Rochdale experiment in Manchester (1844) is considered the founding experience of the co-operative movement, which set the basic principles of all subsequent initiatives. In 1852 the first legislation was actually enacted in the UK, providing a legal framework for the operations of co-operatives (González *et al.*, 2003). Charles Owen was also quite influential in linking the co-operative movement to trade unionism and making co-operatives an element of socialist emancipation. Although producer co-operatives were never a truly successful experience, consumer co-operatives were rather popular throughout the UK and remained effective until the Second World War.

Mutualism and co-operativism were very strong in Germany as well. The movement originated within the bourgeois-liberal philosophy, but further developed the utopian dimension of communal work and ownership. A determinant influence was played by characters such as Lassalle, founder of the German Workers Brotherhood and leader of German unionism, as well as Raiffeisen and Schulze-Delitzsch, who supported the development of the German co-operative movement, implementing initiatives respectively in peasant credit unions and in the commercial credit system. In the Bismarck years (1880s) and during the Republic of Weimar (1919–33) building co-operatives played a prominent role in German housing programmes. Specific legislation was enacted in 1889 and housing co-operatives experienced a boom, as a viable alternative to the capitalist housing market (Gerometta and Haussermann, 2003).

The co-operative movement was quite popular also in Belgium, where it developed a strong organisational apparatus, partly within the Catholic social reformism movement, but also in the socialist camp, linked with the Trade unions and workers' organisations. Belgian co-operatives were historically active in production (craft and skilled manufacturing), credit (especially Raiffeisen type of rural credit unions, but also middle class urban credit co-operatives) and services. Quite original was the Belgian pharmacy co-operative experience (Christiaens and Moyersoen, 2003).

In Italy the co-operative movement took off later than in the other countries and was confined to the Northeastern regions, as an expression of both the Catholic political organisations (the 'white' co-operatives) and the left-wing political organisations (the 'Red' co-operatives). During the second half of the twentieth century the 'Red' network of co-operatives (*Lega delle cooperative*) became a major economic actor, at the national and international scale, both in production and distribution, somewhat losing its initial idealistic stance.

[a] The building societies of the twentieth century somehow replicated that experience, although they concerned housing and the lower-middle class, rather than the working class.

agendas (Hofmann, 1971). In the last decades of the nineteenth century the first modern socialist parties were formed in many countries.

Together with its maturation, however, scientific socialism split into different philosophical, political and national trajectories, which we can roughly group into three main approaches to changing society: a) anarchist; b) communist; and c) social-democratic (see Table 2.1). The anarchist and communist movements both aimed at a revolutionary transformation of the capitalist social order, the former without and outside the state, the latter through the state and the dictatorship of the proletariat. In contrast, the social-democratic movements and parties aimed at a progressive democratisation and transformation of society through the state and legislative reforms. All these trajectories are considered expressions of the first 'modern cycle of contention' (Tarrow, 1998), with their specific repertoires of collective action: marches and public demonstrations, public meetings and assemblies, barricades and violence. Each of these trajectories experienced specific national and regional declinations.

But beyond national and philosophical differences, what characterised all the nineteenth-century workers' organisations and movements – in contrast to the other social philosophies reviewed earlier and with the possible sole exception of the anarchist initiatives – was their strong political dimension, their class-based (rather than community- or trade-based) constituency, the fact that they aimed at changing society as a whole and, thereby, had a broader scope and scale of action (regional, national and even international reach). Their visions, repertoires, and organisational forms are a basic legacy that can be found in many twentieth-century movements, including what has been called the 'new cycle' of contention after the Second World War.

The 'new' Post-Second World War cycle of contention

In the course of the first half of the twentieth century, owing also to the establishment of universal suffrage, the scattered workers' movements of the nineteenth century were progressively institutionalised into formal political and/or mass-based organisations[18] in the majority of the Western and Northern European nations.[19] But a new wave of social movements – in the meaning put forward in the first section of this chapter – flared up, starting in the 1960s and spreading throughout the capitalist countries, in what has been labelled a 'new cycle of contention' (Tilly, 1993; Tarrow, 1998),[20] 'New Left' movements (Touraine, 1968; see Staggenborg, 2008), or new 'Urban' movements (Castells, 1972, 1973; see Mayer, 1997, 2009).

A new context

Although their ideologies, repertoires and organisational models had unequivocal roots in the 'old' social movements, the new wave of social movements occurred in a very different context and exhibited quite different features (Hobsbawm, 1995; Tilly, 1995; Tarrow, 1998; Staggenborg, 2008).

Box 2.4 National trajectories of the workers' movements

The UK was historically the most advanced in unionisation (see Appendix), also owing to its precocious industrial revolution. On the other hand, precisely because of the early liberal turn, the socialist trajectory in this country took a distinctive 'parliamentary' and 'reformist' character. This is evident in the Chartist movement, in the Fabian political organisation and, later, in the political doctrine of the Labour Party.

In France, because of the more repressive conditions, the workers' movement was from the beginning cast in a more revolutionary frame of action. Political opposition was no longer driven by the bourgeoisie, but by the masses and strongly embedded in the Republican movement. A number of revolts in the textile factories of Lyons in the early 1830s had led to the prohibition of any collective bargaining process. French workers' associations thus had to work on a clandestine basis. This, indirectly, contributed to rather radical ideological elaborations, on the one hand, and a number of quite innovative experiments in the revolutionary episodes of 1830, 1848 and 1871 on the other (see Appendix).

German society was more backward than the British and French at the beginning of the nineteenth century, as few liberal-bourgeois reforms had been implemented, while at the same time new conflicts were brewing within the emerging industrial society. Political rights and co-operativism were thus the two complementary pillars of the German workers' movement (Hoffman, 1971).

In Italy, the workers' movement was significantly behind its foreign counterparts. The country was still working on its unification and the industrial revolution was limited to the northern regions. Workers' associations were scattered and clandestine, mostly acting within the Carbonari secret society and under the influence of the Republican movement led by Giuseppe Mazzini, who was against class struggle. Only after the unification of the country (1861) did the workers' movement begin gaining autonomy (Villari, 1977).

Among the different workers' movements, the Anarchist stream, although minor in comparison with the more structured socialist organisation, represents an interesting historical legacy in a number of countries. It was particularly strong in Spain and in Belgium, despite the recurring political splits.[a] In their utopian and 'direct action' initiatives anarchist groups implemented quite innovative forms of organisation without hierarchy and without centralisation of decision-making, which resurface, for example, in many contemporary Belgian initiatives (Christiaens and Moyersoen, 2003).

[a]   In the First International Congress of 1864 the mutualists inspired by Proudhon separated from the collectivists following Bakunin; in the Hague Congress of 1872 the anarchists left the International; in 1880 the anarcho-communist current and later the anarcho-syndicalism current separated from the others.

A first major difference was that the new movements occurred in a context of relative economic affluence. The Fordist model of production and consumption had spread from the US to Western Europe, bringing almost full employment and unprecedented levels of income for large portions of the population – including the working class. Second, the new wave of mobilisation occurred in a relatively progressive political context. Starting in the late 1950s and 1960s, many Western states had shifted towards the left, with either social-democratic parties or centre-left coalitions in government. In many European countries the 'corporatist' state formula was established – with the state acting as a centralised intermediary between capital and unions – and social reforms were enacted, leading to the establishment of the so-called welfare state in the 1970s.[21]

Thus, while the nineteenth-century movements had developed in times of extreme material hardship and social exploitation, the new wave of contention began at the height of the post-Second World War economic boom and in a context of relative democracy. It was a 'post-industrial' (Touraine, 1968) and 'post-materialist' type of contention, more focused on culture and values, as well as on greater emancipation and participation. This apparent contradiction is explained by the silent social and cultural revolution that had taken place: the further urbanisation of society, the growth of a salaried middle class, the secularisation of values, the spread of education, the decline of the traditional patriarchal family and the parallel emancipation of women, the development of national and international communication media and cultural industries (TV, music, movies).

Different also was the main actor of the movements, namely, young people (Hobsbawm, 1994),[22] among whom students and women played a major role, although workers and intellectuals also joined in what is now recognised as a very broad, trans-class wave of contention (Mayer, 2009). Youth 'culture' was the vanguard and the vehicle of youth 'protest'.[23] It criticised the system, starting with anti-conventional personal behaviour (disrespect for bourgeois values, casual clothing, sexual freedom) and artistic expression (music, graphical arts). Thus, individual liberation translated into social emancipation and then political struggle, involving other social groups – women, workers, intellectuals, marginalised ethnic groups – and diversifying throughout the 1970s and 1980s into several different trajectories and models of contention, in the US as well as Europe. Claims no longer concerned basic material needs, but enlarged rights and greater democracy, as well as broader cultural and ethical change: women and minority civil rights, greater decision-making power, better services, environmental safety, peace (Mayer, 1997, 2009; Staggenborg, 2008). For the first time, 'the agitation resulting from the aspirations of the alienated were linked, if tenuously and in constant tension, with the demands of the materially exploited' (Marcuse, 2009: 188). Moreover, many of these movements became deeply rooted in, and expressed, decidedly urban concerns (Castells, 1973, 1983; Mayer, 1997).

Another difference was the increased amounts of resources available to the new generation: knowledge and time, but also organisational and financial resources (from foundations, government, business, civic associations), as well as new technologies. Many innovations were introduced into repertoires and organisational forms, owing to the development of new media such as TV and the culture industries that provided new vehicles for communication and the diffusion of ideas. On the other hand, there were also striking elements of continuity with the past: as first argued by Tilly and Tarrow, the new movements basically employed 'enriched' repertoires that were essentially derived from the 'old' social movements.

In our SINGOCOM survey of national movements belonging to the 'new' cycle (Martinelli *et al.*, 2003) we have identified three main philosophical/ organisational models: a) niche, alternative, self-standing actions; b) mass movements; c) community initiatives[24] (see Table 2.2).

Niche, alternative, self-standing demonstrative actions

These were the most spontaneous and creative initiatives, reminiscent of the nineteenth-century self-help, utopian experiments, but also very much in tune with the anarchist doctrine. What characterised this model, in fact, was the refusal of hierarchy and the emphasis on direct action, both independently of and, some times, against authority.[25] They attempted rather 'libertarian' experiments of alternative lifestyles, consumption, production and/or community organisation: from communal housing in abandoned or empty buildings (the 'squatters' movement), to co-operative organisation of production and services, to artistic reinterpretation/re-appropriation of themes, objects and places. The common trait of these actions was that they did not seek to make structural change. Actions had a demonstrative aim, showing an alternative to both the state and the market. They were implemented outside and beyond more structured reform movements, although they found interstitial spaces of existence within the system and sometimes even exploited state resources.

Organised mass movements

In many places and instances the youth protest movement contributed to the revival of the workers' movement – which over the twentieth century had been institutionalised into hierarchically structured organisations (political parties and unions), oriented to formalised bargaining procedures, and significantly bureaucratised. For this reason they have been labelled 'New Left' movements (Tarrow, 1998; Staggenborg, 2008).

They combined the old organisational forms with new ones,[26] using more decentralised forms of mobilisation and exploiting the opportunities offered by the new media (Tilly, 2004). They had broader social constituencies and aims, as students and workers rallied other social forces (women, intellectuals, portions of the middle class, various minorities). They fought for, and in many instances achieved a variety of social and political objectives: from greater democracy in the workplace to peace, from cheap housing provision to abortion legislation, from anti-nuclear policy to equal opportunities, from sustainable energy policy to greater social security coverage, from alternative urban planning to improved collective consumption. They extensively tapped – although in a creative way – into the repertoire of the nineteenth-century workers' movement, enriched with non-violent resistance tactics as experimented with in the US Civil Rights Movement of the 1950s.[27]

In their diverse declinations in time and space, these movements shared a number of characteristics that set them apart from both the niche, self-standing actions reviewed in the previous model and the community-based initiatives of the next (see Table 2.2): they had a mass, often inter-class base; they had broad societal objectives that did not solely benefit the narrow constituency or community, either through straightforward antagonism with the state or within and through existing institutions; they were highly organised, either as political formations, around editorial initiatives, or as associations. As stressed by Mayer (2009), many 'New' urban movements were capable of articulating the structural contradictions of late-capitalist societies with specific social and urban concerns and bring about – by involving also labour unions and political parties – broader changes in politics and society.

Community-based initiatives

Apart from the 'niche', self-standing alternative initiatives of anarchist inspiration and the organised mass movements just described, we have identified a third trajectory, which includes all those structured initiatives with a strong community orientation, often implemented with public support or within state programmes. These initiatives were in strong continuity with both the bourgeois-liberal and Christian top-down community initiatives, on the one hand, and the bottom-up mutual aid associations and co-operative movement, on the other, in as much as they were a mixture of exogenously and endogenously engineered action, through voluntary as well as professional work.

From an organisational point of view, community initiatives struck a varying balance between informal, ad hoc, self-standing associations and formal hierarchical structures (Tarrow, 1998), often operating under state programmes or loose church umbrellas. They also often benefited from the leadership of professional social workers, political or religious leader figures. But the main characteristic of this type of initiative was its strict orientation to defend, solve the problems of, and/or provide benefits to, the community. Aims and actions were diverse (see Table 2.2), sometimes oriented to single issues and sometimes carrying out integrated approaches, but always with a definite community (social, ethnic) and/or place (neighbourhood, city) dimension.

Table 2.2 The post-Second World War cycle of contention

	Niche, alternative, demonstrative communal initiatives	Organised (mass) movements	Community, grassroots, neighbourhood initiatives
Philosophical roots ('frames')	Utopian communities; self-help initiatives; libertarian and anarchist tradition (refusal of hierarchy and centralised organisation).	Workers movements.	Bourgeois and Christian community initiatives, mutual aid associations, co-operative movement.
Movements and initiatives	Squatting. Self-contained (hippy) communes. Occupation and self-management of public premises and services. Demonstrative actions.	Civil Rights movement (US African Americans). Anti-war movements. Student mobilisation. Workers movements. Civil rights and equal opportunity movements (abortion, divorce, greater democracy). Feminist movements. Gay movements. Anti-nuclear and environmental movements.	'Urban' movements (against top-down planning decisions, for specific services and/or programmes). Neighbourhood and community – 'grass-roots' – organisations (for the redevelopment of specific urban areas, for the defence of specific ethnic communities, etc.).
Aims	Alternative reproduction (life style) and production (arts, crafts); social utopias; outside both the state and the market. Symbolic disruption.	Political and social changes: in the work place, in the reproduction sphere (family legislation, housing, education, social services), in terms of participation (to planning decisions, to the management of schools), in terms of equal opportunities and civil rights; in the area of culture and the environment.	Urban, neighbourhood, and/or community-related issues. Against top-down decision-making; to obtain specific rights, services and/or programmes; for the enhancement, redevelopment, preservation, defence of specific areas, social groups, or cultural identities.

	Niche, alternative, demonstrative communal initiatives	Organised (mass) movements	Community, grassroots, neighbourhood initiatives
Actions ('repertoire')	'Squatting', occupation of public premises, and alternative communes; creative and artistic production/appropriation/ reinterpretation of objects, places; demonstrative actions.	Creatively revisited 'old' repertoire: strikes, demonstrations, sit-ins, petitions, etc.	Revisited 'old' repertoires of mutualism and self-help: voluntary work, self-managed organisations.
Recipients (beneficiaries)	Solely the members of the initiative; symbolic messages to society at large.	Broad social groups (students, workers, parents, women, minorities, etc.) and society at large.	Members; the community (place-based or social).
Organisations ('mobilising structures')	Loose, ephemeral, self-contained, non-hierarchical organisations; strictly oriented to achieve the set aim.	Structured local, regional or national associations and/or political organisations often rallied around a newspaper or a cause.	Self-help and mutual aid associations; co-operatives; social economy; non-profit organisations, third sector.
Approach	Libertarian; bottom-up; demonstrative. Self-help, self-defence.	Highly organised approach, often with hierarchical structure.	Bottom-up, participatory. Often with professional or voluntary external support (church, parish, social workers).
Relationship with the system	Does not really challenge the system. Symbolic disruption. Demonstrative. 'Interstitial' (exploits/fills 'folds' or 'cracks' of the system). Sometimes using public resources.	Reformist. Seeks changes in legislation and policy, through confrontation but also through and within state institutions.	Strongly critical of the system but no intention to overturn existing order: change through self-defence/ help and single-leverage initiatives, often with help of state institutions and funds.
Scope of action (spatial reach)	Enclosed community; local.	Urban, regional, national, international.	Local, community.

Source: Author

Box 2.5 National trajectories in the 'new' cycle of social movements

Nationwide, mass-based political movements

Many of the 'new' movements had quite a large, transversal, often nationwide impact. They involved the whole Western world, from the US to Europe. In the US they started with the Black civil rights movement and evolved into the anti-Vietnam War movement on the university campuses, as well as into the 'hippies' movement and a related musical and performing arts revolution. In Europe they began with the anti-Algerian war in France and exploded later into the French and Italian student movements of 1968–69, which then spread to other countries. In Germany they took an anti-nuclear and environmental turn. Throughout the 1970s and early 1980s, the cycle was rekindled with new issues and claims, diversifying into several different trajectories and models of contention (Mayer 1997, 1999; Staggenborg, 2008), before subsiding in the 1990s.

In Italy, the new movements were very political from the beginning; with students allying with factory workers and involving other social groups, they lasted longer and had deeper consequences on society and politics than in other European countries (Tarrow, 1989). A major Italian specificity right after the Second World War was the mobilising capacity of political parties, especially the antagonistic 'white' Christian-Democratic Party, on the one hand, and the 'red' Communist Party, on the other, with their respective nationwide mass organisations (Tarrow, 1989; Lembi and Vicari Haddock, 2003). The Communist Party, in particular, strongly contributed through the workers' mobilisation of the 1960s and the involvement of other social classes in the 1970s, to the achievement of social reforms in the domain of civil rights and equal opportunities (divorce, abortion, family legislation) and the establishment of the welfare state. Also active were some Catholic organisations, which played quite an innovative and progressive social role in the 1970s, especially after the second Vatican Council. Some of the student movements were co-opted into these broad national reformist movements, where they contributed innovative ideas and practices, whereas many others remained autonomous, feeding more antagonistic and libertarian actions (for an excellent account of the 'New Left' cycle of protests in Italy, from 1965 to 1975, see Tarrow, 1989).

Alternative, niche, libertarian initiatives

In Italy, parallel, but also strongly related to the above mass mobilisation, a host of less structured, more dispersed and more 'libertarian' political movements and social initiatives developed as well (Tarrow, 1989; Lembi and Vicari Haddock, 2003). The latter were generally more antagonistic vis-à-vis state institutions and hierarchies. Actions of diverse origin and various foci converged in this model: from militant catholic initiatives to neighbourhood associations, from civil disobedience to self-managed social centres, from women's self-help collectives to agricultural communes.

In France, the strong utopian communitarian tradition resurfaced in the 1960s and 1970s with the diffusion of alternative 'communes' of production and consumption, including 'hippy' experiments, both rural and urban, an important 'squatting' movement, and many loosely related social economy initiatives, such as micro-credit and local exchange trade (LET) networks (Ailenei, 2003).

In Germany (Gerometta and Haussermann, 2003), the centralised and authoritarian post-Second World War urban renovation policy ('pull-down renovation') partly explains the development of the 'squatters' movement in the majority of large German cities during the 1970s. Together with other initiatives, such as LETs, these alternative experiments merged with the self-help and civic association traditions inherited from the nineteenth century and engendered many community-oriented, neighbourhood-based associations, attempting to introduce more participatory practices in the prevailing top-down urban policy, whether negotiating with the state or as an alternative to the state (Della Porta, 1995).

In Belgium, the 'new' urban movements of the 1970s focused especially on the reproduction sphere and greater participation in political decision-making. With regard to the first, in the wake of the 'situationist' movement of the 1950s and 1960s, the dimensions of creativity and artistic expression were introduced in the struggle against capitalist alienation and in the affirmation of alternative ways of life. Concerning the latter, an important neighbourhood resistance movement developed against centralised urban renewal policy (Christiaens and Moyersoen, 2003).

(Social economy) and community/neighbourhood initiatives

Similar to Italy, post-Second World War socio-political organisations in Austria followed a nationwide 'black'/'red' divide, with the Social-Democratic Party implementing a rather top-down reformist approach in the context of a typical 'corporatist' state, centralising bargaining procedures. However, the 1980s are considered a period of significant social innovation, with the development of numerous decentralised, bottom-up and more participatory social initiatives in the domain of urban governance and with a community development approach. In these initiatives, a new content-oriented 'project culture' contributed to by-passing the traditional black/red divide and accommodating new 'green' instances. The experimentation was ephemeral, however, because of the return of a renewed paternalistic and authoritarian government style (Novy and Hammert, 2003).

In Italy, the third sector, linked to neighbourhood initiatives, gained momentum only in the 1990s, when specific legislation was enacted.

But it is in the UK that the community approach – a clear offshoot of both the philanthropic voluntarism and self-help traditions – has reached its most institutionalised form. Already in the 1950s the training of social workers was somewhat formalised. In the 1960s, there was a revival of voluntary work in deprived neighbourhoods, as the Gulbenkian Report opened the way for community organising, social planning, and community development projects (quite similar to US experiences), which led to the institutionalisation of community work as a profession. But contrary to the early paternalistic approach, these initiatives had a distinct 'radical' edge. Throughout the 1960s and 1970s, community work in the UK merged with welfare rights movements, neighbourhood resistance to authoritarian planning and redevelopment projects, the 'squatters' movement, union activism, ethnic minority organisations, feminist groups, movements for devolution, etc. Most importantly, community work was supported by government policy. In the late 1970s and early 1980s it was a major component of the New Urban Left experience, which experimented with more participatory and innovative community projects within the existing institutional framework (González *et al.*, 2003).

From social movements to social innovation

In this last section we address three questions. First, do the social movements and initiatives presented and analysed in the remainder of this book belong to a 'newer' cycle of contention, that is, are they different from the 'New Left' and 'Urban' movements of the 1960s and 1970s? Second, how does the historical legacy of previous cycles affect contemporary local trajectories? Third, what is the relation between social movements and social innovation?

A post-Fordist new cycle?

The 1980s are considered a watershed between the end of the so called Fordist–Keynesian regime of accumulation and the establishment of a post-Fordist, not to say postmodern, course, with its neoliberal regulatory corollaries of flexibility, deregulation, and privatisation.[28] Major components of this economic, social and institutional transition into what is often called the 'second modernity' (see Chapter 1), were the further deindustrialisation of Western economies, only partially compensated by the growth of service activities, the increase in immigration flows, the growing fragmentation of society, coupled with a decline of the welfare state and the crisis of traditional representative politics and parties. The 1990s then witnessed the firm establishment of the neoliberal paradigm across European societies, with relevant consequences on their regulatory framework. The Fordist–Keynesian institutions had been inspired by 'egalitarian' principles, in line with the reformist approach inherited from Liberalism, as amended by the social-democratic philosophy. In the new course, individualism resurfaced (Bauman, 2000; Sennett, 2006), together with a resurgence of inequality – now called 'social exclusion' – while, at the same time, the 'safety net' provided by the welfare state in the 1960s and 1970s, especially in the deprived neighbourhoods of large metropolitan areas and in lagging regions, progressively, albeit unevenly, shrank.

With regard to social movements, over the 1980s the great wave of transversal social mobilisation around the workers' and students' claims that had characterised the late Fordist phase progressively waned, as a result of several concurrent factors, internal and external: the institutionalisation of some organisations and their relative bureaucratisation, the segmentation of society and diversification of needs, the further assertion of hedonism and return of individualism,[29] the re-emergence of right-wing reaction. In this decade, according to many observers (Taylor-Gooby, 1994; Fraser, 1995; Mayer, 1997), social movements progressively moved away from broad-based universalistic 'redistributive' claims and focused on more narrow issues of 'recognition'and diversity. In the 1990s, despite the reappearance of material hardship (i.e. mass unemployment and poverty), the decline of the industrial working class, coupled with new and renewed social cleavages (between, e.g. tenured and temporary employment, skilled and unskilled workers, native and immigrant citizens, older and younger generations, men and women), hindered the transversal aggregations achieved in the 1960s and 1970s, while unionisation rates declined. By the end of the millennium, the class-based and, later, inter-classist social solidarity that had characterised the workers' movements in their long trajectory throughout the nineteenth and twentieth century eventually evaporated. Social movements 'splintered' into different types and directions (Mayer, 2009).

In fact, the 1990s' movements are more heterogeneous and fragmented, if not antagonistic, than those of the 1960s and 1970s (Mayer 1997, 2009; Staggenborg, 2008). A discussion has developed about how much these diverse post-Fordist movements – feminist, gay, for independent living, for peace, for environmental and social justice, for creative self-expression, against real estate-led redevelopment programmes, etc. – can be considered a distinct 'newer' cycle, especially in relation to social policy (see Martin, 2001 for a survey).

The 'postmodernist' view (e.g. Melucci ,1989) puts the emphasis on the 'post-material' concerns of these movements and their focus on contested identities, symbols, and disputed meanings, as opposed to the equality and redistributive concerns of old – the 'recognition–redistribution' dilemma, in Fraser's words (1995). Critics of the 'postmodernist' perspective argue that the purported 'novel' features of contemporary movements were present in the nineteenth-century movements as well (Callhoun, 1995) and that 'material' issues have actually come back on the agenda, enhanced by the neoliberal urban regimes (Mayer, 2006). Moulaert (2000) highlights the strong 'redistributive' approach of many neighbourhood development movements of the 1990s.

The national surveys carried out in the SINGOCOM project (Martinelli *et al.*, 2003) confirm that, although mass mobilisation came eventually to an end, social movements found indeed new impetus during the two decades of neoliberal restructuring, albeit in a more focused way. New and renewed grievances emerged in reaction to the growing economic and social hardship, the dismantlement of redistributive policy and/or the (re)enforcement of authoritarian institutions. In the context of a retrenching welfare state, solutions to new and old human needs were sought outside both the state and the market, through grass-roots, self-help and community-based initiatives, which also contributed to re-create identity and solidarity on a 'place' basis.

Can we then speak of a new 'post-Fordist' or 'postmodern' cycle of social mobilisation? In the SINGOCOM research and in this book we defend the view that not only is there a common European heritage from the nineteenth century, but there is also a strong *continuity* between that legacy, the 'new' cycle of the 1960s and 1970s, and the innovative initiatives we investigated in the third millennium. The social, political, economic and cultural contexts may have changed, but the grievances, repertoires, mobilising structures and visions of current social movements still have their firm roots in the philosophical trajectories reviewed earlier in this chapter, *throughout* the 1960s and 1970s.

Thus, if it is true that contemporary grievances are no longer voiced through mass-based, reformist movements and organisations, and the workers' movement trajectory may have subsided, our case studies clearly show strong continuities with the other two trajectories we identified within the 'new' cycle of contention of the 1960s and 1970s – namely, the libertarian, niche, demonstrative actions rooted in the utopian–anarchist tradition, on the one hand, and the social economy, self-help neighbourhood- and community-based initiatives, rooted in the mutualist tradition, on the other (see Tables 3.1 and 14.2 in the corresponding chapters).

We also believe – as others (Williams, 1992, 1999; Martin, 2001; Mayer, 2009) – that the antagonism between late-Fordist and postmodern movements in the debate of the 1990s is pointless: current claims are both materialist *and* post-materialist, for both redistribution *and* recognition and diversity. Alongside the 'new' needs put forward in the 1960s and 1970s cycle (personal freedom and self-expression, participatory democracy and bottom-up decision-making, recognition of diversity and self-determination), 'old' demands for basic needs (housing, jobs, collective consumption) and universal rights have returned to the contentious agenda with a vengeance. Contemporary movements may be more defensive, fragmented, diversified and fluid; but they do challenge the established order; they are neighbourhood-centred, but they also conjugate community and identity concerns with – implicit or explicit – claims for equality, collective consumption and universal rights. While they may reflect the existence of an increasingly diversified society, they all struggle for recognition and empowerment, thereby challenging the established distribution of *power* and the existing governance structures. Moreover, although with a strong local focus, thanks to the internet technology, they have the potential for bridging local action with international networking at a global scale (Mayer, 2000, 2006).[30]

The territorial declinations of a common heritage

Although contemporary social movements and initiatives tap into a common European heritage, they are also strongly conditioned by the specific national, regional and local institutional contexts in which they occur. In other words, social movements are strongly path- and place-dependent and plug into the diversity of needs and challenges of particular communities, within their specific institutional dynamics. This is a major claim of the post-disciplinary ALMOLIN approach (see Chapter 3), which we were able to confirm in the case studies.

The country surveys carried out in the SINGOCOM project (see Martinelli *et al.*, 2003) do show that there is a 'Western European' common philosophical heritage in the historical deployment of social movements. Born in the Renaissance's urban societies, it was rekindled by the principles of Enlightenment and the French revolution, although still in a liberal-bourgeois frame, took full speed with the Industrial Revolution and the workers' movements of the nineteenth century, and was passionately revived during the post-Second World War economic miracle. Indeed, all the countries investigated experienced social movements belonging to most of the philosophical trajectories identified earlier.

On the other hand, those surveys also confirm that there were important national and regional declinations, related to the influence of specific thinkers and leaders, the peculiarities of development of the local productive and social forces, and hence the cumulative construction of territorially rooted social capital. This is apparent in our case studies, where different traditions resurface in the neighbourhood initiatives and are enabled, as well as conditioned, by the specific features of the state at its different scales.

From social movements to social innovation

In reviewing the main features and dynamics of social movements in this chapter, we highlighted the conditions that make social grievances evolve into social movements, as well as the differences and continuities in the different historical cycles of contention. But the central concern of the SINGOCOM project was social innovation in urban communities. It is therefore necessary to briefly make the bridge between social movements and community-generated social innovation, that is, highlight when and how contentious action has a socially innovative impact.

As we stressed earlier, this is obviously related to the actual 'outcome' of movements and initiatives. In our study we therefore considered initiatives that had some sort of 'successful' and relatively 'lasting' effect at the level of the community and beyond. As we will fully explain when we present the ALMOLIN analytical framework in the next chapter, we argue that social innovation occurs when collective action achieves three main forms of change, alone or in combination: a) the satisfaction of human needs (material and immaterial) not otherwise met or considered; b) the empowerment of margin-alised social groups, through the enhancement of capabilities and the (re)creation of identity, thereby increasing their visibility, recognition, access or voice rights; c) changes in social, power and/or governance relations within the community and between the community and society at large (i.e. among citizens, civil society organisations, business interests, government institutions, at different spatial scales).

These three dimensions are strongly related. As we shall see, the first (content-oriented) is often the medium to achieve the latter two (more process-oriented). The mobilisation to obtain social services in a deprived neighbourhood can, for example, provide jobs, create solidarity, increase the visibility and participation to decision-making of marginalised groups, improve interaction among different institutions, etc. But while these dimensions of social innovation are transversal to our case studies, the research also shows that their actual form, dynamics and impact are highly contextual and depend on the place-specific socio-economic structures and institutions, as well as on the latter's temporal trajectories.

Notes

1 For Tarrow (1998: 3), 'the irreducible act that lies at the base of all social movements, protests, and revolutions is "contentious collective action"'.

2 In the Marxist doctrine, the primary foundation of social movements was class, and the factory or the mine was the basis for the workers' collective identity and solidarity. In twentieth-century social movements, identity has been increasingly based on other social categories, such as ethnicity (e.g. the Civil Rights movement in the US), gender (e.g. the feminist movement), locality (e.g. community claims), as well as on transversal aggregations focusing on specific purposes (e.g. the environment).

3 By 'naming grievances, connecting them to other grievances and constructing larger frames of meaning that will resonate with a population's cultural predispositions and communicate a uniform message to power holders and others' (Snow and Benford, 1992: 136).

4 Tarrow (1998) stresses how violence is the easiest form of collective disruptive action, especially from small groups, to initiate contention without incurring major

coordination costs. On the other hand, many actions that started violently have been progressively institutionalised. A good example is the strike, which began historically as a violent confrontation and has now become a highly institutionalised and conventional form of bargaining.

5 Tilly (1995) points out a major difference between eighteenth- and nineteenth-century 'old' repertoires that were 'parochial, bifurcated and particular' (e.g. food riots, seizure of land, burning of houses), and 'new' repertoires that are 'cosmopolitan, modular and autonomous' (e.g. strikes, demonstrations, public meetings, etc).

6 This is for example the case of the nonviolent sit-ins introduced by the Civil Rights movement in the US – borrowed from Ghandi – which became a standard form of action in the 1960s' and 1970s' social movements.

7 Kriesi (1996) proposes a typology based on two variables: a) mode of participation (direct vs. indirect); b) orientation (own constituency vs. authority).

8 The increasingly relevant role of communication technologies must also be emphasised. Media such as television in the 1960s and 1970s and the internet starting in the 1990s were crucial in the rapid diffusion of frames and repertoires, in creating consensus and in enlarging support.

9 Tilly (1995) speaks of 'orientation to power holder' to stress the difference between patronised and autonomous movements.

10 For Tarrow (1998) the first 'modern cycle' started in 1848 encompassing several European countries, whereas the 'New Left' cycle, which began in the 1960s, both in the US and Europe, continued throughout the 1970s with a variety of movements.

11 On co-optation see Moulaert *et al.* (1997).

12 On the other hand, it must also be stressed that the relationship between the evolution of social movements and the behaviour of the state is not linear. Sometimes greater political access may contribute to defusing social movements by institutionalising claims, whereas political repression, rather than crush resistance, may lead to revolution (Kriesi *et al.*, 1995, Tarrow, 1998).

13 In nineteenth-century Liberalism, the principle of 'equality' did not include equal political rights, but only equality in front of the law. In other words, bourgeois liberalism was fiercely opposed to democracy – which presumed equal political rights. Only people who had initiative and capabilities should be enabled to achieve success, whereas the place of the masses in society was to work in the fields and factories and live up to the norms set by the bourgeois legal system. Only in the second half of the century did bourgeois liberalism evolve towards a more democratic vision, but by then the enemy was no longer democracy, but socialism (Villari, 1977; Lo Surdo, 2006).

14 In the enlightened bourgeois camp, we can mention the vision of Adriano Olivetti and his experiment of a model company community in Ivrea, Italy, during the 1950s.

15 Hofmann (1971) classifies social philosophies of the nineteenth century according to this 'one aspect' leverage.

16 Often involved in insurrectional and secret societies' activities.

17 Enlightened bourgeois-Christian social reformism and utopian socialism had developed during the industrial revolution. When Marx published his analysis of capitalism the changes engendered by the industrial revolution had fully emerged. Marx not only provided a coherent account of the class-based conflict inherent in industrial capitalism, but also clearly prefigured the alternative society of the future. In the second half of the nineteenth century the social and political questions at the centre of early reformism became a class question and the scattered social movements evolved into a working-class movement of national and international reach.

18 Political parties and unions, all characterised by a federated, hierarchical organ-
    isational structure.
19 The nationalist-socialist regimes in Italy and Germany actually interrupted these
    developments, trading some corporatist social legislation for very repressive and
    authoritarian measures.
20 As opposed to the 'first modern cycle of contention', which started with the
    widespread revolutionary events of 1848 across many European countries.
    According to Tilly and Tarrow, it was in the first cycle that social and political
    issues were integrated and the modern 'repertoire' of collective action established.
21 By the end of the 1970s more than 6 per cent of public spending in Italy, Belgium,
    France and West Germany went to welfare services and the largest part of civil
    service employment was in social services (Hobsbawm, 1994).
22 As stressed by Hobsbawm (1994), in the 1960s young people represented a very
    large autonomous social force. They were the fruit of the post-war baby boom,
    most of whom students as a result of compulsory education and the increased
    affluence of the working class, who had no notion of hardship and tribulation, no
    inclination towards sacrifice and compliance with rules, and plenty of free time to
    think and discuss alternative values and models of life.
23 The youth culture of the 1960s was 'demotic', i.e. inspired by popular values, and
    'antinomian', i.e. against established rules (Hobsbawm, 1994).
24 It is interesting to note that Tarrow (1998) makes a similar tripartite typology, but
    he strongly contrasts the 'social-democratic solution' of mass movements with the
    'anarchist counter-model', stressing the hierarchical and bureaucratic organisation of
    the former in opposition to the violent, destructive and clandestine character of the
    latter. His third model is the 'community-based organisation', which strikes a
    delicate balance between formal structure and spontaneity. In our typology, however,
    we consider the legacy of the anarchist model in a more positive perspective, stressing
    its niche, demonstrative, 'outside the system' character. Moreover, we do not
    consider the community model to be an 'intermediate' form.
25 It is true that in the repertoire of this model there were many unlawful initiatives
    (e.g. squatting and occupation of public premises, civil disobedience) and clandestine
    activities, with extreme cases of terroristic actions; but on the whole this trajectory
    was characterised by very creative and unconventional, albeit disruptive
    experiments.
26 For example, Leninism and Maoism (Tarrow, 1989).
27 There is wide agreement in placing the origin of the protest wave of the 1960s
    in the civil right movements of the African American people in the US (see
    Staggenborg, 2008). The repertoire of that movement – bus boycotts, freedom rides,
    sit-ins, demonstrations – and the main themes of its ideological frame – human
    rights, freedom and justice – were formed in the Black church networks and spread
    to the universities through the 'Freedom Summer' student campaigns, becoming
    the basis of the subsequent anti-Vietnam War and 'New Left' movements.
28 There is by now a very large literature on the Fordist and post-Fordist regimes.
    See among others: Boyer (1986), Boyer and Saillard (1995) and, for a recent survey,
    Jessop (2005).
29 The revolts of the 1960s and 1970s had targeted, among other demands, the
    suffocating 'moral restraint' of the capitalist socio-cultural order of the time. The
    more libertarian and romantic currents of such movements had claimed (and
    successfully achieved) affective liberation and greater individual freedom. Conserva-
    tive constraints were thus replaced by the imperative to enjoy, but the latter was
    then progressively incorporated – and de-politicised – in what Boltanski and
    Chiapello (2007) call the 'New Spirit of Capitalism' (see also Sennett, 2006). This
    'cultural' transformation features a neutralisation of originally counter-hegemonic

demands for greater freedom, creativity and autonomy by new organisational and managerial forms of capitalism (Mouffe, 2009).

30 This does not mean, of course, that community- and neighbourhood-based movements do not run the risk of loosing the 'societal' perspective by 'retreating' into the local dimension, thereby overlooking the fact that social exclusion is largely determined at higher spatial scales; but we will fully address this issue in Chapter 3 and Chapter 14.

References

Ailenei, O. (2003) 'Visions and movements in the urban social economy of France', in F. Martinelli, F. Moulaert, E. Swyngedouw and O. Ailenei (eds) *Social Innovation, Governance and Community Building – SINGOCOM. Scientific Report Month 18*, Contract HPSE-CT-2001-00070 funded under the key action 'Improving the Socio-economic Knowledge Base' of FP5, European Commission – DG Research, Lille: IFRESI-CNRS. Online. Available: http://users.skynet.be/frank.moulaert/singocom/index2.html (Accessed 1 June 2009).

Bauman, Z. (2000) *Liquid Modernity*, Cambridge: Polity.

Boltanski, L. and Chiapello, E. (2007) *The New Spirit of Capitalism*, London: Verso.

Boyer, R. (1986) *La théorie de la régulation: une analyse critique*, Paris: Editions La Découverte.

—— and Saillard, Y. (eds) (1995) *Théorie de la régulation: l'état des savoirs*, Paris: La Découverte, English transl. (2001) *Regulation Theory: State of the Art*, London and New York: Routledge.

Callhoun, C. (1995) '"New social movements" of the early nineteenth century', in M. Traugott (ed.) *Repertoires and Cycles of Collective Actions*, Durham, NC: Duke University Press, pp. 173–215.

Castells, M. (1972) *La question urbaine*, Paris: Maspero.

—— (1973) *Luttes urbaines et pouvoir politique*, Paris: Maspero.

—— (1983) *The City and the Grassroots*, London: Edward Arnold.

Christiaens, E. and Moyersoen, J. (2003) 'Social innovation in Belgium: philosophical roots, social practices, and local experiences', in F. Martinelli, F. Moulaert, E. Swyngedouw and O. Ailenei (eds) *Social Innovation, Governance and Community Building – SINGOCOM. Scientific Report Month 18*, Contract HPSE-CT-2001-00070 funded under the key action 'Improving the Socio-economic Knowledge Base' of FP5, European Commission – DG Research, Lille: IFRESI-CNRS. Online. Available: http://users.skynet.be/frank.moulaert/singocom/index2.html (Accessed 1 June 2009).

Della Porta, D. (1995) *Social Movements, Political Violence, and the State: A Comparative Analysis of Italy and Germany*, Cambridge: Cambridge University Press.

Facchi, A. (2007) *Breve storia dei diritti umani*, Bologna: Il Mulino.

Fraser, N. (1995) 'From redistribution to recognition? Dilemmas of justice in a "post-socialist" age', *New Left Review*, 212: 68–92.

Gamson, W. (1990) *The Strategy of Social Protest*, 2nd edn, Belmont, CA: Wadsworth.

Gerometta, J. and Haussermann, H. (2003) 'Visions and traditions of socially innovative area development: Germany and Berlin in a historical perspective', in F. Martinelli, F. Moulaert, E. Swyngedouw and O. Ailenei (eds) *Social Innovation, Governance and Community Building – SINGOCOM. Scientific Report Month 18*, Contract HPSE-CT-2001-00070 funded under the key action 'Improving the Socio-economic

Knowledge Base' of FP5, European Commission – DG Research, Lille: IFRESI-CNRS. Online. Available: http://users.skynet.be/frank.moulaert/singocom/index2.html (Accessed 1 June 2009).

Ginsborg, P. (1989) *Storia d'Italia dal dopoguerra ad oggi. Società e politica 1943–1988*, Torino: Einaudi.

Giugni, M. (1998) 'Social movements and change: incorporation, transformation, and democratization', in M. Giugni, D. McAdam and C. Tilly (eds) *From Contention to Democracy*, Lanham, MD: Rowman and Littlefield, pp. xi–xxvi.

González, S., Thomas, H. and Court, L. (2003) 'United Kingdom', in F. Martinelli, F. Moulaert, E. Swyngedouw and O. Ailenei (eds) *Social Innovation, Governance and Community Building – SINGOCOM. Scientific Report Month 18*, Contract HPSE-CT-2001-00070 funded under the key action 'Improving the Socio-economic Knowledge Base' of FP5, European Commission – DG Research, Lille: IFRESI-CNRS. Online. Available: http://users.skynet.be/frank.moulaert/singocom/index2.html (Accessed 1 June 2009).

Hobsbawm, E. (1962) *The Age of Revolution: 1789–1848*, London: Abacus.

—— (1975) *The Age of Capital: 1848–1875*, London: Abacus.

—— (1987) *The Age of Empire: 1875–1914*, London: Abacus.

—— (1994) *Age of Extremes: The Short Twentieth Century: 1914–1991*, London: Abacus.

—— (1995) *French Revolution*, Phoenix, AZ: New edition.

Hofmann, W. (1971) *Da Babeuf a Marcuse. Storia delle idee e dei movimenti sociali nei secoli XIX e XX*, Milan: Arnoldo Mondadori Editore, original title *Ideengeschichte der sozialen Bewegung des 19. und 20. Jahrunderts*.

Jessop, R. (2005) 'The regulation approach on economic and social development', Discussion Paper, *Development Models and Logics of Socio-Economic Organisation in Space, DEMOLOGOS*, Specific Targeted Project, Contract CIT2-CT-2004-505462, funded under FP6, European Commission – DG Research. Newcastle: GURU. Online. Available: http://demologos.ncl.ac.uk (Accessed 1 June 2009).

Klandermans, B. (1997) *The Social Psychology of Protest*, Oxford: Blackwell.

—— Kriesi, H. and Tarrow, S. (eds) (1988) *From Structure to Action: Comparing Social Movements Research across Cultures* (International Social Movement Research, 1), Greenwich, CT: JAI Press.

Kriesi, H. (1996) 'The organisational structure of new social movements in a political context', in D. McAdam, J. McCarthy and M. Zald (eds) *Comparative Perspectives on Social Movements: Political Opportunities, Mobilising Structures, and Cultural Framings*, Cambridge: Cambridge University Press, pp. 152–84.

—— Koopmans, R., Duyvendak, J.W. and Giugni, M.G. (1995) *New Social Movements in Western Europe: A Comparative Analysis*, Minneapolis, MN: University of Minnesota Press.

Lembi, P. and Vicari Haddock, S. (2003) 'Italy', in F. Martinelli, F. Moulaert, E. Swyngedouw and O. Ailenei (eds) *Social Innovation, Governance and Community Building – SINGOCOM. Scientific Report Month 18*, Contract HPSE-CT-2001-00070 funded under the key action 'Improving the Socio-economic Knowledge Base' of FP5, European Commission – DG Research, Lille: IFRESI-CNRS. Online. Available: http://users.skynet.be/frank.moulaert/singocom/index2.html (Accessed 1 June 2009).

Lo Surdo, D. (2006) *Controstoria del liberalismo*, Roma-Bari: Laterza.

Marcuse, P. (2009) 'From critical urban theory to the right to the city', *City*, 13(2–3): 185–97.

Martin, G. (2001) 'Social movements, welfare and social policy: a critical analysis', *Critical Social Policy*, 21(3): 361–83.

Martinelli, F., Moulaert, F. and Swyngedouw, E. (2003) 'The legacy of history in contemporary social movements: in search of socially innovative mechanisms?', in F. Martinelli, F. Moulaert, E. Swyngedouw and O. Ailenei (eds) *Social Innovation, Governance and Community Building – SINGOCOM. Scientific Report Month 18*, Contract HPSE-CT-2001-00070 funded under the key action 'Improving the Socio-economic Knowledge Base' of FP5, European Commission – DG Research, Lille: IFRESI-CNRS. Online. Available: http://users.skynet.be/frank.moulaert/singocom/index2.html (Accessed 1 June 2009).

Mayer, M. (1997) 'Les mouvements sociaux comme acteurs politiques dans les villes européennes: leur évolution entre les années soixante-dix et quatre-vingt-dix', in A. Bagnasco and P. Le Galès (eds) *Villes en Europe*, Paris: Éditions La Découverte; English transl. 'Social movements in European cities: Transitions from the 1970s to the 1990s' in A. Bagnasco and P. Le Galès (eds) *Cities in Contemporary Europe*, Cambridge: Cambridge University Press, pp. 131–52.

—— (1999) 'Urban movements and urban theory in the late 20th century', in S. Body-Gendrot and B. Beauregard (eds) *The Urban Moment*, Thousand Oaks, CA: Sage, pp. 209–39.

—— (2000) 'Urban social movements in an era of globalization', in P. Hamel, H. Lustiger-Thaler and M. Mayer (eds) *Urban Movements in a Globalizing World*, London: Routledge, pp. 141–57.

—— (2006) 'Contesting the neo-liberalization of urban governance', in H. Leitner, J. Peck and E. Sheppard (eds) *Contesting Neoliberalism. The Urban Frontier*, New York: Guilford, pp. 90–115.

—— (2009) 'The "Right to the City" in the context of shifting mottos of urban social movements', *City*, 13(2–3): 362–74.

McAdam, D., McCarthy, J. and Zald, M. (eds) (1996) *Comparative Perspectives on Social Movements: Political Opportunities, Mobilising Structures, and Cultural Framings*, Cambridge: Cambridge University Press.

McCarthy, J.D. and Zald, M.N. (1977) 'Resource mobilization and social movements: A partial theory', *American Journal of Sociology*, 82(6): 1212–41.

Melucci, A. (1989) *Nomads of the Present: Social Movements and Individual Needs in Contemporary Society*, London: Hutchinson Radius.

Mouffe, C. (2009) 'Einige Ideen zu Radikalpolitik Heute', Paper presented at the Seminar *Updating Radical Democracy – Uber Hegemonie und radikale Demokratie*.

Moulaert, F. (ed.) (2000) *Globalization and Integrated Area Development in European Cities*, Oxford: Oxford University Press.

Moulaert, F., Delvainquière, J.-C. and Delladetsima, P. (1997) 'Les rapports sociaux dans le développement local: le rôle des mouvements sociaux', in J. Klein, P.-A. Tremblay, and H. Dionne (eds) *Au-delà du néolibéralisme: Quel rôle pour les mouvements sociaux?* Sainte-Foy: Presses de l'Université du Québec, pp. 77–97.

Novy, A. and Hammer, E. (2003) 'Austria', in F. Martinelli, F. Moulaert, E. Swyngedouw and O. Ailenei (eds) *Social Innovation, Governance and Community Building – SINGOCOM. Scientific Report Month 18*, Contract HPSE-CT-2001-00070 Funded under the key action 'Improving the Socio-economic Knowledge Base' of FP5, European Commission – DG Research, Lille: IFRESI-CNRS. Online. Available: http://users.skynet.be/frank.moulaert/singocom/index2.html (Accessed 1 June 2009).

Rochon, T.R. and Mazmamian, D. (1993) 'Social movements and the policy process', *Annals of the American Academy of Political and Social Science*, 528: 75–87.

Rucht, D. (1996) 'The Impact of National Contexts on Social Movement Structures', in D. McAdam, J.D. McCarthy, M.N. Zald (eds) *Comparative Perspectives on Social Movements: Political Opportunities, Mobilizing Structures, and Cultural Framings*, New York: Cambridge University Press, pp. 185–204.

Sennett, R. (2006) *The Culture of the New Capitalism*, New Haven, CT and London: Yale University Press.

Snow, D. (2004) 'Social movements as challenges to authority: Resistance to an emerging conceptual hegemony', *Research in Social Movements, Conflicts and Change*, 25: 3–25.

—— and Benford, R.D. (1992) 'Ideology, frame resonance and participant mobilization', *International Social Movement Research*, 1: 197–217.

Staggenborg, S. (2008) *Social Movements*, Don Mills, Ontario: Oxford University Press.

Tarrow, S. (1989) *Democracy and Disorder: Protest and Politics in Italy, 1965–1975*, Oxford: Oxford University Press.

—— (1998) *Power in Movement: Social Movements and Contentious Politics*, 2nd edn, Cambridge: Cambridge University Press.

Taylor-Gooby, P. (1994) 'Postmodernism and social policy: a great leap backwards?', *Journal of Social Policy*, 23(3): 385–404.

Tilly, C. (1975), 'Reflections on the history of European state-making', in C. Tilly (ed.) *The Formation of National States in Western Europe*, Princeton, NJ: Princeton University Press, pp. 3–83.

—— (1978) *From Mobilization to Revolution*, Reading, MA: Addison-Wesley.

—— (1984) 'Social movements and national politics', in H.C. Bright and S. Harding (eds) *Statemaking and Social Movements*, Ann Arbor, MI: University of Michigan Press, pp. 297–317.

—— (1993) *European Revolutions: 1492–1992*, Oxford: Blackwell.

—— (1995) *Popular Contention in Great Britain: 1758–1834*, Cambridge, MA: Harvard University Press.

—— (2004) *Social Movements: 1768–2004*, Boulder, CO: Paradigm.

Touraine, A. (1968) *Le mouvement de mai ou le communisme utopique*, Paris: Seuil.

Villari, R. (1977) *Storia contemporanea*, Bari: Laterza.

Williams, F. (1992) 'Somewhere over the rainbow: universality and diversity in social policy', in N. Manning and R. Page (eds) *Social Policy Review*, 4: 200–19.

—— (1999) 'Good enough principles for welfare', *Journal of Social Policy*, 28(4): 667–87.

Zald, M.N. (2000) 'Ideologically structured action: An enlarged agenda for social movement research', *Mobilization*, 5(1): 1–16.

3 ALMOLIN

How to analyse social innovation at the local level?

Sara González, Frank Moulaert and Flavia Martinelli

Introduction

This book focuses on the analysis of social innovation dynamics at the 'local' level, and especially within neighbourhoods and local communities, as an integral and vital part of wider urban dynamics. In the first chapter, we reviewed different theories of social innovation and situated our own understanding of this concept within different strands of the literature and in connection with the notion of community. In the second chapter, we traced the historical roots of social movements in Europe as a key to understanding some of the features and dynamics of our contemporary socially innovative experiences. This third chapter, then, attempts to bridge those theoretical and historical discussions with the empirical case study chapters that will be presented in the remainder of the book. To this end, it spells out the analytical framework that we mobilised to identify dynamics of social innovation at the local level.

First, we explain why the 'local' was chosen as the privileged 'entry' scale in our research. Second, we present our post-disciplinary 'alternative' analytical model – *ALMOLIN – ALternative MOdel of Local INnovation* – and the way it guided our empirical analysis of socially innovative initiatives and organisations at the local level. Third, we highlight the main features and dynamics of the social innovation process. Finally, we introduce our case studies explaining the logic for their choice and our approach to comparative urban analysis.

Social innovation at the local level

In the previous chapters, we discussed the concept of social innovation in theoretical, ethical and historical terms. Here, we specifically address its *empirical* meaning at the *local* scale, that is, at the urban – mostly neighbourhood – spatial scale, and as part of particular community dynamics, which was the main focus of the SINGOCOM project.

Our interest in the local stems from the view that the local scale can be a more 'tangible', a 'better', or 'more just' and democratic level at which to organise change, including social and political activity (see Chapter 1). In addition, communities seeking change often have a local territorial basis. In so focusing, however, we have purposefully avoided the uncritical 'localism' drift (Moulaert and Leontidou, 1995) or 'local trap' (Purcell, 2006). There are at least three dangers associated with the local trap, which we sought to overcome in our research (Moulaert *et al.*, 2005). *First*, there is the danger of 'socio-political' localism that holds an exaggerated belief in the power of local level agency and institutions to improve the world, thereby ignoring or disavowing the inter-scalar spatiality of development mechanisms and strategies. *Second*, there is the danger of 'existential' localism – the idea that all needs are best satisfied within the local *heimat*, by local institutions or – pushing the localist argument even further – by drawing mainly on local resources. This of course does not make sense, for economic, social, cultural and political reasons. *Third*, there is the fallacy of 'misunderstood subsidiarity', an increasingly hegemonic discourse, which hides the fact that the higher-scale state and corporate capital levels tend to unload their budgetary and other responsibilities onto the hierarchically lower, and especially the local, scales.

In our research we have been able to avoid this trap by using two methodological strategies. First, while the local is our empirical entry point into the research field, we fully acknowledge that processes – including social exclusion and inclusion, as well as social innovation dynamics – occur at a multi- and trans-scalar level. This means that any socially innovative initiative at the local level is inevitably embedded in a broader geographical scaffolding that is continually restructuring (Brenner, 2004; Jessop, 2000; Moulaert, 1995; Swyngedouw, 1997). For example, global finance crises can trigger local surviving initiatives such as credit unions or time-share schemes. New national regulations and policies can create situations in the face of which socially innovative actions emerge. Moreover, innovative projects that are initiated in one place can also diffuse to other localities and/or develop in a trans-scalar manner through regional, national or international networks. We have also avoided 'one-dimensionalism', as identified by Jessop *et al.* (2008), by including the spatial, scalar, territorial and networked dimensions of the socio-spatial relations involved in the making of social innovation strategies.

Our second methodological strategy was never to lose sight of the fact that the local scale, like any other scale, is socially and politically produced and therefore does not exist 'out there' by itself, waiting to be discovered by the researcher (Swyngedouw, 1997; Marston, 2000). Moreover, in many of our case studies, the particular local scale was actually 'constructed' through the socially innovative experience, that is, was a consequence of the collective action that led to place-building or of the institutional dynamics that were spurred through socially innovative networking. In the case of the *Ouseburn Trust* in Newcastle, for example, a group of campaigners effectively gave meaning to a place that was off the radar of the local council and had lost much of its identity. In the case of *City Mine(d)* in Brussels, activists created new 'malleable' spaces for civic engagement. And *Olinda* in Milan managed to involve a diversity of social groups from the city and beyond, and for a while the local authorities also, in their wider networks.

New spaces, scales, territories and networks are thus constructed or re-created locally through social innovation, often embedded into or connected to regional, national and international scales and networks. In other words, in this book, we analyse social innovation at the local level, and often within particular area-based communities, as a 'window' into wider scalar processes. Our theoretical underpinnings and case studies engage thus with a relational conception of scale and space (Massey, 2004: 5); one in which space is not seen as rigid and static but 'as internally complex, essentially un-boundable in any absolute sense, and inevitably historically changing', and taking into account the power structures that constrain the relational possibilities of change-agencies (Moulaert and Mehmood, 2010).

This perspective also permits a more balanced use of the concept of 'community' (see Chapter 1). Far from the concept being monolithic and homogeneous, in our research we use it as a complex and multidimensional phenomenon. The local community is never identifiable as a single entity; there is always a variety of groups claiming some kind of identity or ownership. What is more, it is not only those who are physically present locally who feel attachment and responsibility towards a place (Amin, 2004), but also those linked to the locality through other relationally constituted means.

ALMOLIN: an alternative model for analysing local innovation

To carry out our comparative analysis of case studies within the SINGOCOM project, we developed an analytical 'model' called *ALMOLIN – ALternative MOdel of Local INnovation*, which provided both the scaffolding through which we framed our empirical investigation and the link to the theoretical under-pinnings of our project (Moulaert *et al.*, 2005). This post-disciplinary model was built using elements from different social science literatures. Critical theoretical perspectives on the role of the state, civil society, community and neighbourhood development and organisations, on the social economy, on economic democracy ('participatory budgeting'), and on participatory planning were 'mobilised' or 'reconstructed'. Together, they permitted an improved understanding of social innovations in local development, particularly as these come forth in response to processes of alienation, exploitation and exclusion of different types (for reviews of these theories, see also the special issue of *Urban Studies* (Moulaert *et al.*, 2005) and the special issue of *European Urban and Regional Studies* (Moulaert *et al.*, 2007).

Figure 3.1[1] synthesises the different elements of ALMOLIN and puts them into a dynamic perspective. It can be seen as a methodological toolkit aimed at digging into the most important dynamics in each of the case studies while at the same time bringing to the fore both common and comparable elements. The figure shows that these dynamics are multifaceted and multidimensional.

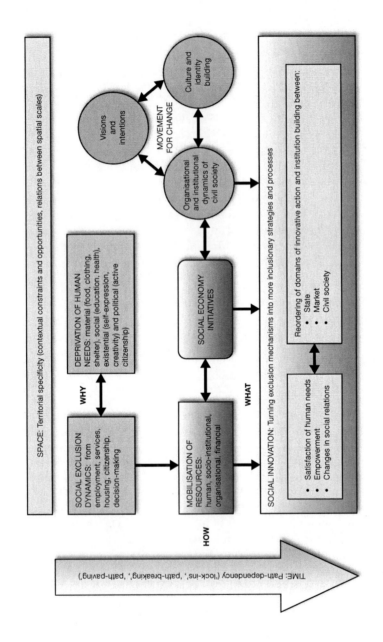

Figure 3.1 Dynamics of social innovation
Source: Authors.

At the core of Figure 3.1 is the interplay between the dynamics of social exclusion and the deprivation of human needs, which are (or ought to be) countered by social innovation dynamics. Social innovation dynamics include reactions to deprivation and exclusion, organisation around some shared vision of change – often in the form of social movements – and reproduction of a culture of change based on the pursuit of a new identity – thereby cutting loose from the depths of humiliation and alienation. Overcoming situations of exclusion always entails citizens mobilising resources within, or against, existing organisational and institutional dynamics. The figure does not show civil society or 'grand' political dynamics; these are indirectly included through path dependency and the institutionally interconnected nature of spatial scales (neighbourhoods, local communities, municipalities, cities, regions . . .). The boxes in the figure use a macro-language but, when applied to case-study analysis, they come to life and adopt a concrete content. What we have sought to stress in the case studies is how, over time, organisations and initiatives seek to determine their particular social innovation content in reaction to exclusion dynamics and situations of deprivation; as well as how initiatives in the social economy are launched, agendas set, institutional dynamics promoted or hampered.

In what follows, we will point out some basic connections between the main elements of the ALMOLIN figure as we have used it in the case study analysis.

a) *Time and space.* These dimensions are shown in the margins of the figure as they affect or interfere with almost any of the elements in the figure. They allow us to see the importance of 'holistic' definitions and theories of social exclusion/inclusion and social economy in historically and geographically specific ways (see section on comparative research methodology later in this chapter). In our analysis we regard the role of path-dependency – and its spatial dimension – as crucial, as it stresses the role of specific opportunities and constraints in the trajectories of particular territories (embedded in their wider spatial scales). Path dependency can work in different directions: it can lead to a 'lock-in' situation, with no immediate opportunities for change; or it can be 'path-paving' in fostering continued social and institutional innovation; or else it can be 'path-breaking' when leading to abrupt transformations of past dynamics. Path-dependency can be structural or institutional. Structural path-dependency means, for example, that community development initiatives in a 'raw' capitalist environment face different challenges from those in a 'welfare state' or 'mixed economy' environment. Institutional path-dependency means that in the context, for example, of a long tradition of private–public co-operation in local development, it will be easier to work for new institution building and social innovation in governance relations, than in places where the state or the market sector are dominant. In other words, we approach social innovation within a strategic-relational framework (Jessop, 2008) where the impact of local institutional histories and cultures can be empowering as well as disempowering, or lead to temporary lock-ins.

b) *Social exclusion dynamics.* These are generally the starting point and may play a determining role in spurring on socially innovative initiatives within specific localities or neighbourhoods. In our research, we observed that social innovation is almost always triggered as a 'reaction' to social exclusion, and emerges only in exceptional cases from a conscious attempt to improve inclusionary dynamics or already existing harmony among social groups. Social exclusion may refer to material needs (poverty, lack of housing), but also to social (limited access to education and health), political (no citizenship, no access to decision-making), and existential (no access to self-expression and creative activities) deprivation. The above processes answer the 'Why?' question in Figure 3.1.

c) *Mobilisation of resources and social innovation.* The mobilisation of social, institutional and financial resources to overcome exclusionary processes (the 'How?' in Figure 3.1) does not have an a priori 'socially innovative' impact or outcome. In reality, there will be (strong) antagonisms between movements for social inclusion and those reproducing social exclusion or in favour of the status quo. For example, local movements, even when allied with local political elites or neighbourhood councils, may have to counter mechanisms of social exclusion stemming from higher-level public or private authorities (e.g. cuts in social security spending or wage cuts and layoffs). In our definition, social innovation occurs when the mobilisation of social and institutional forces succeeds in bringing about the satisfaction of previously alienated human needs, the relative empowerment of previously silent or excluded social groups through the creation of new 'capabilities', and, ultimately, changes in the existing social – and power – relations towards a more inclusive and democratic governance system. Let us examine these three outcomes (the 'What?' in Figure 3.1) in their connections with the other elements of our analytical methodology.

d) *Satisfaction of human needs: mobilising resources, social economy and institutional dynamics.* In the first dimension of our notion of social innovation it is the *dialectics* of the mobilisation of actors and the institutional dynamics of both the state (in its different articulations) and civil society – including social economy initiatives in their different forms and uneven outcomes – that contribute to the actual emergence of social innovation. These intersections are clear in the case of the 'social economy' as revealed in Moulaert and Ailenei (2005).

Moulaert and Nussbaumer (2005) define the social economy as that part of the economy – or the complement to the 'coexisting' capitalist market economy – that: i) organises economic functions according to principles of democratic co-operation and reciprocity; ii) generates a high level of equality in distribution and/or organises redistribution when needed; iii) satisfies basic human needs in a sustainable way. The conception of social economy put forward in ALMOLIN is that of a 'social market' economy, that is, an economy in which the market still plays an important role but has returned to its original social function of needs–satisfying, allocating 'fair' compensation to all production factors in the value-added chain, and making use-value of commodities reflect social and ecological quality. Such a market is of course significantly more regulated than the globally competitive market celebrated and put into practice in the contemporary neoliberal economy.

Therefore, the dialectics involving basic needs satisfaction, the social economy, and organisational and institutional dynamics of both the state and civil society, are very relevant in explaining social innovation at the local scale. In some of our cases, social mobilisation used the state as a vehicle for access to, or better provision of, social services. In other cases, the third sector was a catalyst for socially innovative inclusionary actions. Theories on the relationships between civil society and the state are helpful here in understanding the various configurations that the satisfaction of human needs may adopt (see part 3 of Williams, 2005).

e) *Empowerment: visions, culture and identity building in movements for change.* The capacity to elaborate collective visions and intentions – 'What's to be done' – is a fundamental element in the construction of collective identities, cultural change, and new capabilities. The latter feed movements for change, which, in turn, affect organisational and institutional dynamics (as shown in the triangle 'visions and intentions – culture and identity building – organisational and institutional dynamics of civil society' in Figure 3.1). Movements for change in all their forms and at all spatial scales (neighbourhood associations, community committees, national coordination of locally active civil society organisations) are at the core of the dynamics of social innovation as we view it. Visions may change through strategy development and action; but they can also change as part of institutional transformations. Still, what truly determines social innovation is the 'empowering' character of change movements. As will be shown in the next chapters, the most successful socially innovative initiatives enabled their constituencies not only to be heard, but also to actively pursue and achieve their inclusion in service delivery systems, decision-making processes, or the labour market.

f) *Changes in social relations: the re-ordering of domains between civil society, state and market sectors.* Social innovation ultimately determines durable changes in social – power – relations between social groups, among scales of government, and among civil society, the state and the market sectors. These dynamics, which will be explicitly addressed in Chapter 15, are directly related to those pointed out in the triangle 'visions and intentions – culture and identity building – organisational and institutional dynamics' and form the core of the community-based socially innovative practice presented in Figure 3.1. They involve relations among social groups within the community and beyond, that is, between the community and the broader society, across the different institutional and spatial scales.

But there is also the struggle and reorganisation of relations and power between the state, the (capitalist) market sectors and the social economy, and these in turn are strongly affected by the 'place-specific' opportunities for and constraints on development.

The *state*, as will be shown in most of our case studies, plays an important role here, in its different spatial articulations: the space left by capital for non-market-oriented social innovation is largely dependent on the interpretation the state gives to it – and on the power positions of different social forces within the state as an arena for class struggle (see Chapter 15). The extent to which the state maintains its independence vis-à-vis privatisation and deregulation movements is a key to the definition of the action space of social innovators in various domains.

g) *Territorial specificity*. This is the closing *tessera* in our methodological framework for analysing social innovation at the local level. The specificity of a local territory and its (local) communities is not only defined by the factors identified by the dynamics pointed out above, and by path-dependency as well as context specificity; there is also the role of con-tingency and what we could call casual and micro-agency effects that occur in specific territories and, therefore, become constituents of the 'real' character of the territory. As we shall see, in many of our case studies, existing local organisations, charismatic leaders, traditions of economic solidarity, prior experiences of public–private partnerships all contributed to the strength of local initiatives, to defining their niche in a spatially broader institutional and economic space, and in achieving social innovation.

Social innovation dynamics in the case studies

Socially innovative initiatives are of course present in, and an integral part of, our everyday life. Innovation, differentiation and variation are defining characteristics of capitalism. Indeed, the capitalist mode of production and regulation is marked by all manner of tensions, conflicts, inconsistencies, and the proliferation of spaces of experimentation. As Gibson-Graham (2006: xxxiii) have suggested, by using a different language and 'reading for difference rather than dominance', one can identify a myriad of alternative initiatives proliferating in many places around a wide range of themes, issues, and activities. One of the unanswered questions is, of course, 'What is the impact such diverse initiatives have in terms of social innovation?'

In order to answer this basic question, we must rephrase it according to our early definition of social innovation itself. This problematic thus divides into three questions: 1) Are the initiatives able to provide people with their (alienated) basic needs? 2) Do they empower the dispossessed? 3) Do they change social and power relationships? These are the questions implicit in our definition of social innovation and which have become benchmarks against which to 'measure' the impact of the initiatives we have studied in this book.

Obviously, there are no single or simple answers to these questions. The nature of social innovation initiatives, as we have stressed, is highly place- and space-dependent. Basic needs are not the same in all places and at all times. To be innovative in a bureaucratic, top-down, conservative institutional setting is not the same as in a democratic, participatory, progressive one. However, there are some basic pointers that can help identify the nature and impact of social innovation initiatives, which derive from our analytical framework. We have summarised them under five broad headings: a) *why* did a socially innovative initiative emerge, in reaction to what and/or inspired by which visions or philosophical legacies; b) *how* did it unfold, mobilising which resources, with what organisational structure and in what relation with other institutions and agents (governance aspects); c) *how wide* in spatial terms; d) *what* was the socially innovative content; and e) *how long* and lasting was the 'new'.

Why did social innovation emerge?

Social innovation at the local level can emerge in reaction to a variety of factors: deprivation, alienation, exclusion and exploitation are chief among the triggers for mobilisation. Poverty, poor housing or unemployment; property-led regeneration or other alienating urban renewal programmes; human, social and physical decay of neighbourhoods; exclusion from access to services; lack of recognition, opportunities and rights; capitalist exploitation in the workplace: all these range among the well-documented features of exclusion dynamics. But innovative processes can also arise in response to institutional or governance failures, such as, for example, restrictions in the credit system and reduction of welfare support programmes, decline of social and cultural services, privatisation of public spaces and infrastructure, commodification of leisure, reduction of civil rights and retrenchment of democracy. Eventually, people can also get together to fight for less 'material' causes, such as identity alienation, a crisis in morale or a decline in community spirit.

Understanding why a particular initiative did emerge also raises the question of defining its temporal boundaries. In our analysis of the dynamics of an innovative social initiative, it was often difficult to distinguish the particular moment or date that triggered an action in reaction to the above factors. It proved useful, however, to identify 'turning moments', that is, events – political, economic, social – that generated significant transformative processes and periods, which could be related not only to local situations, but also to the regional, national or international context, such as financial slumps, industrial crises, changes of government, shifts in funding regimes, etc. Changes in urban regimes and policy frameworks, in particular, proved a major conditioning factor – either enabling or constraining – and were used to work out useful periodisations in many of our cases: *BOM* in Antwerpen, *AQS* in Naples, *NDC* in Newcastle, or *Grätzelmanagement* in Vienna.

An important qualifier of the social innovation dynamics is their inspiration – what examples, visions or philosophical legacies served as guidelines in the mobilisation process. Sometimes action in one place is inspired by and taps into the repertoire of other contemporary initiatives. This is, for example, the case of *BOM* in Antwerp and *Olinda* in Milan. But quite revealing in our research was the link between contemporary mobilisation and the historical heritage of social movements. As shown in Chapter 2, European history is very rich in radical and alternative ideas and movements, and although there is a common heritage of values and struggles, these have been significantly influenced by national specificities and the different processes of construction of the nation state. Likewise, within nation states there are regional differences, such as, for example, that between Wales and the north-east of England and between northern and southern Italy. Indeed, we found that most of our local initiatives derived their inspiration from a repertoire of European, national and regional traditions, such as, for example, the nineteenth-century utopian communities, workers' movements, mutual aid and co-operative experiences, social Christianism, or anarchist movements, as well as the 1960s' and 1970s' 'New' Left or 'urban' movements, often themselves in continuity with local historical traditions (see Table 3.1). This does not necessarily mean that the people who launch contemporary social innovation initiatives are consciously borrowing visions and practices from past social movements, but that particular philosophical and organisational resources are more readily available and taken on board in some places than others.

How did social innovation emerge?

Once we had established why social innovation initiatives emerged, that is, in reaction to which needs or events and inspired by which philosophies and visions, it was important to explain how they grew and worked, what resources were mobilised and what organisational models they adopted. In terms of social resources, most of the cases we examined relied on the voluntary mobilisation of local deprived or concerned social groups, sometimes of the whole local community, that is, aggregating different social forces around a common goal, sometimes with the support of professional organisers or local leaders. In a number of cases, the presence of a charismatic leader – whether vicar, planner, doctor or local activist – proved crucial, such as in the *Arts Factory* in South Wales, the *Association Alentour* in Roubaix, *Olinda* in Milan and the *Ouseburn Trust* in Newcastle.

As to financial and institutional resources, some of the initiatives presented in the book were independent of state funding or regulatory mechanisms, but many made use of specific government programmes, whether local, national or European. For example, *BOM* in Antwerp, *Grätzelmanagement* in Vienna and *NDC* in Newcastle were to different extents involved in state programmes and used both local and European funds, but without abandoning their socially innovative features for a long period.

And how wide was the reach of social innovation?

Another interesting question is the spatial 'reach' of these initiatives, that is, how wide they spread. A distinction can be made between: (i) neighbourhood-centred initiatives; (ii) neighbourhood initiatives with a wider spread/impact effect; and (iii) city-wide initiatives (see Table 3.1). But the spatial reach considered in these terms only takes into account the impact of the initiative as such and not the 'parallel' learning and communication dynamics in which most of these projects are involved. From the latter point of view, many of the initiatives examined here, although territorially rooted, have 'scaled up' by networking with other projects and movements, at a regional, national and even global scale, either within formal European arrangements (such as e.g. LA21, URBAN, Antipoverty programmes), or through spontaneous affinity search (e.g. *City Mine(d)* in Brussels, *BOM* in Antwerp, *Leoncavallo* and *Olinda* in Milan, *AQS* in Naples). This networking provided crucial organisational and tactical exchanges.

In assessing the spatial dimension of the case studies two important questions were whether neighbourhood-based strategies work better than city-wide initiatives and whether inward-oriented relations make a stronger impact than network-oriented initiatives. The distinction between neighbourhood focus and wider spatial-scale targeting is indeed a scientifically and politically significant issue and the empirical findings of our research show that a combination of scales, especially for partnering and resource mobilisation, had a positive impact in terms of social innovation.

What was the content of social innovation?

The aims of the socially innovative initiatives reviewed in this book are quite varied. They range from mechanisms to make the economy more social – such as training programmes, initiating economic activities offering new or neglected use-values, enabling social and ethical micro-credit, consulting small and social economy ventures – to artistic and cultural projects. They also put forward wider and less material claims, such as the promotion of active citizenship (social and political rights), the strengthening of identity through the production of cultural and social services, cultural change by fostering recognition, integration and tolerance. Among the latter, for example, we can mention the *Arts Factory* and *Olinda* initiatives, which fostered understanding and respect of diversity through transversal community activities and services.

Beyond such diversity, in each of our case studies we have looked for the impact of the initiative in terms of our *tripartite definition of social innovation* (see Table 3.1). From this perspective, most of our socially innovative initiatives provided for the *satisfaction of basic human needs* that were alienated in one way or another, in qualitatively new forms, content and/or process. As already mentioned, these human needs are not just material, but also relate to the sphere of identity, recognition, equal opportunity and citizenship. Therefore, their satisfaction produced effects not only in economic terms, but also in terms

Table 3.1 Presentation of case studies

Social innovation initiative	Type of community and spatial reach of initiative	Approach and content	Philosophical roots	Dimensions of social innovation
Centro Sociale Leoncavallo Milan, Italy	Located in the north-eastern outskirts of Milan, it caters to a broader community of homeless, immigrants, marginalised people, with a multi-scalar spatial reach and national networking.	Self-managed, informal organisation providing services to the disadvantaged. The provision of meals and shelter, but also cultural events blurs the distinction between suppliers and users and provides for recognition and socialisation.	'New Left', very radical, urban movements of the 1970s, with an anarchist streak.	Satisfaction of basic needs (material and cultural). Empowerment through recognition and changes in social relations within city at large.
Associazione Olinda Milan, Italy	Neighbourhood initiative, involving former psychiatric hospital, but with metropolitan and national reach, through networking with similar initiatives.	Self-help social co-operative initiative. Opening traditional mental health facility to city, combining training and employment for inpatients with services to the city (restaurant, hostel, workshops).	National movement in favour of closing psychiatric hospitals merging with 'New Left' movements in the 1970s.	The satisfaction of basic needs (employment of inpatients) is instrumental to Empowerment, together with changes in social relations through services and cultural activities.
AQS – Associazione Quartieri Spagnoli Naples, Italy	Located in a deprived neighbourhood of central Naples (about 15,000 inhabitants), it is a neighbourhood-oriented initiative, with some broader networking.	Association for the self-production of social services (especially for children and young women) as a means to move away from criminality and acquire capabilities.	Social Christianism merging with 1970s militant left-wing social action.	Basic needs (social services and employment) as a way to empower marginalised youth. Changes in governance relations within the neighbourhood and with external institutions.

Social innovation initiative	Type of community and spatial reach of initiative	Approach and content	Philosophical roots	Dimensions of social innovation
Association Alentour Roubaix, France	Located in L'Epeule, a deprived and socially fragmented neighbourhood (9,000 inhabitants) of West Roubaix. Mostly oriented to the community.	Community-oriented integrated approach: reinforcing social links in the neighbourhood and identity through self-help, social services, local employment initiatives, as well as involvement in local urban management.	Bourgeois philanthropy, but also French tradition in social economy.	Satisfaction of basic needs (social services, training, employment) as a means to change social relations within the neighbourhood (creation of trust) and empower residents in local urban management.
Arts Factory Rhondda Valley, South Wales, UK	Deprived neighbourhood (3,400 inhabitants) in Ferndale Ward, oriented to community members, but reaching out to other places in the Rhondda Valley.	Community-owned enterprise. Through classes, activities and services, provides opportunities for personal development, social contacts, work.	Self-help and mutualist traditions, but breaking away from male-dominated traditional workers' culture.	Through the satisfaction of basic needs (material and cultural), empowerment of residents and change in social relations and cultural attitudes.
Ouseburn Trust Newcastle, UK	Lower end of valley along the river Ouseburn: Ouseburn Ward (4.600 inhabitants). Mostly oriented to community needs.	Local association created to defend community interests against redevelopment pressures.	'New Left' and 'urban movements' of the 1960s and 1970s. Roots in British tradition of community work and Church militancy.	Mainly empowerment of community interests and changes in governance practices by establishing dialogue with local government.

Table 3.1 (continued)

Social innovation initiative	Type of community and spatial reach of initiative	Approach and content	Philosophical roots	Dimensions of social innovation
NDC – New Deal for Communities Newcastle, UK	An institutionally established urban neighbourhood (4,000 households) made up of distinct cultural communities. Neighbourhood dimension, within national programme.	Programme launched by central government to empower communities. Tensions between performance-oriented evaluation criteria and top-down approach by government, and social aims of community leadership.	Self-help and mutualist tradition. Community development approach from the 1970s.	Basic needs (housing, services 'customised' to neighbourhood needs). Empowerment of community, leading to changes in governance practices in the domain of planning.
City Mine(d) Brussels, Belgium	Citywide project, with relevant networking connections at the national and international levels.	Self-organised urban initiative that both fosters (with material, logistical and networking support) and occasionally initiates a variety of self-determined urban actions. Seeks to establish new alliances through multi-scalar organisation and mobilisation.	'New' urban movements, combining aspects of the anarchist tradition with grass-roots social mobilisation and self-organisation.	The satisfaction of needs such as artistic expression and re-appropriation of public space is instrumental in empowering marginalised groups and in changing governance relations.

Social innovation initiative	Type of community and spatial reach of initiative	Approach and content	Philosophical roots	Dimensions of social innovation
BOM-*Buurt Ontwikkelings-maatschappij* Antwerp, Belgium	City-wide initiative involving three large deprived neighbourhoods: North-East Antwerp, South Edge and Canal Area (about 100,000 inhabitants).	Neighbourhood development corporation (partnerships between urban government institutions and civil society organisations, supported by EU funds) for alternative integrated socio-economic renewal of deprived urban areas.	1970s 'urban movements' engaging with community action.	'Integrated' area development combining satisfaction of basic needs (economic, social cultural) and transformation of social relations within the neighbourhood (trust and empowerment) and between neighbourhood and external private and public institutions (change in power relations and governance).
Grätzelmanagement Vienna, Austria	Two working-class neighbourhoods with high presence of immigrants, in the Brigittenau and Leopoldstadt districts. Mostly oriented to residents, but inserted in urban institutional dynamics.	Pilot project, attempting to introduce more participatory governance practices 'from above' and to reform organisational system of urban planning.	'Red' Vienna experience after First World War. Then, top-down 'gentle urban renewal' approach in the 1970s, in the tradition of Austrian controlled modernisation and social integration from above.	Satisfaction of basic needs from above. Changes in relations between different levels of government. Limited empowerment of the community because of bias towards business.

Source: Authors

of social, political and cultural inclusion. The second dimension in our definition of social innovation stresses the impact of the initiative in terms of an
increase in human capabilities and hence the *empowerment* of people, groups
or communities, previously excluded from governance dynamics because of
their lack of consciousness, rights, skills, opportunities, powerful social capital
or political networks. This was the case in the large majority of our socially
innovative initiatives, although to different extents, as we shall see. Ultimately,
most of our initiatives, through the satisfaction of basic needs and/or the
empowerment of people, did contribute to *changing power relations* among social
forces (e.g. between capital and labour, residents and developers, immigrants
and neighbourhood councils), between civil society, the market and the state,
as well as between different scales of government, in the direction of more
democratic and participatory governance practices.

Social innovation was, thus, in many cases about the politicisation of local
communities against, for example, an oppressive (local) state, by fighting budget
cutbacks or promoting actions to maintain local services. It did involve mobilisation against conservative party politics and machines, against real estate
owners and developers, capitalist investment and disinvestment. It did trigger
struggles for greater control of the local economy or more democratic planning
procedures. In some instances, it did support equal rights or empower projects
around immigration, class, gender, sex or refugee issues.

How long and lasting was the 'new'?

Finally, it is important to assess the time frame and durability of innovation –
how long can the 'new' stay new? How long did it take for a common understanding to develop, for formal or informal rules and roles to become established,
for claims to be fulfilled and needs, inclusion, empowerment to be institutionalised? Alternative initiatives often rely on a combination of 'temporary'
factors, such as funding, peoples' time and skills, spaces to meet, and sometimes
they only emerge in response to a temporary situation. Therefore, they go
through different life cycles in which the main principles might be redefined,
roles changed, governance mechanisms redesigned. Typically, initiatives might
start small and local, only to scale up and become bigger. Or they may begin
with a radical and confrontational edge but then be co-opted by the formal
structures of the state or the market or simply exhaust their drive. Here the
tensions between innovation and institutionalisation, on the one hand, and
between success and failure, on the other, are crucial for assessing the impact
and duration of social innovation.

The case studies and the comparative research methodology

The SINGOCOM project built on a research methodology that had been
developed and progressively fine-tuned in previous projects (Moulaert *et al.*,

2003). In presenting the results of that research, this book makes an original contribution to an expanding body of urban comparative work (Ward, 2008). It does so by improving the holistic methodology already used in the URSPIC project (Moulaert *et al.*, 2003).

Holistic research methodology goes back to Smuts (1926) and Diesing (1971) and is inherently comparative (Ramstadt, 1986). As summarised by Moulaert and Nussbaumer (2005) in the starting phase of the SINGOCOM project, a holistic methodology involves the selection of an analytical 'theme' (e.g. people with housing needs), within a particular (territorial) subsystem (e.g. an urban neighbourhood). The theme is then analysed in a number of selected subsystems, checking whether the theme is as relevant for all subsystems and/or whether there are differences. A typology of the theme and its variants is developed. Once the theme is empirically established, other themes and the linkages between them are investigated in the various subsystems. Several 'validated' themes can eventually be connected and interpreted as being part of a coherent pattern model, that is, a holist theory. Such an approach is inherently comparative, in time and space, allowing for specificity, within a general interpretive framework.

In our holistic–comparative SINGOCOM framework the neighbourhoods or local communities in which the innovative initiative developed represented the subsystems. The themes were all related to conditions of social exclusion and socially innovative strategies to overcome it. The sixteen case studies that were investigated 'in depth' in the course of the research were the result of an interactive selection process, out of a larger 'data bank' of innovative initiatives, set up by the local research teams at the onset of the project.[2] The information that was collected for these in-depth case studies was both quantitative and qualitative. The strategy for collecting this information was left to each of the local teams, as each possessed the unique local knowledge about where to find the best sources of information. National, regional or local statistics were gathered, policy documents were analysed, interviews with local experts and, in some cases, participatory research (e.g. the *Leoncavallo* case in Milan and to some extent the *City Mine(d)* case in Brussels) were carried out. In the *Alentour* case in Roubaix a survey by questionnaire was also carried out among the neighbourhood residents, which provided a rich source of additional information. What ensured consistency and comparability across the different cases, and the sometimes different nature and depth of quantitative and qualitative information, was the holistic analytical framework.

Indeed, as nicely put by Nijman (2007: 1), comparative urban research deals with the issue of 'what is true of all cities and what is true of one city at a given point in time'. Our analysis moved between these two poles and, as with any multi-sited research, maintaining comparability between case studies while providing room for the specificity of each context and research strategy, was a challenge. It was clear from the beginning that social innovation although a shared meta-theme, as we had defined it, was going to 'mean' different things in different places. While, for example, collaboration between private and public institutions was 'innovative' in southern Italy, it was suffered as 'conservative' in the UK. But we maintained our holistic 'methodological' consistency across case studies by constantly referring back to the common definition, analytical concepts, and theoretical bases of our notion of social innovation at the local level, as spelled out in the previous sections of this chapter.

In the end, besides ensuring comparability, the analytical power of ALMOLIN allowed us to identify and assess — across the different case studies — those features and dynamics of alternative initiatives that were most conducive to the introduction of lasting social innovations, either by responding to basic social needs in innovative ways, by empowering excluded or marginalised social groups, or by changing the power relationships between different actors and/or scales of government, always in the direction of a more democratic, more inclusive and more equitable society.

In the next chapters of this book we present ten of the sixteen case studies investigated in the SINGOCOM project. These cases were selected because they represented to a good extent the full spectrum of the socially innovative experiences we examined and they also allowed some interesting cross-country comparison, highlighting how the different historical and institutional contexts influence the nature of social innovation. The basic features of their socially innovative impact, historical roots and spatial reach are charted in Table 3.1, whereas their detailed features and dynamics, as framed by the ALMOLIN analytical approach, are recounted in the chapters that follow. In this presentation, the pendulum — to use Nijman's (2007) words — certainly shifts towards explaining what is true of one place at a given time; but then, in the last two chapters of the book, we shall return to the realm of what is consistently manifest across all cases.

Notes

1 Figure 3.1 is an improved version of the chart published in Moulaert *et al.* (2005: 1982).
2 Each local team carried out a survey of innovative local initiatives in each of the nine cities, based on the 'questions' put forward in our methodology. Out of this broader database the final cases were selected in a collegial meeting of the research project teams. The full SINGOCOM data bank can be consulted at http://users.skynet.be/bk368453/singocom/index2.html.

References

Amin, A. (2004) 'Regions unbound: towards a new politics of place', *Geografiska Annaler*, 86: 33–44.

Brenner, N. (2004) *New State Spaces*, Oxford: Oxford University Press.

Diesing, P. (1971) *Patterns of Discovery in Social Sciences*, Chicago: Aldine-Atherton.

Gibson-Graham, J.K. (2006) *A Postcapitalist Politics*, Minneapolis: University of Minnesota Press.

Jessop, B. (2000) 'The crisis of the national spatio-temporal fix and the ecological dominance of globalizing capitalism', *International Journal of Urban and Regional Research*, 24: 323–60.

—— (2008) *State Power*, Cambridge: Polity Press.

—— Brenner, N. and Jones, M. (2008) 'Theorizing sociospatial relations', *Environment and Planning D: Society and Space*, 26: 389–401.

Marston, S. (2000) 'The social construction of scale', *Progress in Human Geography*, 24: 219–42.

Massey, D. (2004) 'Geographies of responsibility', *Geografiska Annaler: Series B, Human Geography*, 86: 5–18.

Moulaert, F. (1995) 'Measuring socioeconomic disintegration at the local level in Europe: an analytical framework', in G. Room (ed.) *Beyond the Threshold, the Measurement and Analysis of Social Exclusion*, Bristol: The Policy Press.

—— (2007) 'Introduction: Social innovation and governance in European cities. Urban development between path-dependency and radical innovation', *European Urban and Regional Studies*, 14: 195–209.

—— and Ailenei, O. (2005) 'Social economy, third sector and solidarity relations: a conceptual synthesis from history to present', *Urban Studies*, 42: 2037–53.

—— and Hamdouch, A. (2005) 'Alternative models of local innovation (ALMOLIN)', in F. Moulaert (ed.) *Social Innovation, Governance and Community Building – SINGOCOM*, Final Report, Contract HPSE-CT-2001-00070 Funded under the key action 'Improving the Socio-economic Knowledge Base' of FP5, European Commission – DG Research, 78–101. Online. Available: http://cordis.europa.eu/fetch?ACTION=D&SESSION=&DOC=1&LAN=EN&RCN=9080&CALLER=DOCS_LIB (Accessed 27 December 2007).

—— and Leontidou, L. (1995) 'Localités déintégrées et stratégies de lutte contre la pauvreté: une réflexion méthodologique post-moderne', *Espaces et Sociétés*, 78, 35–53.

—— and Mehmood, A. (2010) 'Analysing regional development and policy: a structural-realist approach', *Regional Studies*, 44(1): 103–18.

—— and Nussbaumer, J. (2005) 'Defining the social economy and its governance at the neighbourhood level: a methodological reflection', *Urban Studies*, 42: 2071–208.

—— Rodríguez, A. and Swyngedouw, E. (eds) (2003) *The Globalized City: Economic Restructuring and Social Polarization in European Cities*, Oxford: Oxford University Press.

—— Martinelli, F., Swyngedouw, E. and González, S. (2005) 'Towards alternative model(s) of local innovation', *Urban Studies*, 42: 1969–90.

Nijman, J. (2007) 'Introduction – Comparative Urbanism', *Urban Geography*, 28: 1–6.

Purcell, M. (2006) 'Urban democracy and the local trap', *Urban Studies*, 43: 1921–41.

Ramstad, Y. (1986) 'A pragmatist's quest for holistic knowledge: the scientific methodology of John R. Commons', *Journal of Economic Issues*, 20: 1067–105.

SINGOCOM databank. Online. Available: http://users.skynet.be/bk368453/singocom/index2.html (Accessed 1 June 2009).

Smuts, J.C. (1926) *Holism and Evolution*, New York: The Macmillan Company.

Swyngedouw, E. (1997) 'Neither global nor local: "glocalization" and the politics of scale', in K. Cox (ed.) *Spaces of Globalisation*, New York: Guilford.

—— (2004) 'Globalisation or "Glocalisation"? Networks, Territories and Rescaling', *Cambridge Review of International Affairs*, 17: 25–48.

Ward, K. (2008) 'Editorial – Toward a Comparative (Re)turn in Urban Studies? Some Reflections', *Urban Geography*, 29: 405–10.

Williams, C. (2005) *A Commodified World? Mapping the Limits of Capitalism*, London: Zed Books.

4 Social innovation in the wake of urban movements

The *Centro Sociale Leoncavallo* in Milan: a case of 'flexible institutionalisation'[1]

Andrea Membretti

The history: path-dependency as the basis for innovation

The *Centro Sociale Leoncavallo* is the most popular 'centro sociale' (social centre) in Italy, with more than thirty years of activity in the town of Milan. As to its connection with social movements and civil society, the history of the Centre can be divided into three main phases: this sequence shows how the Social Centre has always been part of larger urban and national movements, even if in a dialectical and innovative relationship.[2]

The beginning: Leoncavallo as a territorial expression of the 1970s' urban movements

The *Leoncavallo Social Centre* was born in Milan in 1975, in a town still eminently industrial, through the initiative of a group of young people, coming from the so-called 'extra-parliamentary left'. During that period in Milan, as in many other Italian towns, the wave of social movements emanating from the 1968 mobilisation was still in full swing (Della Porta and Diani, 1997). For this reason, it was impossible to identify anything akin to a local civil society, as the field of social aggregation was mainly political action, even if based on the expression of human needs, such as the claim for a house to live in or for city spaces for free culture (Pickvance, 2003).

The founding act of *Leoncavallo* was the illegal occupation of a former pharmaceutical factory, in Leoncavallo Street, located in the north-east of Milan, just inside the core of the Casoretto blue-collar district. As with many other similar experiences around Italy, the Centre was set up with the aim of creating a self-managed place, able to couple the bottom–up supply of socio-cultural services to the neighbourhood (e.g. child care, classes, concerts) with a wider political action and claim (Ibba, 1995). In that period, self-managed social centres represented what has been defined as a 'movement area' (Melucci, 1984) – a network of (g)local actors sharing a common counterculture and communicating/interacting one with the other, even if not unified by a strong ideology or clearly defined common goals. They represented the territorial and physical expression of a social and cultural milieu, claiming new rights of citizenship as these were defined as a result of the so-called 'new movements' of the 1970s (ibid., 1984). Such social centres were strongly rooted in their neighbourhoods, in a relationship of osmosis.

'Ebb tide': the dramatic end of a movement era

The end of the mobilisation wave at the end of the 1970s drove the Centre to a phase of 'regression'. Milan was changing dramatically, both in its social composition – with the decline of the working class and related neighbourhood communities – and in its urban structure – with the closure of factories and the beginning of residential suburban sprawl.

After the last spark of the 1977 youth countercultural movement (Balestrini and Moroni, 1997) – in which the Social Centre once again played an important role – *Leoncavallo*'s activists, as in many other social centres around Italy, drifted into a long period of crisis, characterised by drug abuse problems, but also by urban violence (street fights against groups of fascists) and by police repression. The political action of the Centre increasingly focused on very narrow and radical interventions, for example, the liberation of 'Red Brigade' prisoners in jail.

On the neighbourhood side, it was a period of self-exclusion: in a territory changing dramatically under the pressure of gentrification, *Leoncavallo* became extremely dogmatic in its ideological approach, in strong opposition to every kind of political and socio-cultural institution at the local and national scale. The defence of a 'residual' and in some ways a 'tribal' identity seemed to be the main reason for the activists to hold on to the Centre.

New movements in town, a renewed role for the Social Centre

In the mid 1980s, an inversion in these 'regressive' dynamics occurred (Mayer, 2000). *Leoncavallo* gradually reverted to its original openness to the city, overcoming its late social and political marginality. Through the organisation of countercultural public events, the Social Centre became once again – and with a wider reach – the melting pot for different social and cultural milieus. At the same time, prompted by these dynamics of differentiation and enlargement, new organisational and professional skills were deployed by activists, setting the basis for the subsequent debate about social enterprise and the role of *Leoncavallo* in urban social change. In this sense, the original idea, at the root of the occupation in 1975, of a 'territorial' community organising a self-managed response to the needs of the neighbourhood, was revived and re-invented on a metropolitan scale. In a way, it was the beginning of a new 'glocal' identity.

The year 1989 was a major turning point: in a political climate dominated by neoliberal thinking, the mayor of Milan accepted the request by the owners of the building occupied by *Leoncavallo* to evict its occupants. The violent intervention of the police and the strong resistance of the activists produced wide social support for the Centre, in Milan and Italy at large, thanks also to the media that amplified the event. After a couple of days the building, which in the meanwhile had been partially destroyed by bulldozers, was reoccupied and rebuilt, brick by brick. Indeed, the period of socio-political isolation of *Leoncavallo* ended in 1989 and a new era of social rooting, not only in the neighbourhood but in the city as a whole began, based on a wide network of supporters mobilised in the earlier days.

This new role was confirmed in 1990 when another wave of student mobilisation arose against the privatisation of culture and research. This perceived social centres – and *Leoncavallo* above all – as relevant 'models' for political action and for sociality and cultural production in particular. Exposure to this movement pushed *Leoncavallo* further into a process of de-ideologisation: although a strong leftist connotation remained, a growing pragmatism, first of all in the relationships with other political and socio-cultural institutions, became a main element of the Centre's identity. Associations, political parties, journalists and intellectuals, who as representatives of the 'institutional establishment' were strongly opposed by the Centre just a few years before, now became interlocutors. A network of relationships began to grow and develop, which represents today a major asset in the socio-political legitimation of *Leoncavallo* and its claims (Moroni *et al.*, 1996).

Gaining legitimation, facing institutionalisation

In 1994, a right-wing campaign was initiated against *Leoncavallo* and the occupants were forced to leave the building. However, the support coming from different sectors of a growing, protesting civil society was even more effective on this occasion.

A massive people's demonstration was called by *Leoncavallo* in Milan, and afterwards a new site was illegally occupied: a really large former printing factory, not so far from the previous site, which has become the current location of the Centre. The *Leoncavallo* case, with its high symbolic and political implications, was even discussed in the national parliament, where many members of leftist political parties supported and declared the importance of this social actor in Milanese cultural and political life. Wide social support among intellectuals, political groups and artists became widespread in defence of the Centre. Eventually, and partly because the owners of the building did not formally request it, the police and local institutions decided not to evict the occupiers of the printing factory in the belief that *Leoncavallo* would be able, in the future, to become a formalised organisation and pay rent. In the year 2000, however, since no agreement had been reached with the owners, the Court of Milan ruled that the Centre must leave the building. At the same time, however, the sentence was suspended because of the public interest status accorded to *Leoncavallo* by the very same court.

In 2001, in order to gain greater public visibility for the Centre and have a voice inside the institutional political arena, one of the informal leaders of *Leoncavallo* was elected to the city council as an independent representative of a left-wing party (Rifondazione Comunista).[3] A few months later the assembly of the Centre decided to establish the '*Leoncavallo* Foundation', which was intended to involve many political, social, cultural and economic actors from Milan and other cities. The Foundation was designed as an instrument to allow the legal use of the building and the promotion of legal activities within it, although the Centre, through its informal groups and structures, would continue to promote a wide range of services and activities on the borderline between formal and informal status. The new structure was finally implemented in May 2004, with an initial capital of €100,000, thanks to the participation of associations, political parties, intellectuals and individuals interested in promoting active citizenship in Milan. As of 2009, the Foundation was still working to find an agreement with the owners of the building concerning the conditions of occupation.

Towards a 'flexible institutionalisation': organisational dynamics and relationships with civil society

The story of *Leoncavallo* just sketched here clearly shows how the Social Centre has gone through a process of public legitimation and organisational consolidation based on actions and approaches that were the fruit of nearly thirty years' experience. It therefore represents a particular model for the organisation of resources, the management of social and political relations and the interpretation of a reality, whose major characteristic is the continuous tension between the need for structure and the need for flexibility. On the one hand, it moves in the direction of a stronger internal division of labour, a clearer differentiation of competences and more intense bridges with institutions (social, cultural, political); on the other hand, it aims to maintain informality, the osmosis with the movements, and individual versatility within the organisation. In other words, it is possible to speak of 'flexible institutionalisation' (Membretti, 2003), meaning not a state, but a process of constant re-balance of conflicting forces.

This process of consolidation, strongly linked with the main dimensions of social innovation as defined in Chapter 3, is based on two main elements:

- the reflexive skills developed by the Social Centre, which enable its activists to give periodic criticism of the organisation's basic principles and innovative adaptation to the changes of the external milieu (urban regime); this flexibility is reflected in innovation in social relationships, both at the organisational inner level and at the broader territorial level (relationships with the neighbourhood, with the users, etc.);
- the net-like and self-managed structure that enables the Social Centre to maintain a constant link with socio-political and cultural movements; this

flexibility is strongly linked with innovation in governance processes at different spatial levels and with their articulations.

The current situation of the Centre clearly reflects the above tensions; the *Leoncavallo* Foundation project, which was able to manage the Centre's institutional relations – especially with the landlords, to whom rent would be paid – represents the highest point reached so far in the dialectics between movement and institution (Alberoni, 1981). A further dialectic element comes in the form of the presence, since 2001, of a leader of *Leoncavallo* on the Milan Town Council and, since 2006, in the national parliament. This enables the expression of the movements' voice in local institutions and the consolidation and intensification of the Centre's relations with other institutional actors.

From this point of view, the relationship with civil society and social movements, which was built up over the years, nowadays represents a resource that *Leoncavallo* tries to use in the dialectics with political and administrative local institutions: the institutionalisation of the Centre should thus be interpreted as the construction of a socio-political actor, able to face and deal with both the political and the economic institutions of Milan and the nation. This strategy, even if not explicit, attempts to overcome a typical weakness of social movements, that is, their difficulty in mobilising resources in a long-term perspective (Della Porta and Diani, 1997; Vitale, 2007). 'Flexible institutional-isation' seems, therefore, to be the adaptive and winning response, in terms of innovation in governance and in social relationships, of a movement actor facing dramatic changes, both in the local urban regime and in the socio-cultural and political frame.

Bottom-up innovation: the collective definition and satisfaction of human needs

From the beginning of its history, *Leoncavallo* has been dealing with human needs: since 1975, the Social Centre has operated on the basis of welfare services, culture and sociality, with special attention to their territorial dimensions. Given its continuous involvement in different waves of urban social movement, consideration of the satisfaction of human needs means in the first place an analysis of the processes of people's involvement in the definition/satisfaction of their needs as a socio-political action. In these dynamics of empowerment, the physical space plays a strong role, and this starts with the articulation of a variety of spaces inside the Social Centre: spaces in which different services are supplied and where they intermingle, producing important 'contaminations' between different needs and different people.[4]

Satisfying human needs: culture, sociality and welfare

In different ways and at different scales, *Leoncavallo* has provided social services for thirty years. It has contributed to the definition of and response to two

Table 4.1 Sociality, cultural and welfare needs

Sociality and cultural needs	Since the beginning of the 1990s, the Centre has been responding to the growing demand for occasions and spaces for the production of an autonomous and non-commercialised culture. At the same time, *Leoncavallo* has been offering opportunities for social exchange, under the auspices of non-exploitative relationships among people.
	Sociality and cultural needs seem to cross traditional class boundaries: the last survey (2001) carried out among users of *Leoncavallo* cultural services (Membretti, 2003) shows that attendance at concerts, plays, debates and exhibitions is largely diversified by age, sex, work conditions and place of residence. Moreover, the needs appear to be quite widespread, as proven by *Leoncavallo*'s quite large number of users, about 100,000 people per year.
Welfare needs	*Leoncavallo* also operates in the field that we can define as 'civil welfare' (de Leonardis, 1998): these are services strongly related to the citizenship dimension, i.e. the concrete response to those basic rights (right to food, clothing, housing, health, security, etc.), without which a human being not only cannot be defined a citizen, but also does not even have the dignity of a person. The demand for these services comes from migrants, the homeless, psychologically impaired people and, more generally, people below the poverty threshold. Since the mid 1990s the Centre has been offering these people free meals, short-term hospitality and protection from the persecutions of the police and of xenophobic groups. Particular consideration is given to migrants: legal assistance to help regularise their position in Italy, information about job opportunities and, in some cases, direct supply of jobs in the Social Centre. The self-managed style of the Centre (*autogestione*) and its spatially versatile organisation also create opportunities for socialisation and the development of face-to-face community relationships, thereby responding to a demand for 'human recognition' (Taylor and Habermas, 1998) from people who daily live the condition of non-citizens and 'non-persons' (Dal Lago, 1999).

Source: Author

different but related categories of needs: culture and sociality, on the one hand, and welfare and social needs, on the other.

Looking at the organisational dynamics of such services as detailed in Table 4.1, in the *Leoncavallo* case we can speak of a 'joint construction' of both needs and responses, that is, more than just responses to needs: the Social Centre is not just a supplier of services, but a physical and socio-cultural space in which – and because of which – a collective discussion about human needs and the means to satisfy them is nourished. The Social Centre's welfare services are therefore to be interpreted as spheres of activation and of qualification of the actors – individual and collective – that apply for them. Through a recognition and empowerment process, human needs turn into actual rights, which are defined by a space and a group of actual interpersonal relationships. In this sense, 'empowerment' tends to coincide with a process of 'active citizenship construction': to enable people is therefore to give them the opportunity to develop socio-political capabilities, both as individuals and as citizens.

Defining human needs: enabling the users

Human needs find a response, or even better, a sphere of collective definition and collective response, inside the physical, relational and symbolic settings within which *Leoncavallo*'s services and activity are organised. The self-management organisational approach tends, in fact, to give priority to informal practices, rather than to the role of the subjects who activate them, or to formalised procedures. Therefore, the dimension of informality and horizontality in interpersonal relationships makes the distinction between supplier and user in a self-managed service far less rigid, as compared with that in state- and market-provided services. In this new approach, services are open to the participation of users, who can co-operate with their management in some way. During large events, for example – such as big concerts, art exhibitions, etc. – it is possible for some users (10–15 each time) to work as volunteers in the bar or in the self-service restaurant inside the Centre. In this way, working for the Centre becomes the opportunity to experiment with the 'other side' of the services, destructuring the dualistic idea of a rigid distinction between staff and customers.

Another peculiar characteristic of the services provided is their symbolic frame, which has an essentially political nature: the service is a channel for the communication of socio-political content, a means for user activation towards involvement in action or, at least, support for the Social Centre's action (Membretti, 1997). The process of institutionalisation of services is therefore a process of institutionalisation of collective mobilisation, or, in other words, of citizen activation.

For these reasons it seems appropriate to use the term 'enablers' instead of the term 'suppliers' for individuals and groups managing these services: they are actors who facilitate user empowerment through the management of services and spaces. The enablers are, in our case, informal groups and associations that operate in the Social Centre and that autonomously manage the spaces in which they operate and where services are provided. From this point of view, the spatial dimension is fundamental: *Leoncavallo*'s physical configuration, in fact, seems to be a multiple frame for the dialectical definition of human needs that are discussed and faced. Those spaces enter, therefore, a process of 'enactment' (Weick, 1995) of a milieu that consists of them, of the users, of the symbolic meanings, of the practices and of the connections with the outside world. From this point of view, the joint construction of the demand and the response to social needs can be thought of as a process of sense-making, of construction/interpretation of a shared reality, within an activated space.

Framing human needs: the role of spaces

The definition and response to human needs – cultural, socio-political and of socialisation – originate from a plurality of physical spaces inside the Social Centre, in which different activities and services develop. These spaces, however, are not clearly distinct on the basis of their function: in fact, the culture/sociality and welfare macro-dimensions are continuously mixed up in them. Roles are multidimensional and multifaceted and relationships based on reciprocity, rather than exploitation, are promoted.

Spaces are in fact 'enacted' in different ways (Weick, 1995), depending on the actors that operate inside them and on the services organised: for example, in the same space and at the same time several activities can coexist: a restaurant service – whose customers are first of all the users of cultural services such as concerts and debates – a free-meal service for the homeless and immigrants and also a dining room for the activists of the Centre, all of them mixed together inside and throughout the physical space and the organisational procedures. In this particular example, the space represents a very concrete occasion to put different kinds of services and populations into a mutual relationship, in the direction of a 'contamination' between users and activists of the Centre. Labelling processes, typical of both private and public socio-cultural services, are reduced in this approach; on the contrary, spaces become the physical element for different processes of framing (Goffman, 1974) each time these are enacted from different interactions and from the related sense-making processes of symbolic interpretations.

The abandoned areas of the former printing office occupied in 1994 were – and still are – involved in a continued definition of the functions, the goals and therefore the identity (or, better, the many identities) of the social actors who work in them and identify with them. The development of such reflexive abilities produces a vision of *Leoncavallo*'s space based on the binomial 'introvert-extrovert'. The tension between these two opposite poles has therefore become – in the actual management of services – the experimentation field of an actual idea of society and social relations, a space considered as a meeting point between community and society, and between several communities. In this sense – both symbolically and actually – the court and the square (or, better, the courts and the squares) coexist in the Centre and interface continuously through the practices carried out by the different actors involved. Openness towards the outside and an inner 'protection' are therefore elements that coexist in the Centre and its services (Membretti, 2004).

The resources for a 'glocal' socio-political action

Finally, it is important to stress the role of resources in *Leoncavallo*'s social and political action. Nowadays, the Centre can rely on a set of different resources, accumulated over time (see Table 4.2): individual and collective skills and capabilities (also in the organisational field), social capital, public consensus and, only minimally, financial funds. Last but not least, it should be borne in

Table 4.2 Resources for 'glocal' socio-political action

Human resources	Eighty people work regularly in the Social Centre: half receive a minimum salary, called 'solidarity token'[a]; the rest of the group consists of 'pure volunteers'. The social composition of these two groups varies with respect to skills and expertise, with a mix of specialisation and social background. In this sense, socio-political participation in the Centre's activities becomes a means to increase both individual capabilities (Sen, 1992) and networks of relationships (Granovetter, 1983).
Organisational resources	Since its foundation, the Centre has always based its operation on the self-management (*autogestione*) principle and practice (Membretti, 2007b, 1997; Ritter, 1980). These involve horizontal relationships (lack of hierarchy), informality (lack of fixed roles) and assembly democracy (search for unanimous consent). Every inner space of the Social Centre is self-managed by a group of activists, with considerable autonomy. Thus, *Leoncavallo*'s organisation consists of a network structure with a high degree of organisational flexibility and decentralised decision-making.
Financial resources	In order to preserve its autonomy, the Centre is based on a self-financing principle. The two main sources of revenue are entrance tickets for cultural events and the takings from the bar and self-service restaurant. It must be stressed that profits would be non-existent if the Centre paid taxes on the sale of its services. Moreover, the economic survival of the Centre would not be possible without the illegal occupation of its premises. Therefore, the building is a major 'financial' asset of *Leoncavallo*.
Political resources	*Leoncavallo* has always been connected to social and political movements – urban, national and international – linked to the so-called 'extra-parliamentary left'. The strong bonds with the movements have always represented an important political resource to be used in periods of conflict with the institutions. The recent wave of anti-globalisation has significantly influenced the Social Centre, which is still a point of reference for various campaigns against neoliberal order. Also important is the support from a section of public opinion now awakened to the problem of self-managed social spaces and to the fight against neoliberal privatisation of metropolitan space and socio-cultural services.
Cultural and artistic resources	From the beginning the Centre has given a central role to the cultural and creative expression dimensions and it has always been crossed by various artistic trends, connected with wider national and international cultural movements. In the last decade, the Centre has further consolidated this role and has become a landmark in Milan – and in national and international milieus – for many countercultural trends (music, theatre, comics, publishing, etc.). This is possible not only because of the network of personal and direct ties to the main milieus of countercultural production, but also to some more institutionalised actors of the art and culture industries.

[a] In 2001, the amount of the 'solidarity token' ranged between €400 and €500 per month. At the end of 2001, a discussion developed and the initial notion of the 'solidarity token' – meant as a reimbursement and based on the principle of reciprocity – has been evolving in the direction of a notion of 'income': in this sense the 'symbolic' value of the token is moving into the sphere of workers' 'rights', even if within a communitarian frame.

Source: Author

mind that the occupied building is the *conditio sine qua non* for the very existence of the Centre, thereby representing a fundamental material resource.

Citizenship as an innovative service: a process of social, political and economic 'reintegration'

The analysis of organisational dynamics in the case of *Leoncavallo* is evidence of an important connection between the three main building-blocks of what, following the definition given in Chapter 3 of this book, we consider as social innovation: a) the definition and satisfaction of human needs; b) the changes in social relationships; c) the empowerment and participation processes. This connection has developed through a path-dependent institutionalisation of the services offered by the Social Centre, in a dialectical relationship between movement and social enterprise.

Looking at the first building-block, *Leoncavallo* was born as an innovative and bottom-up response to socio-cultural and welfare needs: from the outset, the response to these kinds of needs was self-managed within the Centre through a process of collective definition of their nature, their content and, especially, the way to approach them. In so doing, *Leoncavallo* has avoided the establishment of procedures that risk creating dependence in the users of the services and has developed a dialectic between individual needs and a collective horizon of rights. Thus, the real meaning of *Leoncavallo*'s actions has always been highly political in its connection to the sphere of citizenship and universal rights. Citizenship, in this empirical approach, becomes the 'product' of different services and enacted spaces: it is the main output, but also the main input for innovation and social change.

This shift from the individual to the collective dimension has been possible first of all because of the peculiar characteristics that the service relationship assumes inside the Social Centre. These characteristics are related to the second building-block of social innovation. *Leoncavallo*'s services are in fact meant as an interface between community and society: they tend to overcome the distinction between suppliers and users and to disrupt the established settings typical of standard service provision (both public and private). The processes that tend to be activated here are 'reciprocity' (Polanyi, 1974), but also the 'gift' of a universalistic matrix (Mauss, 1950) – that is, an aversion to any hierarchy of relations and positively inclined to the construction of universalistic forms of identity. On the one hand, services are the milieus for the construction of communities (of activists and users); on the other hand, they are vehicles of inclusion, of a relational 'surplus', potentially enjoyable by everyone and linked to the proximity and informality dimensions. In this way, community relations are open to the outside world, while reciprocity and gifts are activated with basically non-particularistic goals.

Therefore, self-management of socio-cultural and welfare services not only responds to individual and collective needs, but also represents an important field of innovation in social relationships, with particular regard to groups characterised by strong risk of social exclusion. Social innovation here is strictly connected to the internal organisation during the last thirty years: the practice of *autogestione* – which comes directly from the experience of the movements in the 1970s – has generated, in a recursive way, innovation based on the widening and diversification of the networks in which *Leoncavallo* has been connected –thanks also to new electronic media.

This has been possible mainly due to the third building-block of social innovation, concerning the empowerment dynamics related to individual roles in the collective self-management process. In fact, the acquisition of competences and the assumption of individual 'functions' – even in the generalised atmosphere of informality and horizontality – have represented not only a form of individual empowerment and validation for the actors involved, but also, and especially, a process of collective empowerment for the whole organisation.

From this perspective, self-management represents an innovative approach to the flexibility, the versatility and the creative adaptation required by the contemporary socio-economic system at all levels. Moreover, the self-management of services – and more generally of the whole Social Centre – represents a space for the learning of co-operation and for the exercise of actual forms of citizenship. In this sense, it is not only an exploitable practice for the organisation, but it also assumes the characteristics of an 'identity good' (La Valle, 2001), as a process of collective sense-making, through which a shared feeling of belonging is created.

The empowerment dimension, as stressed earlier, develops not only through the participation of the user in the definition and management of the services, but also through work experience, which involves several activists of the Centre. Work in *Leoncavallo*'s services is a multipurpose means to answer various needs. It is a field of enlarged participation and from this perspective is an open field for the definition of the nature of the services provided. It is also the core element of a strategy of inclusion for some categories of weak subjects (especially immigrants). For these people, the job opportunity is also a mode of recognition: a practice aiming to validate them above all as men and women, and then as citizens. Moreover, work at the Centre is a means and a place for the acquisition of knowledge and practices that are only partially used within it but become a personal and collective asset to be spent outside.

The three building-blocks of social innovation that we have just considered in the case of *Leoncavallo* are – in different ways – strictly connected to its approach to the relationship of service provision: inside this peculiar relationship the dimensions regarding economic, social, cultural and political spheres are mutually interactive. Through the relationship of service, and thanks to the peculiar physical and symbolic frames represented by the *terrain vague* of the inner spaces of the Centre, it is possible to identify what we could call a comprehensive process of 'reintegration', a kind of 'procedural recombination' (based on organising/sense-making processes), that the Centre puts into effect with respect to the social, economic, political and cultural dimensions.

In this sense, we are dealing with the ongoing consolidation of practices and cultures, which aims to create a particular kind of public institution, that is, metropolitan but also national/international spaces for debating and acting on issues of common concern. The 'flexible institutionalisation' of *Leoncavallo* represents, therefore, a collective action aiming at the creation of a dialectic between the informality of the movements and the 'structuring' of the institutions, in a physical space 'in continuous redefinition'.

Fuelled by the services and framed by the spaces, citizenship is, again, the main output of all these processes.

Notes

1   This chapter is a re-elaboration of: Membretti, A. (2007a) '*Centro Sociale Leoncavallo*: building citizenship as an innovative service', *European Urban and Regional Studies, Special issue: Social Innovation and Governance in European Cities*, 14(3).
2   For a general background to this section, see De Leonardis *et al.* (1994), Laville (1994; 1995), Mela (1996), Vicari Haddock (2004).
3   In 2006, the same leader was elected to the national parliament, supported by several social centres around Italy.
4   All the information presented or used here was collected by the author between 2001 and 2004, through several interviews with leaders and activists of *Leoncavallo*, or through field observation. This information and related quotations are available from Membretti (2003).

References

Alberoni, A. (1981) *Movimento e istituzione*, Bologna: Il Mulino.
Balestrini, N. and Moroni, P. (1997) *L'orda d'oro 1968–1977, La grande ondata rivoluzionaria e creativa, politica ed esistenziale*, Milano: Feltrinelli.
Dal Lago, A. (1999) *Non-persone*, Milano: Feltrinelli.
De Leonardis, O. (1998) *In un diverso welfare, Sogni e incubi*, Milano: Feltrinelli.
—— Mauri, D., and Rotelli, F. (1994) *L'impresa sociale,* Milano: Anabasi.
Della Porta, D., and Diani, M. (1997) *I movimenti sociali*, Roma: NIS.
Goffman, E. (1974) *Frame Analysis*, New York: Harper & Row.
Granovetter, M. (1983) 'The Strength of Weak Ties: A Network Theory Revisited', *Sociological Theory*, 1: 201–33.
Ibba, A. (1995) *Leoncavallo 1975–1995: venti anni di storia autogestita*, Genova: Costa & Nolan.
La Valle, D. (2001) *La ragione dei sentimenti, Una teoria dello scambio sociale*, Roma: Carocci.
Laville, J-L. (1994) *L'économie solidaire*, Paris : Desclée de Brouwer.
—— (1995) 'Services de proximité et politiques publiques', Paris : Centre d'Etude de l'Emploi.
Mauss, M. (1950) 'Essai sur le don, Forme et raison de l'Echange dans les sociétés archaïques', *Année Sociologique*, 1.
Mayer, M. (2000) 'Social movements in European cities: transitions from the 1970s to the 1990s', in A. Bagnasco and P. Le Gales (eds) *Cities in Contemporary Europe*, Cambridge: Cambridge University Press, pp. 131–52.
Mela, A. (1996) *Sociologia delle città*, Roma: Carocci.

Melucci, A. (1984) *Altri codici. Aree di movimento nella metropoli*, Bologna: Il Mulino.

Membretti, A. (1997) 'Centri sociali autogestiti: territori in movimento', Unpublished Degree Thesis, Pavia (Italy): University of Pavia.

—— (2003) *Leoncavallo SpA: spazio pubblico autogestito. Un percorso di cittadinanza attiva*, Milano: Leoncavallo.

—— (2004) '*Centro Sociale Leoncavallo*, Soziale Konstruktion eines offenlitchnen Raums der Nahe', in G. Raunig (ed.) *Bildraume und Raumbilder, Repräsentationskritik in Film und Aktivismus*, Wien: Verlag Turia + Kant.

—— (2007a) '*Centro Sociale Leoncavallo*: building citizenship as an innovative Service', *European Urban and Regional Studies – Special issue: Social Innovation and Governance in European Cities*, 14(3): 252–63.

—— (2007b) 'Autorappresentanza e partecipazione locale nei centri sociali autogestiti, Milano e il Cox 18', in T. Vitale (ed.) *Partecipazione e rappresentanza nelle mobilitazioni locali*, Milano: Franco Angeli.

Moroni, P., C.S Cox 18, C.S Leoncavallo and Consorzio AASTER (1996) *Centri Sociali: geografie del desiderio*, Milano: Shake.

Moulaert, F., Alaez Aller, R., Cooke, Ph., Courlet, Cl., Häusserman, H. and Da Rosa Pires, A. (1990) *Integrated Area Development and Efficacy of Local Action, Feasibility Study for the European Commission*, Brussels: EC, DG Social Policy.

—— Martinelli, F., González, S., Swyngedouw, E. (2007) 'Social innovation and governance in European cities: urban development between path dependency and radical innovation', *European Urban and Regional Studies – Special issue: Social Innovation and Governance in European Cities*, 14(3): 195–209.

—— Rodriguez, A. and Swyngedouw, E. (2003) *The Globalized City: Economic Restructuring and Social Polarization in European Cities*, Oxford: Oxford University Press.

Pickvance, C. (2003) 'From urban social movements to urban movements: a review and an introduction to a Symposium on urban movements', *International Journal of Urban and Regional Research*, 27: 102–9.

Polanyi, K. (1974) *La grande trasformazione*, Torino: Einaudi (translated from *The Great Transformation*, Free Press, New York, 1944).

Ritter, A. (1980) *Anarchism: A Theoretical Analysis*, Cambridge: Cambridge University Press.

Sen, A. (1992) *Inequality Re-examined*, Oxford: Clarendon Press.

Taylor, C. and Habermas, J. (1998) *Multiculturalismo, Lotte per il riconoscimento*, Milano: Feltrinelli. (Translated from: Gutmann, A. and Taylor, C. (eds) (1992), 'Multiculturalism and the "Politics of Recognition"', Princeton University Press, Princeton; in Habermas, J. (1996), 'Kampf um Anerkennung im demokratischen Rechtsstaat', in *Die Einbeziehung des Anderen*, Suhrkamp, Frankfurt am Main.)

Vicari Haddock, S. (2004) *La città contemporanea*, Bologna: Il Mulino Paperbacks.

Vitale, T. (2007) *Partecipazione e rappresentanza nelle mobilitazioni locali*, Milano: Franco Angeli.

Weick, K. (1995) *Sensemaking in organizations*, Thousand Oaks: Sage.

5 Building a shared interest

Olinda, Milan: social innovation between strategy and organisational learning

Tommaso Vitale

Introduction

Olinda is both a voluntary association and a social co-operative that was created with the aim of transforming a large, enclosed psychiatric hospital (PH) in the northern suburbs of Milan into a more open and therapeutic environment for patients as well as for ordinary citizens of the whole metropolitan area.[1]

The history of *Olinda* can be divided into three stages. In the first, a group of trainers was able to develop practices of vocational training focusing not on patients' weaknesses but on their capabilities, in an effort to 'co-produce' mental health. In 1995 the group created the *Olinda Association* in order to mobilise more human resources for the vocational training of inpatients. In the second stage, starting in 1996, *Olinda* organised a big summer festival (with music, sports, theatre, etc.) which included many third sector groups and involved several different local authorities. During the first festival, thousands of ordinary citizens entered the hospital for the first time; the hospital space became a stimulus for collective action and part of the wall around the hospital grounds was symbolically removed. The festival legitimised *Olinda*'s therapeutical innovations and enabled the first large debate about the continued existence of the psychiatric hospital, otherwise bound to be closed under a national law. In the third stage, *Olinda* started a social enterprise, in an effort to combine services for the city with services for mental health: multifarious activities were set up in the buildings of the former hospital – a restaurant, a carpenters' workshop, a bar and a hostel – which are still functioning, together with the annual summer festival.

Olinda used conflicts from both within and outside the organisation in order to advance public discourse and to raise visibility with regard to their decisions and actions. This case demonstrates (1) the role of outsiders in introducing new ideas, skills and social capital and, especially, how the bringing together of different types of people can generate new insights, developments, possibilities; (2) how much sociability and cultural productions/events really are a turning point in building a shared interest in innovative action; (3) the relevance of the effort to give legitimacy and dignity to those who were previously outcasts; and (4) the importance of involving the public administration and creating innovative institutional arrangements.

Olinda is the story of a reflexive organisation which does not run away from contradictions. It tries to transform its experimental practices in the mental health field into a broader social innovation, while at the same time fighting against social exclusion.

Innovation within the psychiatric hospital

To understand the main dynamics of innovation at the beginning of *Olinda*'s story, it should be remembered that a PH is a place that renders its inmates powerless and increases their chronic dependence upon the institution (Goffman, 1961). It is also a place that gathers in those refused or abandoned by other social assistance institutions: those who are believed to be intractable, chronic cases, those with accumulated problems. The PH is an institutional device, which reproduces its self-justification by making itself indispensable. Against this backdrop, *Olinda*'s path was not an easy one, due both to institutional difficulties connected to the deinstitutionalisation of the PH and to relationships with the surrounding neighbourhood.

The first innovations in the Milan PH coincided with the arrival of a psychiatrist from Rome with previous experience in vocational training for people with mental problems and involved in the network of the Italian renewal of psychiatric practices, the so-called 'deinstitutionalisation' movement. He brought his own skills, experiences and network relations. He had the legitimation needed to propose innovative activities and his arrival simultaneously permitted (a) the constitution of a new team interested in the exploration of new therapeutic practices, notably linked to vocational training, and (b) the definition of the situation of the PH as problematic, thus opening a phase of observation and study on how change could be achieved within the institution. These two dynamics jointly produced a process of '*intéressement*' (Callon, 1986), meaning that the actors defined each other's roles. The external leader and his first team, acting as innovating actors, contributed to the redefinition of the actors they tried to include in their policy network, as well as the intervention of those they wanted to exclude. An alliance was formed with some of the PH's doctors and social workers, some private entrepreneurs, a few university professors, as well as some people in the artistic business community. It was not a big network, but its boundaries were completely different from those of the traditional Milan advocacy coalition network involved in mental illness policies and services.

Olinda began empowering people in the circuit of social assistance, transforming them from passive beneficiaries into actors. *Olinda*'s work within the walls of the former PH consisted of the transformation of services that 'respond to a need' into services as 'processes of capability building'. In addition, the production of such services adopted an approach of 'doing with' rather than 'doing for', in order to make possible the valorisation of the personal competence of the former inpatients. In this sense, rather than recognising needs, *Olinda* recognised rights and specifically a particular type of right: the right to exercise capabilities (Sen, 1992), namely, the capability of work and the capability of finding a voice (Dean *et al.*, 2005). For those deprived of the status of actors, stripped of subjectivity and a presence on the economic, political and even social scene, no organised agency existed; *Olinda* treated them as a resource to be supported.

Innovation without: involving outside interests

The main problem of the first phase was the perception of *Olinda* as a 'critical situation', namely a situation where people, while acting, had to justify the reasons, means and goals of their practices. In other words, *Olinda* practices were so innovative that they created problems of legitimisation.

Enhancing the degree of legitimation of a practice requires a justification, but the criteria for legitimating such innovative actions had not yet been established. Thus, *Olinda* had to cope with problems of coordination with the other actors in the PH, trying to set up evaluation criteria. It tried to do so by connecting its practices with the experiences made in Gorizia, Trieste and other PHs involved in the 'Basaglia movement' (Basaglia, 1987). But this quasi-legitimacy was weak and disputed – as in every innovation/exploration, which has not yet gained a high degree of acceptance. In the second phase, *Olinda* departed from the narrowness of therapeutic codes (and disputes), implementing a 'generalization process' (Boltanski and Thévenot, 2006) – a process able to build a higher level of generality, thus widening publicity for its activities. This was indeed the main outcome of the Summer Festival organised by *Olinda* in 1996.

Few actors were involved in the first stage. Organising the festival was a test to mobilise, and in some way also represent, a larger population of actors. Because of the separateness of the PH and the narrowness of the former policy network, there was no common interest that could involve citizens in discussion about the PH. There were no social actions and transactions that could generate externalities and consequences for the population outside the PH. Without any perceived externality to create an interest and act as a mobilising force to exercise control over the action, no issue can emerge that may come to be regarded as a legitimate right (Coleman, 1987). It is a situation with no social capital, a system of 'each for himself', where no conditions exist for a collective action (ibid., 1987: 153).

In a situation with no spontaneous common interest, no moral shock (Jaspers, 1997), nor shared indignation to kickstart any action, *Olinda* launched a process of 'intéressement' (Callon, 1986), that is, a process of involving and combining interests in order to establish a durable relationship with new partners and establish common ground. Initially, the gratuitous character of the idea of realising a festival, without any instrumental reasons, attracted participants: a festival, nothing more than a festival. The informal and horizontal character of the operational meetings was very important to the inclusion of all types of participants, and also to the enactment of innovative ideas.

The process of involving different interests was realised through practices of participation in which different actors learned to trust and work with one another and to act collectively for common ends (see Chapter 3 in this volume). Three main rules were established, with the aim of ensuring that everyone could propose activities for the festival, but had to find someone else to work with in partnership on the proposal: (1) 'never alone'; (2) 'never with the usual partners' (so that all initiatives were implemented through new partnerships); (3) 'be interactive' (not only co-production among the existing organisers, but also with future participants). These rules were chosen not only in accordance with *Olinda*'s aims and values, but also for strategic reasons: they were incentives for the mobilisation of participants. More precisely, they were the only kinds of incentive that *Olinda* could offer to spur on a mobilisation.

In fact, because of the high level of difference in the political cultures of the participants, *Olinda* could not use norms and shared values –the typical incentives of clans and communities (Ouchi, 1980). Neither could it use an incentive system based on cost–benefit calculations or on the maximisation of actors' utility, because of its lack of resources. In this phase, *Olinda* was unable to provide even expressive benefits (prestige, sense of belonging, recognition, etc.) coming from its own internal organisation. Thus, the main mechanism supporting participation was the construction of partnerships, implementing a model based first on membership-building through trust and reciprocity and then on purposive benefits (Clark and Wilson, 1961). We can talk of 'trust through tests of co-operation' – creating a system of interdependence among a variety of groups, organisations and individuals, without any sharing of a strong collective identity.

The collective actors involved were rather heterogeneous: there were big corporations and small NGOs, professionals and political groups, and also many individuals with no affiliation, with a good balance between old and young participants, and between women and men. We lack precise data on the socio-economic status of individual actors, but we can say that they belonged to different political cultures (Catholics, extreme left-wing, social–democrats and greens). This means that they had different grammars of engagement and very different evaluation criteria, both factors that most of the time prevent the coordination of collective action. The participation of professionals from cultural fields was very important as they played the role of brokers (Diani, 2003), linking previously unconnected social sites and opening up the network outside the narrow policy sector. We believe this individual participation was possible precisely because of 'tests of coordination' as we have called them, which provided not only trust resources but also paths for participation.

Within the larger network, there was also the legitimate membership of groups of compulsory psychiatric inpatients who were usually considered a threat to the social order. The festival offered opportunity for voices to be heard and deliberation to occur, the making of what Nancy Fraser (1997: 81) has termed 'counter-publics', defined as 'parallel discursive arenas where members of subordinated social groups invent and circulate counter-discourses which in turn permit them to formulate oppositional interpretations of their identities, interests and needs'. During the festival, the former inpatients in particular produced these counter-discourses through a combination of actions and discussions. It also provided a way to develop solidarity, political consciousness and organisational infrastructures, that is, not only social capital but also collective consciousness (Mayer, 2003: 119).

In the policy process, before the first festival, the deinstitutionalisation of the PH was a non-agenda item. In fact, it was cast in the traditional practice of secrecy and invisibility, in which the PH concealed its activities. In contrast, during the festival itself the PH was represented not as the symbolic core of social exclusion but as a place of resources, a potential cultural pole in the suburbs, a workshop full of projects designed with (and not for) the 'guests' of the PH, and for the whole town. All the cultural activities of the festival were effective means of conveying information about the PH to officials, supporting the urgency of its dismantling, and highlighting its perverse effects. With the festival *Olinda* established an open involvement context, by which the public as a whole, and not only people implicated in the former policy network of mental health services, was the potential target of the mobilisation effort. This process opened up the possibility of public debate on the quality of psychiatric services in Milan and reduced the space for opportunistic, routine action of the health authorities and their governing boards. By imagining an alternative use for the premises of the PH, by opening it as the venue for a festival and bringing in thousands of citizens, the real possibility arose of conceiving both the space and the care offered there from a different point of view, of 'dismantling' the mental hospital in order to create something else.

The fact that the space of the PH was accessible to the public was very important because this permitted its recognition as a stake, as a public good, as an object in need of regulation and governance. There were some conflicts with other NGOs: on the one hand, a radical anti-psychiatric movement contested *Olinda*'s strategy as too moderate and as practising internal censorship in order to retain public support; on the other hand, two clubs affiliated to a large nationwide association (ACLI and ARCI), and traditionally working within the PH, fought against the innovations promoted by *Olinda*, notably even suggesting to local authorities the dangerousness of the festival for the patients. But the festival proved that it was not an egoistic mobilisation for the sole defence of particularistic interests (e.g. those of the professionals of the mental health sector).

The closing of the PH was finally obtained in 2000, 22 years after the Basaglia Law. This certainly did not occur just because of the mobilisation described earlier. In the mid 1990s there had been a broader nationwide process aimed at the rapid phasing out of the PH system. What was really important in the case of the *Olinda* festival was the introduction of a strong discontinuity into the mainstream policy process. With thousands of people involved within the PH, things could not be taken for granted, and the overall normative foundation of the PH was challenged. This opened a stage of 'epistemic choice' (Ostrom and Ostrom, 2004), where actors discussed criteria and vocabularies for analysing and assessing, and in this way discovered new possibilities. The festival provided the conditions for raising some controversies about shutting the PH and, most of all, about different projects for the use of the PH premises. This happened thanks also to the attention of local mass media, to the diffusion of a booklet advertising the festival, but also to the presence within the PH of thousands of people, who could walk, ask and talk with the inpatients and the workers of the PH itself. In particular, the presence of such quantities of people within the boundary of the PH obliged the entire policy network to produce justifications that were valid 'in all generality' (Boltanski and Thévenot, 2006) to support their policy programme for shutting the PH. Moreover, starting with the health authorities, every policy actor was asked to make a declaration about how to cope with people still living in the PH.

Before the above mobilisation, the PH was ignored and perceived just as a source of trouble in the neighbourhood. But the legitimation of the claim permitted a larger public to assess the trouble as a complex problem and to 'concatenate' (link together) in a public grammar (a) issues of mental health with (b) issues of quality of life and public responsibilities of the administration. Thus, *Olinda* played a mediation role in the generalisation process (Boltanski, 1999) of the PH issue, producing a new advocacy coalition with very heterogeneous actors that pushed forward out of the impasse and the closeness of the former policy network.

The networking and the involvement of diverse interests were not able to change the existing solid basis of power relations or to gain strong control over the policy process, but they permitted the emergence of a public discourse, the recognition of a sense of possibility in dealing with mental health problems and legitimating new practices and claims. They permitted the definition of the PH as a visible issue, a public problem of general interest for the whole Milan metropolitan area.

Beyond strategies: contradictions and organisational learning in a social enterprise

Olinda used visibility as both an instrument and a strategy. This does not mean that *Olinda* was always a strategic collective actor, capable of long-term planning on how to reach its goals, and rationally calculating costs and benefits. During the third stage, *Olinda* started playing games of which it did not know the rules beforehand, exploring scattered opportunities in an adaptive way, playing just to learn the rules. In fact, *Olinda* was challenged by many political and moral contradictions and dilemmas in its practices, without having any criteria to assess and prioritise them (Boltanski, 2002). Thus, *Olinda* is still keeping up its activities in respect of its institutional mandate and the pursuit of its social goals – changing the PH culture, taking care of inpatients and enhancing their working skills – trying to translate fundamental dilemmas in pragmatic tensions and compromises. In our view it was precisely the capability of continuing to work on both poles of the contradiction that permitted the most important process of social innovation carried out by *Olinda* – the transformation of a specialist innovation into a broader social innovation. Thus, we will argue that what characterised *Olinda* in the third stage was its resilience and learning capability.

After the first festival, *Olinda* continued working to develop ways of integrating various interests and networks within collective strategies and a weak but long-term mobilisation. But the problem of building issues of general interest remained, given its anchorage in a specific policy sector. Thus, *Olinda* continued the strategy of combining specific interests and generalisation processes, not only organising a summer festival each year, following the path designed in the first one, but also combining economic and social objectives within it, that is, using the premises of the former PH as a site both for the production of specific services and as a public space for cultural events and socialising opportunities, with strong emphasis on strategic communication. On the one hand, the criteria for economic success were pursued with great attention to business management for economic consolidation and expansion; on the other hand, the criteria for social success were pursued with particular attention to the social quality of the care activities. This way, economic activities and market tests constituted a crucial base for the autonomy of mentally ill people.

Tensions as resources

These were good strategies, but although necessary, they were still insufficient to sustain social innovation (Bifulco and Vitale, 2006). Organisational factors, such as 'reflexivity' and resilience, learning and adaptation were also needed. Ultimately, we will argue that *Olinda* is an example of innovation achieved through conflict and challenge, which succeeded in transforming episodes of conflict (notably with the local authorities, with the neighbourhood and with other non-profit organisations) into opportunities for public debate and collective learning and – at the same time – for organisational learning and resilience.

A few examples will illustrate the point. *Olinda*'s initiatives had established a right to use the public space of the former PH. This had led to a social demand driven by youth and families with children to find places for self-expression and self-organisation in the former PH spaces. There was also a political dimension to this process, as the spaces of the former PH became a resource for collective action (Gieryn, 2000), occasionally promoting initiatives with a political connotation (against war, for solidarity with immigrants, against certain national government policies, and the like). In the previous stage it was the expressive dimension, strictly linked to membership and involvement in the practical activities, which provided the reasons for participation; in this new stage, we believe that normative incentives played a greater role. It was involvement in big issues (most of them defined in terms of the common good), which permitted partnerships with many different NGOs in Milan, and the mobilisation of people on more or less every value-based collective issue of contentious politics: the environment, world peace, third world development, anti-poverty, anti-racism, anti-GM/pro-organic food, pro animal rights, pro asylum seekers. It also supported different interest-based collective demonstrations, such as protest against the decline in quality of health services, initiatives to maintain the community character of the neighbourhood and to improve its quality of life, and other urban struggles. Recently, it also operated as a basis for improvements in alternative lifestyles and organisations (e.g. fair trade business and LETS schemes). However, alongside these occasional initiatives, *Olinda* continued to foster acknowledgement of the political and public nature of the work done in terms of social services and the issues dealt with by them. The culture of its organisation remains based on the opposition to traditional mental health services and on the effort to continue collaboration with mentally ill people (voice, no exit).

All of these features led *Olinda* to be almost constantly involved in organisational dilemmas. The multilevel action taken by *Olinda* was always marked by the constant tension between institutional co-operation and co-operation with left-wing grass-roots movements. This tension was used as an opportunity for learning and for broadening *Olinda*'s options. On the other hand, over the past few years, relationships with the local council have become rarer, since the latter does not seem to value *Olinda*'s work and criticises it for being excessively leftist. Certain indifference has also developed within the Milan Municipality, which has changed its social policies towards cancelling all projects involving public–private partnership and, in our specific case, limiting the occasions for exchange and co-operation with *Olinda*. This municipal pullout significantly reduced the opportunity for *Olinda*'s initiatives to contribute towards a public discourse.

The results of all these different kinds of conflicts and issues have created many dilemmas for *Olinda*. In analytical terms we could argue that in order to fight social exclusion, *Olinda* has attempted to create connections between opposites (de Leonardis, 2001), endeavouring to make practical connections between: a) the individual experience and subjectivity of those suffering exclusion (the specific nature of individual cases), on the one hand, and the shared quality of urban life, on the other; b) the need for help and assistance and for the provision of welfare, on the one hand, and the need for investment, both financial and in terms of creative energy, in the economic field of production, on the other; c) the specific nature of the neighbourhoods adjoining the psychiatric hospital and the resources distributed in the metropolitan area; (d) the consensus towards institutional projects (as condition for engagements in partnerships) and disagreement and conflict (disengagement as a condition for criticising, denunciations and other political activities); (e) the grammar of care and the grammar of mobilisation. What is really interesting is the way in which

Olinda during these years was able to translate these dilemmas into dialectic tensions and then to find compromises with some temporary arrangements.

Notably, *Olinda* managed to define some new conventions (devices/rules), to build up stable and predictable routines of commitment (in its voluntary activities but also in its spring and summer cultural events). These 'devices' are ties that bind production and care, grand mobilisations and daily activities. They are organisational choices, which show the learning capability of *Olinda*. The tensions between different practical constraints are at the same time precious resources for the resilience of this organisation. The pursuit of temporary compromises that allow tensions to be overcome is at the heart of its functioning, of its organisational learning and then of its strategic action.

Organisational choices

It is useful to dwell briefly on the main organisational choices that have sustained *Olinda*'s 'reflexivity' and learning capabilities. First of all, *Olinda* has chosen to keep itself small and not to open branches in other cities. This small operational scale arose from the choice to set up and nourish the construction of the enterprise starting out from the individual operators and former users. Second, the organisation is characterised by extreme independence of management and decision-making in each service sector and, at the same time, by a strong sense of belonging and sharing of collective identity: the tension between belonging to *Olinda* as a whole and to a specific sector seems to generate learning and not fracture. Third, the presence of an 'association' alongside the co-operative represents: (a) a way of circulating ideas, sharing problems and successes and re-elaborating a shared identity and mission within the organisation itself; (b) a means of raising visibility and communicating with the different contexts where action is taken, as well as a tool for cultural exchange and attracting resources, within the broader environment; (c) a solution that makes it possible to keep the links between entrepreneurial objectives and social aims open and alive.

Another feature that characterises *Olinda* is the style of planning. *Olinda* is organised 'by projects'. The social responses to conditions of hardship are structured as projects to be implemented, rather than a formal structure for the provision of services. This style of planning (1) favours gradual processes, open to ongoing correction and modification and (2) attracts resources from outside the organisation, while creating arenas for involving and making the most of each contribution to the projects (both in financial terms and in terms of voluntary work).

What is clear in the *Olinda* case is the considerable circulation of cognitive resources and knowledge within the organisation. Crucial to the process is the strong emphasis on learning and on reflexivity, but also the ability to involve and combine human resources coming from spheres traditionally far removed from that of social assistance, that is, from the fashion, design, art and entertainment domains. Therefore, *Olinda* is a learning organisation, always giving particular attention to what is feasible, with a high degree of reflexivity: it learns from its strategies and from its contradictions, and is resilient not only due to the presence of a leader but also to internal institutional arrangements, notably the distinction between the association and the co-operative and the connections with the university and networks of similar organisations. During these years it has been able to recognise what could help manage the tensions and it is still learning how to combine better the rhythms of each worker with the market constraints.

Cultural activities for wider networking

The case of *Olinda* clearly shows the different meanings of social innovation in terms of changing social relations. *Olinda*'s initiatives have legitimised new practices and claims, because they pushed forward the recognition of people with mental and social problems as active citizens. This happened thanks to the daily work with the disadvantaged, but also because of the continuous action geared to changing the public discourse, to defining new issues and to pushing forward inclusive solutions in the locality, in the media and in the political agenda of local administrations. Moreover, *Olinda* has been able to promote inter-organisational change, multiplying resources, inventing and implementing new modes of articulated co-operation between public health agencies and the non-profit sector. Over the years, *Olinda* has succeeded in activating, extending and coordinating a diverse set of people, exchanges, actions, communication and conflicts surrounding the production, the recognition and the use of the premises of a former PH as a public area, open to all citizens and accessible to, and by, them.

Olinda created opportunities for social innovation through the strategic choice of combining economic and social objectives. It set in motion processes of collective learning that have increased its social capital, tapping into the wealth of knowledge and practical experience of professionals outside the circuit of assistance and also making the most of contributions from a number of university teachers, as well as those from the artistic, design and fashion worlds. At the same time it has enacted, coordinated and put into circulation the hidden and non-conventional resources of the former PH, that is, the former inmates themselves who learned new skills and started using them in outside activities. It has created a more intense sociability, giving rise to joint projects and economic exchange, enacting spaces and networks of relationships at a metropolitan level first and then at a neighbourhood level. It has contributed to the opening of the former PH as a public urban park and created new connections between formerly separate actors, thanks to its capability in coordinating actors and institutions without ignoring the conflicts, compromises and contradictions.

All these are very relevant social innovations as they affect more than the actors directly involved; the positive externalities also favour social cohesion and changes in social relations beyond the organisation itself. On the other hand, the processes are weak and reversible, as is often the case with social innovations. During the last year, *Olinda* has been trying to stabilise these innovations, establishing a number of conventions in full acknowledgement of its activities, with the formalisation of lease agreements, a partnership set up in order to obtain public social workers and resources, and the acceptance of new standards of psychiatric care. The latter, which is the real challenge for *Olinda*, is in our opinion the hardest, as it bears on the institutionalisation of a social innovation.

Note

1   For constructive comments and criticism, the author is grateful to Michela Barbot, Marion Carrel, Ota del Leonardis, Nicolas Dodier, Andreas Duit, Nina Eliasoph, Thomas Emmenegger, Sara González, Hartmut Haeussermann, Marilyn Hoskins, Jacques Nussbaumer, Elinor Ostrom and Serena Vicari.

References

Basaglia, F. (1987) *Psychiatry Inside Out: Selected Writings of Franco Basaglia*, New York: Columbia University Press.

Bifulco, L., and Vitale, T. (2006) 'Contracting for welfare services in Italy', *Journal of Social Policy*, 3: 1–19.

Boltanski, L. (1999) *Distant Suffering: Morality, Media and Politics*, Cambridge: Cambridge University Press.

—— (2002) 'Nécessité et justification', *Revue économique*, 53: 275–90.

Boltanski, L., and Thévenot, L. (2006) *On Justification: The Economies of Worth*, Princeton: Princeton University Press.

Callon, M. (1986) 'Some elements of a sociology of translation: domestication of the scallops and the fishermen of St. Brieuc Bay', in J. Law (ed.), *Power, Action and Belief: a New Sociology of Knowledge?* London: Routledge, pp. 196–223.

Clark, P. and Wilson, J. (1961) 'Incentive systems: a theory of organizations', *Administrative Science Quarterly*, 6: 129–66.

Coleman, J. S. (1987) 'Norms as social capital', in G. Radnitzky and P. Bernholz (eds), *Economic Imperialism: The Economic Approach Applied Outside the Field of Economics*, New York: Paragon House Publishers, pp. 133–53.

Dean, H., Bonvin, J.M., Vielle, P. and Farvaque, N. (2005) 'Developing capabilities and rights in welfare-to-work policies', *European Societies*, 7(1): 3–26.

De Leonardis, O. (2001) *Le istituzioni. Come e perché parlarne*, Roma: Carocci.

Diani, M. (2003) 'Leaders or Brokers? Positions and Influence in Social Movement Networks', in M. Diani, and D. McAdam (eds), *Social Movements and Networks: Relational Approaches to Collective Action*, Oxford: Oxford University Press, pp. 105–22.

Fraser, N. (1997) *Justice Interruptus: Critical Reflections on the 'Postsocialist' Condition*, London: Routledge.

Fung, A. (2004) *Empowered Participation: Reinventing Urban Democracy*, Princeton: Princeton University Press.

Gieryn, T. (2000) 'A space for place in sociology', *Annual Review of Sociology*, 26: 463–96.

Goffman, E. (1961) *Asylums*, New York: Anchor Books.

Jaspers, J. M. (1997) *The Art of Moral Protest: Culture, Biography, and Creativity in Social Movements*, Chicago: University of Chicago Press.

Mayer, M. (2003) 'The onward sweep of social capital: causes and consequences for understandings cities, communities and urban movements', *International Journal of Urban and Regional Research*, 27: 110–32.

Ostrom, E. and Ostrom, V. (2004) 'The quest for meaning in public choice', *The American Journal of Economics and Sociology*, 63: 105–47.

Ostrom, V. (1993) 'Epistemic choice and public choice', *Public Choice*, 77: 163–76.

Ouchi, W. G. (1980) 'Markets, bureaucracies, and clans', *Administrative Science Quarterly*, 25: 129–41.

Sen, A. (1992) *Inequality Re-examined*, Oxford: Clarendon Press.

6 How to make neighbourhoods act?

The *Associazione Quartieri Spagnoli* in Naples

Lucia Cavola, Paola di Martino and
Pasquale de Muro

Introduction

This chapter focuses on social innovation in the Quartieri Spagnoli neighbourhood in the historic centre of Naples – an area with a high level of physical and social degradation, and insufficient municipal social services, neglected by local and national governments – where at the end of the 1970s a voluntary-based initiative, predominantly inspired by dissenting Catholic movements, started supporting the resident population in their needs for social services, housing and solidarity.

The *Associazione Quartieri Spagnoli* (*AQS*) was formally established in 1986 and committed itself to building a new identity for the area by creating new institutions for social aid and reinvigorating social relations (see Table 6.1 for a brief chronology). In the beginning, in fact, *AQS* activity was mostly centred on establishing trust-based relationships, involving the resident population in reconstructing the social fabric. This allowed the association to become firmly embedded in the local context, to act in the area by working from the inside, and to establish itself as a constant presence and a place to turn to when experiencing insecurity and hardship.

After this first period of fertilisation, a second stage began and continued throughout the 1990s, when the association attracted the attention of public institutions and started new neighbourhood development projects funded by central and local government, as well as by the European Union. As a result, *AQS* has become a landmark for the residents of the neighbourhood and has played an increasingly important and successful role in influencing the formulation of municipal social policy.

The association participated in urban rehabilitation programmes, collaborated closely with municipal, national and European institutions, obtained European funding to carry on social activities and established links with the University Federico II and other extended networks, including the Régies de Quartier and Quartieri in Crisi (Neighbourhoods in Crisis). This was a period of true institutionalisation in which *AQS* intervention in the area became stronger

Table 6.1 AQS chronology

1978	A group of volunteers begins social work in the area.
1980	Earthquake. Urban policies come to a standstill.
1985	The Naples City Council resumes its social policies.
1986	The *Associazione Quartieri Spagnoli (AQS)* is formally established.
1991	AQS receives financial support from central government (Act 216/91) and city council (provision of premises for a youth centre).
1992	AQS becomes part of the European networks of the 'Régies de Quartier' and 'Quartieri in crisi'. First European funding (Poverty Projects and first edition of INTEGRA, HORIZON, NOW projects). A 'Neighbourhood committee' is set up in the Quartieri Spagnoli to discuss local policies.
1993	Mr Bassolino is elected as Mayor of Naples. Establishment of the Department of Dignity and Respect (Councillor Mrs Incostante) in charge of social policies.
1994	AQS becomes a member of the CNCA – Coordinamento Nazionale delle Comunità di Accoglienza (National Coordination of Shelter Communities).
1995	AQS collaborates with the city council in planning and implementing the URBAN project in the Quartieri Spagnoli.
1997	AQS takes part in outlining the 'Piano Comunale per l'Infanzia' (Municipal Plan for Children, Municipal Act 285/97).
1999	Convention with Naples City Council for the social tutoring of families in the Minimum Income Category (Legislative Decree 237/98). Change in power at municipal government; Bassolino (mayor) and Incostante (councillor) leave.
2001	The city council approves the first three-year Social Plan for the District.
2002	New AQS initiatives for immigrants ('Children Parking') co-financed by the Fondazione Banco Napoli foundation. A group of social workers, which had collaborated with the AQS, set up the 'Passaggi' co-operative.
2003	The 'Mothers' Crèche Association' is set up.

Source: Authors

and a warrant for continuity in development strategy. Encouraged by these results, the municipal government has adopted some of the intervention models conceived by members of the association and has applied them in other areas of the city.

As far as results are concerned, AQS has contributed significantly to the improvement in the standard of living and in bringing about changes in attitude, mentality and culture for the residents who have been involved in the association's projects: they have not only attended training courses, found jobs and managed to satisfy other, previously unmet, needs, but have also become protagonists of change and no longer consider themselves as passive and disheartened onlookers.

Quartieri Spagnoli: a privileged laboratory for designing and testing urban social policies

The social context: a history of poverty and deviance

The Quartieri Spagnoli is an area of the city of Naples, situated behind the Town Hall and the centrally located commercial street, Via Toledo. Since the quarter was built in the sixteenth century, it has always been characterised by severe social problems, but it is also known for its vitality and for a wide range of small-scale activities, such as craft workshops, retail shops, stores and other businesses, often in backyards and garages. The architectural heritage of the area, which includes buildings of special historical and artistic value, often dating back to the seventeenth century, has deteriorated over the years. The earthquake of November 1980 caused many buildings in the area to be declared unsafe, increasing the hardship and further affecting the social fabric. Some of the population migrated to other areas, whereas new inhabitants took up residence in the neighbourhood. Nowadays, behind the neighbourhood's overrated image of urban degradation, a number of social styles and models and a mix of different social groups, some of which also belong to the middle class, can be identified (Laino, 2001a).

The residents of the area – mostly indigenous Neapolitans or coming from the province of Naples, with only a limited and recent presence of immigrants from developing countries – lead a lifestyle characterised by intense informal – sometimes illegal – economic activities and transactions. These social relations constitute an important territorial resource, contributing to local identity, vitality, mutual help and sense of belonging, and have also given rise to a peculiar system of rules for existence and coexistence. Prostitution used to be one of the most widespread activities in the area, although now it has almost disappeared; usury is still common as a way of tackling financial difficulty. Nonetheless, neighbourhood livelihood strategies have fuelled social exclusion dynamics, particularly for children, young people and women. Early pregnancies are commonplace; many young children live in a state of abandonment, especially if one or both parents are in prison or in hiding, and the school dropout rate is high. Training is inadequate and survival strategies lead young people towards precarious jobs and illegal employment. Women, in particular, are excluded from any training or work programmes and often become grandmothers before they reach the age of forty.

The political, institutional and governance context

At the end of the 1970s, a wide range of state and private organisations and institutions were involved in providing assistance and tutoring to deprived families in the Quartieri Spagnoli. They included municipal social service workers, priests, dynamic teachers of the five schools attended by the local youngsters, and members of a few non-profit organisations. In fact, the problems affecting the Quartieri Spagnoli had attracted the attention of voluntary movements and organisations, which sought to implement social initiatives. However, this flourishing of innovative social activities came to a standstill when the earthquake struck the city in November 1980.

Only in 1985, thanks to national funding, did Naples City Council resume its social policies, and begin encouraging the development of social services in all urban districts. The range of policy tools was also enlarged and initiatives began to combine financial support with socialisation processes and community activities (workshops, cinema), often in collaboration with or on the initiative of private social organisations. Collaboration between different private and public groups became particularly intense in the Quartieri Spagnoli because of the willingness of people involved in social work to develop networking dynamics. An innovative form of partnership between the different groups operating in the area – a sort of neighbourhood social network, in which many actors (social services, advisory centres, schools, parishes and local organisations in the third sector) could discuss local policies – was experimented with and the AQS was formally established in 1986.

In the 1990s, a radical change in municipal social policies came about with the election of Antonio Bassolino as mayor of Naples in 1993 and the establishment of the municipal Department of Dignity and Respect that remained responsible for social policies until 2000. In this climate of change, in 1995 the EU-funded URBAN programme was launched in the Quartieri Spagnoli and the collaboration between AQS and Naples City Council channelled a significant part of the programme funding into social services (Laino, 1999).

In 1999, a further change occurred in municipal policies and transformed governance and planning. Bassolino became the governor of the Campania Regional Government and left the mayor's office. Mrs Incostante, the councillor for Dignity and Respect also left the council for the region. From that moment, a gradual reduction in the municipal government's level of receptivity to local actor input was observed and the innovative interaction and participation achieved in the previous years by the civil society in governance processes were progressively stifled, with the re-emergence of the bureaucratic culture and the administrative routine of old. The new organisational set-up that relegates local actors to a purely advisory role, shows the new city council's intention to 'leave all authority and power to make decisions to its traditional and natural political and administrative "place" (department or service), in order to avoid discussion and conflict with local actors' (Lepore, 2002a: 155).

The *Associazione Quartieri Spagnoli*: from volunteerism to neighbourhood development agency

Cultural and ideological origins

AQS is based on a project that was spontaneously launched towards the end of the 1970s by a group of friends consisting of students, clerical workers and teachers linked to the religious communities who based their work on Charles de Foucauld's experiences and philosophy. The approach was also inspired by the philanthropic solidarity of critical Catholic movements established between the 1950s and 1960s: they viewed themselves as 'a group of dissenting Catholics, enrooted in an area of hardship and poverty that represents a privileged place for developing a horizon of sense' (Laino 2001a: 31). They chose this form of civic commitment because they felt unable to identify with traditional political practice, that is, with parliamentary and extra parliamentary parties, codes and protocols.

On a social-philosophical level, similarities can also be found with the Movimento di Cooperazione Educativa (Movement for Educational Cooperation) inspired by the Popular Pedagogy of Célestin and Elise Freinet, whereas on an organisational level, it is more akin to the work of militant neighbourhood groups belonging to left-wing parties that were establishing themselves in the suburbs or run-down areas in the same period.

Thus, the project was conceived as living and working in the area in close contact with groups of inhabitants who risked social exclusion or were already in a deprived position, aiming at the creation of social, educational, and training services and the revival of economic activity – artisan and small-scale production in particular.

The first stage: fertilisation and experimentation (1978–90)

During its first years of activity, *AQS* activists were involved exclusively in becoming part of the residents' lives, listening to their problems and consolidating their knowledge of social exclusion dynamics and escape strategies in the area. *AQS* focused its attention on the difficulties faced by children and young people who abandoned compulsory education or interrupted their studies early and spent most of their time in the streets. It then became involved in the problems of informal work, a widespread phenomenon throughout the small workshops in the area, and the limited employability of young people due to poor training and lack of qualifications.

Initially, the volunteers' activities were mainly self-financed. The promoters of the initiatives worked free of charge and also covered overhead expenses. They sometimes benefited from small external contributions from different sources, including, above all, private supporters. However, the most important resource consisted of the close web of relations with the external world, an extensive informal network that involved the university and other research institutes, as well as similar initiatives launched in other parts of Naples, Italy and worldwide by other individuals belonging to the same religious movement. At the same time, the main obstacle the group faced was the cultural, professional and political inertia of government institutions that might be willing to listen but contributed little or nothing on a practical level.

The association was formally established in 1986, when the informal group of friends decided to provide the voluntary activities with a formal legal structure. The association's activities began thereafter to receive financial support from the state and from Naples City Council. It also succeeded in securing the use of the municipal premises that became the base for *AQS'* first social economy project: a multi-purpose youth centre called Via Nova, where educational and socialisation projects and pre-learning activities were organised for resident children and young people (preschool activities, scholastic support, creativity labs for photography, music, pottery, sports activities). At the same time, a project targeting the 'emersion' of undeclared employment was launched with the co-operation of young workers and local artisans. The Parco del Lavoro (Labour Park) was conceived, a complex project involving the training and insertion of young people into local businesses and, for the first time in Naples, courses for 'street teachers' were proposed, and introduced an innovative formula of social work involving close contact with the children of very distressed families.

The second stage: transforming into a neighbourhood development agency (1991–99)

In 1991 the *AQS* entered a period of major development and experienced progressive institutionalisation, assuming the more permanent role of an agency promoting neighbourhood development and playing an active part in designing social policies for the city as a whole.

Until then, the *AQS* had based its activity on a strong territorial embeddedness and a firm commitment to listening and speaking to the population of the area. It now began to develop a special ability to link people, experiences and resources at different spatial scales. The association became a member of the Coordinamento Nazionale delle Comunità di Accoglienza (National Coordination of Shelter Communities). It also established contacts with European organisations such as the Union Nationale des Foyers et Services pour Jeunes Travailleurs, with specialised prevention groups, and with the European network of the Régies de Quartier. Through these channels and the people it became acquainted with, it discovered new opportunities offered by national and European policies for innovative projects.

One of *AQS'* founding members, who had also embarked on a university career, worked from 1995 to 1999 as a consultant for the municipality's Social Policies Department; consequently the strategies and work style of *AQS* also had a significant impact on other neighbourhood and urban planning actions. In line with the philosophy and methods of intervention developed by *AQS*, the URBAN programme in Naples was particularly attentive to the social dimension of public space rather than just the physical rehabilitation aspect (Laino, 2001a). Moreover, *AQS* did much more than other programmes to promote small-scale economic activity, and conceived training – co-funded by the European Social Fund – as a socio-educational service, with stable features, sensitive to the specific social demand of the area and based on the involvement of the local population.

The projects funded as part of the URBAN scheme, together with several other initiatives related to protection, prevention and social inclusion, for which *AQS* received national and European funding (within the INTEGRA, POVERTÀ, HORIZON, NOW programmes) established innovative social roles and tools, such as 'street teachers', 'mothers' crèches', social meeting points, job centres, foster care tutors, training programmes for job socialisation and services to improve the employability of young people. Some of these projects were then adopted as models in other areas and cities.

At this stage, the association's budget had grown significantly. It organised many well-structured activities and developed strong roots in the community, where it earned a reputation based on trust, as a reliable resource of assistance to people in need. By the end of the 1990s, *AQS* had become the main agent promoting neighbourhood development in the area and put its considerable experience to use in a variety of ongoing projects. However, all these projects needed to be closely followed and defended against increasingly tough competition for resources from other 'players'.

The third stage: assessment and revision (2000–today)

The year 1999 marked a turning-point and the beginning of a downhill trend for *AQS*, caused by significant changes in municipal social policy. In addition to changes in the political climate, the 'third sector' itself had changed considerably. The 'market' for social action had evolved and the economic stakes had increased. There was now strong competition for funding from other actors in the non-profit sector, who were not as competent and forward-looking in neighbourhood development, but were effective at fund-raising and emerged onto the scene to take advantage of the situation. The *cantieri sociali* notion – 'social building sites' of ongoing social work – no longer featured and was replaced by plain 'social services' market niches, where the competitive third sector organisations were increasingly geared towards consolidation rather than community-building. As a result, the association now had to reconsider its role as a development agency and search for new ways to pursue its mission.

Despite the apparent continuity in its social policy, the new municipal government did not consider improvements in social capital as really significant in successful neighbourhood development. In the new administrative scenario, the URBAN project was filed away as a past experience, along with the style of intervention and philosophy that went with it. In addition to such changes in social relations and policies, *AQS* has explicitly deplored the reappearance in the political arena of non-transparent behaviour, opportunistic alliances, power struggles and practices of favouritism.

As a result, the association has been facing a strategic, financial and structural crisis for some years, involving a 'control drift', where attention is focused on finding financial backing for ongoing activities rather than devising new intervention models. The lack of project continuity and renewal of financial resources has led to a sense of precariousness and uncertainty.

Moreover, it should be considered that *AQS* works in a context where a number of problems – such as micro and macro (*camorra*) criminality or garbage disposal – are endemic. Those problems keep attracting public attention, blocking out the demand for social services and the benefits that derived from activities in this field. In other words, the focus – especially by the government – tends to concentrate on recurring 'emergencies' rather than on the valorisation and effectiveness of initiatives for social inclusion.

Notwithstanding all these problems, *AQS* is continuing its activities and remains one of the major suppliers of social services in the area.

Social innovation dynamics in the Quartieri Spagnoli

Capabilities building for self-sustainable social inclusion

The type of social exclusion operating in the Quartieri Spagnoli is not directly linked to the crisis and the subsequent gradual reorganisation of the Italian welfare state after the 1970s. It involves social groups that have historically experienced a marginalisation process, even if they live in the city centre. Their marginality, mainly expressed by their exclusion from the formal economic system and their involvement in informal and/or illegal and criminal circuits, essentially derives from a deprivation of capabilities (see Chapter 2)[1] – both basic (constrained access to economic resources and education) and relational (limited access to agency networks, absence of empowerment), which reinforces the vicious circle of exclusion (*AQS*, 1999).

The crisis and reorganisation of the welfare state have highlighted, among other things, the inadequacy of traditional monetary-based assistance in the fight against social exclusion. When the group of volunteers started to work in the area at the end of the 1970s, they were determined to fight against social exclusion through social work based on new forms of civic commitment, that were different from the traditional involvement of political parties and groups.

The story of the *Associazione Quartieri Spagnoli* is one of a small group of people that went from being a spontaneous group of volunteers to becoming a neighbourhood development agency. The process took over twenty years, a period rich in relationships, experiences, successes and failures; years of hard work full of ideas and projects that were conceived because of the ability to seize the best opportunities, in terms of structures, funding and relations, for achieving the desired objectives. The experience had begun without any long-term project and was based on a very special vision and philosophy: experimenting with development initiatives and policy in the simplest possible way, as a daily civic commitment, living and working in one of the most difficult areas in Naples, to assist the most deprived population groups. From the very beginning the style and methods of intervention were strongly informed by this cultural and ideological inspiration: low-threshold work made possible by territorial belonging; skill and constant commitment of people dedicated to the mission.

The headquarters of the voluntary group (a small *basso*, a single-room ground-level dwelling, leading directly onto the street) soon became a well-known meeting place for families in the area. Activities were channelled towards offering residents, and especially young people, the opportunity to gain the rights of citizenship that had not been granted by the state. To achieve this objective, social bonds had to be developed and the community rebuilt, by reformulating the ways of living, the social roles and the value frameworks, by restoring and redefining the sense of legality and the spirit of solidarity and by fostering forms of active citizenship and associative local democracy. *AQS*' aim was 'to develop the citizens' capability to pass from a passive state to one of mobilisation when confronted with specific activities' (Stanco *et al.*, 1994: 26).

The work of *AQS* in the area has, above all, made people aware of their right to ask for, and receive, support to overcome many of the problems that affect their daily lives. The social policies and projects advanced by the association have prompted important changes in attitude and mentality in the resident population. The latter has learnt to appreciate the benefits of social assistance and has acquired the ability to play a leading role and to take responsibility for its own emancipation (D'Ambrosio *et al.*, 2003).

The neighbourhood development process was based on listening and sharing and then offering targeted support for the collective construction of basic capabilities. Rather than 'community building', since a sense of belonging to the community and some forms of solidarity were already well established, it involved 'capability building'. Thus, a central dimension of social innovation in the *AQS* experience was the 'empowerment' process, beyond the mere provision of primary goods and services, by which residents could find a way out of informal, illegal and criminal circuits. In other words, *AQS* laid the foundations for self-sustainable social inclusion.

Changing governance relations: multi-scalar networking and urban social policies

Another major socially innovative impact of *AQS* was its role as a 'development agency', representing the citizens' interests and acting as a political mediator. From the very beginning, the various partners in the organisation were committed to the construction and consolidation of an extended (in)formal network including voluntary associations, private individuals, local authorities, central government ministries and the European Community. In fact, one of the most important resources that *AQS* mobilised was the close web of relations with the external world, at different spatial scales.

In the end, *AQS* played a crucial role in the governance of the area and of the city, aided by the gradual transformation of the small group of volunteers into a promotional body, with an active role in generating policy proposals and social innovation (Laino, 2001b). *AQS* and its actors have become a landmark in the neighbourhood and in the city at large for the implementation of social policies; with their help, thousands of families have been offered opportunities that they would previously have never conceived. The association has been able to gather and interpret unexpressed needs of the resident population and channel them into community development projects. Through its leadership, it has been able to represent these interests at different political levels (local, national and European) and attract the attention of several government bodies to the neighbourhood. From this perspective, it is also important to stress how the association's participation in European networks generated intensive exchanges between organisers, teachers and social workers, while the neighbourhood and its social activities were publicised on a national and international level. This has encouraged cultural exchanges with other realities and, in many cases, contributed to overcoming the resistance of local people, especially the young, to look beyond the area's boundaries and to live new experiences.

Another major achievement of *AQS* is, indeed, the 'spill-over' and 'dissemination' effects of its initiatives: hundreds of young social workers have begun to bring life into the 'market' of social services provision that in Naples represents an important occupational niche. In its role as agency, in fact, the association also served as a catalyst for human and intellectual resources. Many highly skilled development agents are devoted to its mission, with a high level of motivation, strong leadership, relational skills, creativity, planning skills and listening, mediating, experimenting and negotiating skills (Lepore, 2002c).

The progressive institutionalisation of *AQS* in the 1990s as an agency promoting neighbourhood development and influencing the making of social policies in the city council was certainly affected by the new political climate brought about by the election of Bassolino as mayor (1992–99). In those years the local government was, indeed, quite favourable to, and supportive of, bottom–up development projects (Lepore, 2002b). During the 1990s, extensive collaboration and interaction between social mobilisation and city government initiatives prevailed in the city's political arena; the civil society expressed stronger pressure from below and *AQS* played an active role – along with other associations and groups operating in the municipal territory – in stimulating innovative municipal social policies. Thanks to its strong planning skills, *AQS* conceived, experimented and consolidated at a neighbourhood scale innovative projects aiming not only at an improvement in the standard of living of residents, but above all at an extension of relational networks. Encouraged by the success of these initiatives, the municipal government adopted some of the new intervention models conceived by the members of the association and used them in other areas of the city.

Since 2000, however, *AQS* has complained of the local government's loss of 'strategic view' in social policy. Despite apparent continuity with the previous decade, the most recent social policies exhibit a top–down approach, with much attention being given to image rather than to relationships with the citizens and local networks. There is no longer the same willingness to listen to the suggestions of local actors and to try out partnerships and co-planning. When the city council drew up the three-year Social Plan that was approved in 2001, it changed the existing relations and institutional balances in the bureaucratic structure (among politicians, executives, civil servants) and delegitimised the unofficial team of experts, consultants and representatives of the associations that had co-operated with the previous administration. As a result, the association now had to reconsider its role as a development agency and search for new ways and resources to pursue its mission.

In the opinion of *AQS*, the city's current social policy has returned to a traditional top-down approach to planning in which the role of listening to the local population is grossly minimised and in which the indiscriminate standardisation of social services – ignoring differences between the areas – risks damaging social innovation processes rather than promoting them. The role, if any, of the civil society has currently been confined to a merely advisory one.

Conclusions: whither *AQS*?

AQS' long existence offers the rare possibility of checking the dynamics of innovative processes at every stage of the entire life cycle of the association, from its spontaneous appearance in the neighbourhood in the form of a voluntary action, throughout the period of consolidation and institutionalisation as a development agency, to the present day stagnation, in which its role and philosophy are increasingly questioned and further challenged by a crisis of identity and motivation, a rupture with politics and public institutions, as well as stiff competition from the third sector, which is forced into a behaviour increasingly similar to the private sector.

Whatever possibilities exist for reinvigorating the role of the association, *AQS* currently finds itself in a paradoxical situation: on the one hand, it is suffering from a lack of power and ability to raise funding, due to changes in government and political strategies; on the other hand, its intervention models and the institutional practices it has established over time continue to represent a landmark in social urban collective action leading to new policy, and are even successfully replicated in other neighbourhoods and cities. In other words, the social innovation framework introduced by *AQS* – the intervention models and institutional practices created in the neighbourhood and city at large – have become a 'common good' that should attract more attention and support from public institutions.

Note

1   On the concept of poverty as 'deprivation of capabilities' see also Sen (1999).

References

Associazione Quartieri Spagnoli. (1999) 'Il Progetto Peppino Girella dell'Associazione Quartieri Spagnoli nell'ambito del modello C.Ri.S.I.', *Quaderni del Centro Nazionale di Documentazione ed Analisi per l'infanzia e l'Adolescenza*, 7: 249–54.

D'Ambrosio, R., Pala, V. and Triggiani I. (2003) 'Un Parco dove giocarsi l'occupabilità', *Animazione Sociale,* 169: 62–71.

Laino, G. (1999) 'Il Programma Urban in Italia', *Archivio di studi urbani e regionali,* 66: 69–97.

—— (2001a) 'Il cantiere dei Quartieri Spagnoli di Napoli', *Territorio, Rivista del Dipartimento di Architettura e Pianificazione del Politecnico di Milano,* 19: 25–32.

—— (2001b) 'Condizioni per l'efficacia dei programmi di riqualificazione nell'ottica dello sviluppo locale', *Archivio di studi urbani e regionali,* 70: 1–23.

Lepore, D. (2002a) 'Napoli. Progetti di quartiere', in P.C. Palermo and P. Savoldi (eds) *Il programma Urban e l'innovazione delle politiche urbane. Esperienze locali: contesti, programmi, azioni,* Milan: Franco Angeli/Diap, pp. 155–66.

—— (2002b) 'L'attivazione e l'uso dei progetti-sponda a Napoli', in G. Pasqui and E. Valsecchi (eds) *Il programma Urban e l'innovazione delle politiche urbane. Apprendere dall'esperienza: pratiche, riflessioni, suggerimenti,* Milan: Franco Angeli/Diap, pp. 130–33.

—— (2002c) 'Napoli. Riflessioni sulle esperienze: Giovanni Laino, Consulente scientifico di Urban per il Comune di Napoli', in G. Pasqui and E. Valsecchi (eds) *Il programma Urban e l'innovazione delle politiche urbane. Apprendere dall'esperienza: pratiche, riflessioni, suggerimenti,* Milan: Franco Angeli/Diap, pp. 178–81.

Sen, A. (1999) *Development as Freedom,* Oxford: Oxford University Press.

Stanco, A., Stanco, L. and Laino G. (1994) 'Quartieri Spagnoli: Storia di un intervento', *Zazà, Rivista Meridionale di Cultura,* 5: 26–29.

7 Social inclusion and exclusion in the neighbourhood of L'Epeule, Roubaix

The innovative role of the *Alentour Association*

Oana Ailenei and Bénédicte Lefebvre

Introduction: problematic and theoretical framework

This chapter examines the way in which the association, *Alentour*, is involved in the fight against exclusion in L'Epeule, a former working-class and densely populated neighbourhood of Roubaix, which is the second largest municipality of the Lille metropolitan area, situated in the Nord-Pas de Calais region on France's most western border region with Belgium. From the mid-nineteenth century to the mid-twentieth century, this region was a major industrial centre, contributing significantly to the growth of the French economy, particularly through its powerful textile and mechanical industries. Since the end of the 1960s, however, the entire Nord-Pas de Calais has been seriously affected by the decline of traditional industries. As a manufacturing city, Roubaix had also experienced an important influx of foreign immigrants, originally employed in the textile industry, but now hit and fragmented by structural unemployment problems.

A first general starting point is to place our case study and the city of Roubaix in context. Today's Roubaix is plagued by a galloping spread of poverty, accompanied by a severe alienation of socio-political rights and the destruction of social relationships. The second important contextual feature concerns the changes that have occurred in the role of the state, until recently the central actor in development policies in France. These changes have been accompanied by the emergence of new actors, particularly from the civil society. Under these circumstances, the way in which third sector groups become involved in anti-poverty strategies as insertion-mediating agencies and partners in public policies is gaining more and more importance (Mingione and Oberti, 2003). Within these contextual dynamics we focus on the peculiar role of the *social economy* as a particularly interesting organisational form, in the process of social inclusion that unfolded in L'Epeule.

We chose to focus on the social economy as this is a socio–economic 'sector' defined by specific organisations, practices and institutional dynamics, which

aims at combining the satisfaction of needs with the rebuilding of social relations (Ailenei *et al.*, 2007, 2008; Hamdouch *et al.*, 2009). This objective is pursued through alternative mechanisms to fight the diverse expressions of social exclusion dynamics. From this point of view, social economy dynamics fit well into the theoretical framework developed in the SINGOCOM project (Moulaert *et al.*, 2005) and within the definition of social innovation provided in Chapter 3 of this book, the ALMOLIN model. The latter particularly stresses three crucial dimensions of social innovation and their interaction: (1) the *satisfaction of human needs* that are not currently satisfied, either because they are 'not yet' or because they are 'no longer' perceived as important by either the market or the state, the emphasis being on the satisfaction of 'alienated' basic needs, although it is admitted that these may vary among societies and communities; (2) *changes in social (power) relations*, especially with regard to governance, that both enable the satisfaction of human needs and increase the level of participation of all but especially deprived groups; (3) *empowerment*, that is, increasing the socio-political capability and the access to resources needed to enhance the right to satisfaction of human needs and participation. This model, thus, underlines the links between social exclusion mechanisms and the emergence of social economy initiatives to fight such exclusion – through social innovation – and to contribute to local development – through the empowerment and the inclusion of marginalised groups in governance processes. The social economy approach, in line with ALMOLIN, is based on the concept of integrated territorial development which does not exclude non-commercial practices like voluntary work, reciprocity and donations, and no longer considers the people affected by exclusion as assisted people, but rather as actors able to (re)act (Moulaert, 2000/2002).

This said, in the first part of the chapter we will describe the social exclusion dynamics and the growing heterogeneity of the local social needs, as they represent a challenge for established bureaucratic social welfare models. In the second part, we will explain how the various initiatives of the *Association Alentour* contributed to improving social inclusion and to reinforcing social links in the neighbourhood of L'Epeule. *Alentour*'s method consisted of developing social support and mediation services, providing workplaces for the unemployed and involving people in local urban management, facilitating exchanges and dialogue among the local population, as well as between local associative structures and institutional partners. In the last section of the chapter we will focus on the socially innovating content of the inclusion initiatives of *Alentour* in the L'Epeule neighbourhood, in the context of the urban renewal policies started in Roubaix in the 1990s, which mostly focused on commercial and spatial revitalisation as a strategy to recover attractiveness for investors and middle-class people.

In order to grasp fully the exclusionary dynamics occurring in the neighbourhood, a number of interviews with ten key actors and a survey questionnaire (distributed to a sample of 120 inhabitants (out of a total population of 3,200 households) were carried out (data from Ville de Roubaix, 1999 based on INSEE[1] Census 1999). This empirical enquiry contributed very useful insights into the socio-economic context, the population and its needs, and the associative fabric of the neighbourhood.

Exclusion dynamics and needs in the neighbourhood of L'Epeule

In this section, we outline the social exclusion features and issues, as well as some of the innovative dynamics in the territorial, social, political and economic context of Roubaix and L'Epeule. Several subsequent socio-economic and institutional processes have affected the economic, social and physical characteristics of the area: first massive and brutal industrialisation, together with important foreign immigration flows, which generated a complex urban system (from the end of the nineteenth century to the 1960s); then economic decline, housing crises and degradation of the urban landscape (1970s and 1980s); finally, industrial restructuring, relocalisation and 'tertiarisation' of the local economy (starting in the 1980s). The social exclusion dynamics that arose in the 1970s continue to affect the inhabitants of Roubaix today: high unemployment, impoverishment, weakening of social relations, physical degradation of the neighbourhoods and flight of the middle classes to other municipalities of the Lille metropolitan area.

The institutional reactions to these processes were reflected in several public urban redevelopment strategies: support of new economic activities in the 1970s, such as the redevelopment of central areas through new technology centres and business services; policies against poverty and measures to insert local people into the labour market in the 1980s; urban renewal policies and measures against unemployment in the 1990s, for example, via the construction of commercial spaces, improving the urban landscape and protection of historical heritage.

In addition to these general dynamics and policy strategies, our in-depth fieldwork allowed us to identify other more specific features of the Roubaix city context, such as, on the one hand, the progressive emergence of a 'mosaic of local memories', and, on the other, the rise of a specific multifaceted culture of collective action. As regards the local memory, no strong links exist between the different social groups in Roubaix. Although the 'nostalgic workers' – the unemployed or retired workers from the industrial sector – still form the bulk of the local associations, the new 'bobos' – namely, the 'bourgeois bohemian' class, as labelled by David Brooks (2000) – have become increasingly visible in urban public life through many cultural and artistic initiatives. Moreover, while the two latest generations of immigrants' children are in the forefront of the so-called 'young people's associations' movement, their parents – the former workers in the textile industry from Algeria, Morocco, Tunisia, Portugal, Spain, Italy and Poland – are today quite invisible, staying at home or visiting cafés. Finally, the former industrial entrepreneurs and managers have completely disappeared from the social arenas, whereas the new immigrants –

in particular from Asia, Sub-Saharan Africa and Eastern Europe – are silently filling in the local landscape.

At the same time, however, a very specific local culture of collective action has emerged from the confrontation between the traditional organisations, such as trade unions and other workers' social struggle organisations, the more recent movements, such as the 'committees of neighbourhoods' and the 'young people's associations', and public policies. This new culture is based simultaneously on both horizontal relationships, combining equality and solidarity, and vertical relationships. The latter are useful in obtaining resources from the public authorities by exerting pressure, but they do not encourage the construction of permanent and sustainable solidarities. These vertical relations have indeed both destructive effects on the traditional culture of horizontal relationships, and positive effects because they stimulate and revive the 'old' culture.

This 'mosaic of local memories', together with the new culture of collective action, explain why the local social relationships are difficult and why the local actors (public, associative, private) encounter problems in creating partnerships and in building bridges between the inhabitants' initiatives, those of the local authority actors and the major public programmes.

After examining the general dynamics at the city level, we zoom in on the neighbourhood scale. L'Epeule remains one of the most working-class and densely populated neighbourhoods of Roubaix, with all social functions still represented there (retail trade, work, culture, leisure and sport). The quality of housing is relatively high, although the more unhealthy stock increasingly needs to be renovated. The population exhibits an important social mix, including low-income households and families dependent on social welfare, but also many wealthy people, and embracing a wide cultural diversity – French, Algerian, Moroccan, African, Asian, Portuguese, etc. This social and cultural diversity makes the local socio-economic issues more complex and raises the acute problem of the recognition of multiculturalism.

To complete our analysis of exclusion dynamics, we established a hierarchy of resident needs. According to privileged witnesses (representatives of public institutions and associations), the most serious problems in the district are the exclusion of many inhabitants from the economic system (both production and consumption), and the creation of specific poverty pockets in social housing estates and insalubrious old housing, where a large concentration of immigrants without papers and homeless squatters have congregated. They also highlighted the opposition between the traditional culture of the former workers – nowadays confronted with unemployment – and the newer culture of young people – who have never been integrated into the labour market. Those with the greatest difficulties are the young people and the immigrants, the majority of whom are unqualified employees in local textile factories that are progressively closing down.

In our survey we also asked inhabitants to express their problems and needs. The main problems – ranked in order of importance by the inhabitants – are:

the closing of factories and unemployment; changes in the commercial network, that is, the progressive disappearance of traditional stores and their replacement with Arabian, Asian or African shops; the feeling of insecurity; the dirtiness caused by people, dogs or by the Sunday market; insufficient socio-cultural activities; the lack of playground activities or protected places for children and young people; the lack of useable green areas, because existing ones are either enclosed, monopolised by young people or dangerous for children; the physical decay of the neighbourhood, including degradation of residences; the feeling of being marginalised.

Dynamics of social inclusion and social innovation in the social economy: the role of *Alentour*

After identifying the exclusion dynamics in the neighbourhood and the needs these have engendered, we then focus our analysis on the social innovations implemented by the *Association Alentour* to fight against social exclusion.

The origin of *Alentour* is linked to the activity of AME (Association des maisons de l'enfance), an association created in 1948 by the wife of textile industrialist Albert Prouvost. In the 1960s, AME was involved only in the management of the Roubaix-Tourcoing social housing estate. But in the 1990s, the progressive degradation of the neighbourhood of L'Epeule led AME to initiate a project within the Plan Local d'Insertion et d'Emploi – PLIE (Local Plan for Insertion and Employment). This was a policy tool launched by the European Union to help the long-term unemployed and other disadvantaged groups, mainly through training programmes and insertion agencies. In 1989, Lille was the first metropolitan area in France to create a PLIE, organise its different actors and introduce measures to fight exclusion and unemployment at city level (Moulaert *et al.*, 1999).[2] Among those hired in 1993 by AME to develop this programme was Vincent B., who soon afterwards produced an offspring of AME, the association AME Services, with the specific objective of providing economic activities for people with severe difficulties – the long-term unemployed, the poorly skilled young and victims of ethnic discrimination. In 1999, AME Services adopted the name *Alentour* and became independent of the mother organisation AME from both the legal and the financial point of view.

For ten years, from 1993 to 2003, *Alentour* offered a wide range of social services to the inhabitants of Roubaix. The social restaurant Univers, created in 1993 in partnership with the Restaurants de Cœur, a chain launched in 1985 by the French actor Coluche, remains one of the most successful initiatives. The restaurant offers a hot lunch daily and several personal services (laundry, showering and hairdressing) to about seventy marginalised people (i.e. homeless, those without papers, alcoholics, etc.). In order to improve the social relationships among these excluded people, Univers also organises excursions to other French regions, afternoon dancing, sports or art competitions. Another social service activity, comprising the maintenance of common spaces in social housing and municipal buildings, was developed in 1993, in partnership with the social housing administration Roubaix-Habitat and city hall. A third social initiative, the reading-animation service, which circulates books to about 1,400 children in schools and social centres, was initiated in 1995.

In 1996, because of its rapid growth (the association, by then with ten permanent employees and forty people on 'insertion contracts'), began to face financial difficulties. Fluctuating funding weakened the organisation, which was largely dependent on public employment programmes: special 'insertion contracts' for people with difficulties (Contract Emploi Solidarité, Contract Emploi Consolidé, Contract Emploi Jeune) and 'local insertion plans' (PLIE). For example, in 1995, when the Contract Emploi Solidarité was discontinued, the 'help at home' service, initiated in 1993, was forced to close. It was replaced by two other similar services, but the association's financial situation continued to worsen because of difficulties in obtaining contracts. In fact, the association's budget, while 60 per cent state funded, acquired the remaining 40 per cent from clients or from short-term measures such as the URBAN project with just three years funding, and proved extremely volatile. In 1998, the association was given a new contract – the management of the municipal park Brondeloire – by the municipality in order to help rebalance its finances. However, rather than improving the situation, this new service made things worse for other reasons. Among these were the pressures to employ exclusively young people (through the Contract Emploi Jeune) and the subsequent withdrawal of the municipality from the partnership with a resultant cut in funding.

The three-year funding (1999–2001) under the European programme URBAN was an important opportunity for *Alentour* to consolidate its activities and to maintain its employment levels. The objectives of this European programme were the revival of commercial life and the triggering of neigh-bourhood economic redevelopment through several concurrent initiatives: the renovation of abandoned commercial space and the training of future tradesmen; the transformation of an old factory into a business centre (Hôtel d'entreprises Roussel); improvement of the physical and social environment with the creation of a green space – the park Brondeloire – on the site of industrial waste land; the revival of the traditional neighbourhood festivals and sport competitions; the development of local social services, such as the reading-animation initiative for children, a day centre for homeless people, etc. Despite these efforts, however, the association continued to face financial difficulties and, more importantly, lacked official recognition of the social merits of its activities, which made for a difficult dialogue with institutional and financial partners.

In 2002, the founder and director of *Alentour*, Vincent B., decided to leave the project because of both 'internal' and 'external' failures. On the 'external' front, the main defeat rested, in his opinion, on the progressive transformation of 'social interest' activities into straightforward placement and commercial activities, that is, the loss of the 'social economy' character, which formed the very core of its solidarity activities:

My purpose was to build social links in the territory by developing social utility activities with the unemployed people of the neighbourhood. That is the first failure, after which, I could not continue any more. The idea was not to just create reinsertion, to change the personnel every six months or to try 'to push' them into a market structure.

(Vincent B., interview 2003)

The director also underlined the lack of involvement by local actors in the various *Alentour* projects: 'We have developed social links in our territory ... but (the territorial actors) don't care: to create activities and jobs are the only important issues to them' (Vincent B., interview 2003). Among the 'internal' failures prompting him to leave the association, Vincent B. mentioned the loss of reciprocal trust, arising from the contradiction between two opposite discourses: the (re)insertion of the people into the labour market, on one hand, and the 'social' dimension of the activities on the other. He also mentioned the difficulties of managing such an important number of employees, the growing financial fluctuations, and pressures from residents who increasingly perceived the director of *Alentour* as 'a guy who should give a job to all'. In addition to all these, there were also related personal motivations: 'I'm a developer, not a businessman, and I don't know how to organise things in this context' (Vincent B., interview 2003).

The departure of the founder of *Alentour* forced the actors involved in his project to find alternative solutions in order to avoid the definitive end of the association and the firing of all the staff. The Administrative Council of *Alentour*, with the approval of the municipality and of the Local Insertion Plan (PLIE), decided to reorganise the activities: two services, animation-reading and the management of the park Brondeloire, were transferred to the municipality. The other three services became autonomous associations: the catering service as the Association Univers, the social housing maintenance service as the Association Astuce, and the maintenance of the municipal buildings retaining its activity and the name *Alentour*.

Conclusion: how socially innovative is *Alentour*?

Our empirical research – especially the interviews with privileged witnesses – clearly showed that the key institutional actors never talk in terms of 'social innovation' and that sometimes they even downplay the concept, speaking at most of 'interesting initiatives', good funding opportunities or 'new' ways to answer social needs.

In fact, for the majority of the institutional interviewees *Alentour* represents an unusual initiative that listened to neighbourhood concerns and was able to take advantage of specific procedures and available financial resources to achieve its goals and answer to employment needs in the neighbourhood. Moreover, these interviewees stressed other aspects of social innovation that should be taken into account, such as the durability of the initiatives, the resulting activities and the possible reproduction of the experience in other territories. By contrast, the inhabitant survey showed that they perceived the socially innovative potential of *Alentour* precisely in the fact that, besides creating jobs and services, it allowed the (re)creation of social relationships. The social economy, through new modes of needs satisfaction, not only invigorates new modes of internal and external governance but also the 'empowerment' of users (Ailenei *et al.*, 2008; Moulaert *et al.*, 2005; SINGOCOM, 2005).

The way in which *Alentour* worked, at least until the departure of its founder in 2002, fits rather well with the definition and main dimensions of social innovation as given in Chapter 3: (1) meeting the alienated needs of inhabitants; (2) improving the dialogue between local actors; (3) reinforcing the autonomy of marginalised people. Its socially innovative role responds well to the theoretical categories of social innovation analysis put forward in Chapter 3 (see Figure 7.1); these categories also help to enlighten the association's internal contradictions, and the constraints that affected its sustainability over time. First, *Alentour* played a crucial role in interpreting the L'Epeule neighbourhood social needs and in providing social services through the creation of a local associative-public network. Second, the association not only ensured the satisfaction of basic 'material' needs, but also aimed at developing 'social' links and socio-political capabilities of excluded people, thereby contributing to their empowerment. These goals were met by combining a mix of public, private and civic resources, which found a temporary virtuous balance in the 'co-production' of services for the community. In other words, social services for the neighbourhood were partly produced by their users, who thus simultaneously found employment and social integration. Moreover, the daily contact between service suppliers, institutional actors and users (re)created social relations in the neighbourhood and an arena for dialogue and discussion among different groups.

However, some of our interlocutors consider the *Alentour* social economy experience as not really socially innovative, or even as a *déclin de l'innovation sociale*. In our opinion, this harsh judgement expresses a frustration vis-à-vis the failure to accomplish the original ambitious goals of the association and the anxiety stemming from the decline in financial resources (see Ailenei *et al.*, 2008). Viewed from its ambition to establish a long-lasting public arena to discuss and solve the neighbourhood problems, *Alentour* has indeed failed. But it did manage to provide services of social interest and productive co-operation with other actors involved in territorial development. The frustration of failure must therefore be seen against the original ambitions of *Alentour*: to be recognised as a sustainable social economy organisation, to be evaluated in terms of its social objectives and not exclusively according to its economic outcomes. It was precisely the difficult integration of the different institutional, financial and managerial logics into its ambitious socially innovative project that brought *Alentour* to its limit, despite all the results and efforts to reproduce social activities and to stabilise employment within it.

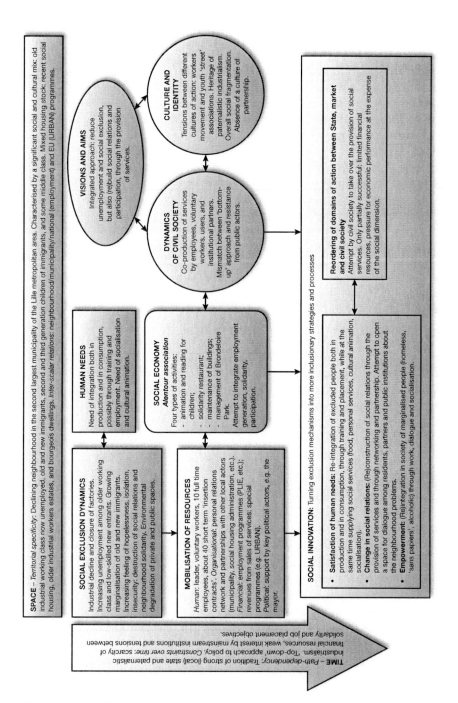

Figure 7.1 Dynamics of social innovation in the case of *Alentour*, Roubaix.
Source: Authors.

Throughout its first ten years, *Alentour* was a vehicle for significant social innovation. Although born within a traditional paternalistic organisation and although it made use of 'top-down' public programmes within a traditionally centralised policy context, the association succeeded – at least initially – in 'reinterpreting' social policy within a relatively innovative 'bottom-up', territorially grounded, and integrated 'social economy' approach. The role of local institutions and authorities was ambivalent. Our analysis has highlighted several individual and institutional attitudes, ranging from support or partnership to conflict or indifference, while showing a tendency to control, or even to reintegrate projects within the established centralised implementation frameworks. In the end, the legacy of the paternalistic bourgeois philanthropy of both the Roubaix industrial past and the centralised French state, constrained the establishment of a true partnership culture.

The originality of the association rests on the fact that it succeeded in mobilising and combining a range of diverse resources: human capital in the form of permanent employees, those with special 'insertion contracts' and voluntary workers; social capital, that is, the social networks of the members, which facilitated or hampered access to other resources; political capital, especially the support of the Mayor of Roubaix; financial resources stemming from special contracts, institutional clients, public programmes, European funding. The role of the Mayor of Roubaix is an interesting mirror, showing the delicate relationship between neighbourhood development and urban policy. The mayor actively supported *Alentour* in its ambition to establish new work sites for maintenance and cleaning (*chantiers de maintenance*),[3] and to obtain funding (as through the URBAN programme, see above). Still, *Alentour* did not really manage to get recognition for its social innovation objectives in its dialogue with the local authorities. Probably there are two main reasons for this.

First, there is the fragmentation of Roubaix society and the way this weighs on new modes of social organisation. The different social groups are poorly bonded, which hampers the formation of wider coalitions. This is also due to ambivalence among social forces in Roubaix with, for example, tension between traditional modernist ways of collective action (worker unionism and struggles) and new ('postmodern') ways of organising in neighbourhood committees and youth organisations. This creates an ambiguous scenario for local actors (public, movements, private) to build partnerships.

Second, there is the direction taken by urban policy in France in general, but also in Roubaix since the 1990s. In his role as a vice-president of the Lille Agglomeration Community (Lille Métropole Communauté Urbaine) the Mayor of Roubaix always supported the interests of Roubaix and Tourcoing (the Nord-East slope of the agglomeration), both considered as 'poor relatives' of Lille, the regional capital. From the 1990s, he became actively involved in urban renewal and unemployment reduction policies in Roubaix – signalled at the outset as badly hit by deindustrialisation and social exclusion since the 1970s. These policies focused on economic and cultural development (business premises, renewal of urban landscape and patrimony, cultural infrastructures and animation) meant to beautify the image of the city for both the Roubaisiens and the outside world. According to some local actors and part of the interviewed local population, this policy lacked social ambitions. Many inhabitants of L'Epeule who participated in our survey expressed a feeling of being abandoned by the local authorities.

Still, in conclusion, we argue that *Alentour*'s most innovative contribution in the neighbourhood of L'Epeule was the 'social' innovation dimension of its initiatives – the co-production of services to satisfy basic needs, to recreate social relations and to empower its residents – rather than purely economic job creation. For this reason, we nuance the judgement of failure conveyed by the founder on his resignation.

Despite its drawbacks, the experience launched by *Alentour* continues and a number of innovative features have been maintained. Alternative solutions to firing all employees were found; activities were redeployed and continue to exist in autonomous organisational forms or as services of the municipality. The various organisations that emanated from *Alentour* have continued the provision of social services, even if this happened under different arrangements and in relatively poor interaction with other social and institutional actors. The social services provided still meet the needs of vulnerable people (isolated persons, children, inhabitants of social housing, young people without qualifications, long-term unemployed, persons without papers, homeless, etc.), while ensuring training and new jobs. The employees still play a certain role in creating social links in the neighbourhood: the employees of the restaurant Univers, for example, still organise trips, parties and society games for users; the agents who work in social housing still ensure a certain degree of security, by continuing to live in the same buildings; the animation-reading initiative still reaches women (in particular housewives) and their children, whereas the animators of the municipal park are young people belonging to the neighbourhood. But, unfortunately, the grand public arena for discussing and organising collective action for urban redevelopment, in a more integrative socially innovative sense, was not established.

Notes

1   Institut National de la Statistique et des Études Économiques (French National Institute for Statistics).
2   The municipalities managed the PLIEs that also benefit from the support of the region and department.
3   *Chantiers de maintenance*, creation of jobs in cleaning and maintenance, as an *action d'insertion* (*insertion par l'économique*).

References

Ailenei, O. (2007) 'Le rôle de l'économie sociale dans les dynamiques socioéconomiques locales. Construction d'un modèle d'analyse et comparaison intra-européenne', unpublished Ph.D. thesis, Université de Lille 1 (France).

—— Hamdouch, A., Laffort, B. and Moulaert, F. (2007) 'Économie sociale, échelles spatiales et processus d'innovation sociale', paper presented at *CRISES Conference 'Créer et diffuser l'innovation sociale'*, Montréal, November 2007.

——, ——, —— and —— (2008) ECOSIN – 'L'économie sociale, plateforme de l'innovation sociale', *Report CPER (Contrat Plan État-Région), MESHS-CNRS, Lille, December 2008*. Online. Available: www.meshs.fr/page.php?r=46&lang=fr (Accessed 1 June 2009).

Brooks, D. (2000) *Bobos in Paradise: The New Upper Class and How They Got There*, New York: Simon & Schuster.

Hamdouch, A., Ailenei, O., Laffort, B. and Moulaert, F. (2009) 'Les organisations de l'économie sociale dans la métropole lilloise: Vers de nouvelles articulations spatiales?', *Revue Canadienne de Science Régionale*, 23(1): 85–100.

Mingione, E. and Oberti, M. (2003) 'The struggle against social exclusion at the local level, diversity and convergence in European cities', *European Journal of Spatial Development*, 1: 1–23.

Moulaert, F. (2000; 2nd edn 2002) *Globalization and Integrated Area Development in European Cities*, Oxford: Oxford University Press.

—— Martinelli, F., Swyngedouw, E. and Gonzáles, S. (2005) 'Towards alternative model(s) of local innovation', *Urban Studies*, 42(11): 1969–90.

—— Rodriguez, A., Sekia, F. and Swyngedouw, E. (1999) 'Urban redevelopment and social polarisation in the city' (URSPIC), *Final report for the EU, DG XII, TSER*.

SINGOCOM (2005) 'Social innovation and governance in urban communities'. Online. Available: www.ncl.ac.uk/ipp/research/projects/singocom.htm (Accessed 1 May 2005).

Ville de Roubaix (1999) Observatoire Urbain de Roubaix, internal document: statistics based on INSEE Census 1999.

8 *Arts Factory* in Ferndale, South Wales

Renegotiating social relations in a traditional working-class community

Sophie Donaldson and Liz Court

Introduction

This case study is concerned with the socially innovative role of a multi-dimensional community-owned enterprise providing for otherwise unmet social needs, in the sense that it offers activities to participants, and services to communities, which would not be supplied by the market. It offers insights into how this role has been carved out, and its relations with the local and wider context. In addition, it discusses the nature of ongoing dynamics, both internal and external – and how these affect the development and impacts of *Arts Factory* (*AF*). In doing so, it sheds light on the following questions: (1) How, in an area of intense policy intervention, can certain needs still go unmet? (2) How, in an area renowned for its socialist political activism, has effective disenfranchisement of much of the population occurred? (3) How do the processes of resource definition and combination affect inclusion and exclusion dynamics? (4) Why is a continuing innovation dynamic necessary?

In fact, as we shall see, in the *Arts Factory* case all three dimensions of social innovation – as put forward in Chapter 3 – are present: responding to basic needs, including personal development, social contacts, community work; empowerment, also through major cultural change; change in power relations within the community and between the community and local authorities.

The case study is based on a number of sources, including interviews with privileged witnesses such as: the co-founder of the *Arts Factory* and two workers within *AF*, as well as a key collaborator with *AF* from the social services department of the local authority, and a local authority and a politician from the national stage who has taken a particular interest in regeneration in that area; the annual review of the *AF* and its magazine; participant observation by our research colleague Kevin Morgan, who has had various contacts with the organisation, including appearing as an 'expert witness' in support of the wind farm planning application. Table 8.1 provides a brief chronology to anchor the subsequent discussion.

Table 8.1 Chronology of the *Arts Factory* case study

1990	Vales Community Business formed.
1995	Ferndale base, Highfields Industrial Estate – *AF* name added.
1996	Garden centre opened at Highfields. First award. First free classes offered.
1997	First social audit – first organisation in Wales to do one. Launched campaign to secure the Trerhondda Chapel for the organisation, saving it from the demolition wanted by the council. British Urban Regeneration Association Award.
1998	Trerhondda Chapel opened – dedicated building for classes and facilities for members.
2000–01	Wind Farm ('Power Factory') idea launched – joint venture with a private company to provide an independent income stream. Also the idea for Parc 21 – a sustainable business park, based on taking on the ownership of a local authority industrial estate – ideally Highfields. The Welsh Assembly Government launched their sustainable development strategy at Trerhondda Chapel.
2002	Rewind, Pause, Fast-forward session – everyone involved in review of the organisation, leading to a new ten-year development strategy.
2003	Application for planning permission for the Wind Farm rejected; appeal procedure invoked, involving decision by Welsh Assembly Government. The BBC featured Trerhondda as a good practice exemplar of viable redevelopment of an historic building in their series 'Restoration' – viewed by three million people.
2005	Appeal against refusal of planning permission won. E.ON replaced United Utilities Green Energy as partner in the Wind Farm project.
2007	Joint venture social enterprise involving the *Arts Factory* and other development trusts in South Wales launched to provide training for local people in building skills while undertaking repairs to social housing. *AF* now employs seventeen staff and forty seasonal workers; it has an annual turnover of over £500,000.00.
2008	E.ON withdraws from the project, as a revised plan means that the Wind Farm falls below the threshold for projects it invests in. A new partner sought. Decision on European Funding is pending.

Source: Authors

Arts Factory in context: telling the story

Arts Factory originated in 1990, as Vales Community Business, to provide work experience and training opportunities for people with learning disabilities through horticultural activities, led by two people who had previously worked for Mencap, a historical UK charity, specifically concerned with learning disabilities. The group wished to challenge their labelling and stigmatisation, which had condemned them to spend their lives essentially being 'looked after' in day centres, on terms defined by Social Services – local authority manage-ment and professional conventions. Instead, they wished to 'get out and do something useful' – which was to be the provision of gardening services, often to elderly social housing tenants.

The approach of Vales Community Business challenged a perception of disabled people as dependent and objects of pity, a perception which was firmly entrenched in a hegemonic political discourse in South Wales, which in other respects was regarded as radical and oppositional to the values and social relations of unfettered capitalism (Hastings and Thomas, 2005; Clavel, 1983). This seems to reflect (or in some cases foreshadow) a number of opportunities and wider developments. First, there were general moves to deinstitutionalise certain populations – the wider mental health movement of 'care in the community' (Means *et al.*, 2003; Chapters 4 (Membretti) and 5 (Vitale) in this book). Second, central government was promoting contracting-out of certain local authority functions (Cochrane, 1993). Third, there was coming to be recog-nition of a greater diversity of needs among local populations (following the ideas of postmodernism and new social movements), as compared to more universal approaches to social welfare, further recognising that social exclusion is something different (only partially overlapping) from economic development or regeneration needs (Sandercock, 2003). More importantly however, these vague sentiments and broader movements were acted upon and operationalised – that is, drawn together in a meaningful and material way – in a particular context. Here the vision of the two leaders was crucial, a vision that had been grounded in their work for Mencap, with its independent ethos and commit-ment to improve understanding of learning disabilities, as well as working with those with learning disabilities to engender positive change in their lives. This then translated to the particular ethos of the group.

The work of Vales Community Business at this early stage already made connections with other socially excluded groups – particularly the elderly or those otherwise unable to maintain their own gardens. While this represented a business opportunity, it is easy to imagine how contact with such groups, and more generally working in a locality in which problems were also manifest both physically and in representations of the area/local people, came to result in a broader vision. This was, and remains, a vision based on an expanded consciousness of the problems faced and on the recognition of the commonalities as well as differences involved. In particular, the trajectory of the organisation's work was prompting a rethinking of the notion of community as it had traditionally been conceived in these old industrial areas – with men of working age in a central position, and others more marginal to the labour market in supportive and/or dependent roles. The advent of women into the labour market in large numbers from the 1960s onwards had begun to challenge this potent political myth, but Vales Community Business was in effect questioning it more radically, by suggesting that disabled people, elderly people and others had value other than in relation to the labour market, and that a notion, and material reality, of community which recognised this could be developed in an area. This vision was not unanimously supported in the locality, and remains contentious, as the history of *Arts Factory* demonstrates.

Unpacking the feelings of helplessness and hopelessness described locally, in an area suffering from the far-reaching and interlocking social and economic consequences of 'deindustrialisation', various needs have been revealed. But equally, it has been recognised that needs can be constructed as opportunities or resources. Out of this recognition developed the numerous community classes and activities, some linked into individual social enterprises, but also tied into a broader agenda of enacting sustainable development and local empowerment – the latter understood as a renegotiation of relations within the community, as well as of relations extending beyond it.

A key element of this strategy has been establishing two physical bases for the activity of *AF*, both involving the re-use of under-used, and in the case of the Trerhondda Chapel, derelict buildings, creating new life where decline all too easily was becoming a self-fulfilling prophecy. The physical location of *AF* also reinforces its philosophy of being a community-based enterprise, because it is both highly visible and extremely accessible to the local community in which it is based. This in turn is reinforced by the involvement of its members – which have rapidly reached over 1,500 in number, given the minimal £1 a year membership fee – in brainstorming new ideas, in decision-making and in volunteering. This reflects the belief that people are empowered through participating in their own transformation, harnessing local knowledge and ensuring local 'ownership'.

The whole approach of *AF* has signalled the fact that it represents a radical break with the standardised and conventional community development schemes of the past and service provision by the local authority in general, which have been marred by the disempowering effect of the local Labour Party. This Party was returned to office in Rhondda Cynon Taff (RCT) in June 2004, after losing the 2000 election, the first time it had ever lost an election in the borough, having been in office for the best part of a century. It had created a conservative labourist culture, which viewed active citizens with a mixture of suspicion and alarm, and was generally perceived to be aloof, paternalistic and closed to new ideas, blind to real local needs (Amin *et al.*, 2002; Mungham and Morgan, 2000).

The Trerhondda Chapel battle between *AF* and the local council in RCT is a perfect illustration of the conflict between such a conservative local political regime and a dynamic social enterprise (compare with Christiaens *et al.*, 2007). The local council wanted to demolish the old building (one of the many nonconformist chapels which were once prevalent throughout the whole of Wales) on the grounds that it was unsafe. In contrast, *AF* wanted to renovate the building on account of its prime location in the community and to promote the cause of sustainable development (through re-use, and community engagement). Eventually the *AF* campaign won the day and the former chapel has been reclaimed for the community.

A continuing struggle, however, is the raising of resources to maintain the range of activities that *Arts Factory* supports. Funding from membership fees is nominal, in line with its accessibility ethos, so *Arts Factory* must rely on various sources each of which have their problems. For example, contracts from the local authority (e.g. for social care provision) and other purchasers (e.g. the Job Centre Plus, the state employment agency) tend to be aimed at specific populations (e.g. those with learning disabilities). Work done by its various individual social enterprises (e.g. graphic design, community consultation, landscape design and improvement) is expected to be at low cost because they are 'not for profit'; while, actually, profit is essential to be ploughed back into community facilities and costs may be higher given the emphasis on social integration. Consequently, some businesses (e.g. a pottery) have had to be shut down, while the inclusive elements of others had to be pared back. To face these problems, the Trerhondda Chapel project engineered an additional funding stream; lettable office space was created and leased to local authority agencies, which appreciated the usefulness of a presence in a well-patronised facility, physically in the heart of the local community. The capital value of the building is now estimated to be £500,000.00, providing a significant asset base. But the problem remains: the other main source of funding – project-funding – is erratic, given funding criteria and the lack of funding for core, day-to-day costs. The European Commission structural fund criteria, for instance, excluded the funding of children's art classes, given that the project did not directly pertain to those of employable age, while lottery funding, although providing for these classes, is not renewable unless a project is substantially different. Ultimately, *Arts Factory* also suffers from competition from the multitude of other initiatives in the region – symptomatic of wide neglect of needs by the mainstream – although it does try to work with them wherever possible, seeing value in collaboration. While *AF* is well placed to respond to the increasing emphasis at national/regional governmental levels that community development projects need, wherever possible, to have robust plans to generate their own income streams, it is often difficult to reconcile a programme of encouraging marginalised groups to discover and express their needs with the demands of seeking revenue in a marketplace.

Deriving from this situation is the innovative and radical proposal to develop a community-owned wind farm ('power factory') – to be at once a solution to the perennial struggle for resources and a key route to advancing the sustainable development agenda locally. This proposal aims to integrate the global and the local by contributing to the green energy needs of the country, a local initiative which also helps to reduce global warming.

The wind farm planning application was initially rejected by the local authority, largely on account of opposition from elected members and a small group of local residents rather than officers – indeed the officers were quite co-operative. A parallel planning proposal, to assume ownership and control of the industrial estate on which some of its activity is based, retrofitting it as an example of sustainable building practices and resource management

(Parc 21), was also refused by the local authority, as its owner, suddenly saw the site as an asset. It is difficult not to see this opposition, which has been doggedly maintained by the local authority over many years, as deriving in part from a desire to 'clip the wings' of an organisation which is increasingly providing an alternative model of governance. Indeed, *AF* clearly shows how residents might relate in a different way to organisations which seek to meet their needs, which demonstrates an ambition tempered by realism and hard-headedness that the authority often lacks, and which has also established its own communication links and working relationships with governance agencies beyond the local authority, notably (but not exclusively) those involved in EU programmes, whether based in Brussels or South Wales. The wind farm idea has at least been salvaged, with negotiations over an alternative site in a different local authority area, which might enable a further development – a visitor centre to educate people about 'green energy' and sustainable development more broadly.

AF has successfully appealed against the planning decision over the wind farm at the higher level of the National Assembly for Wales. *AF*'s practical commitment to sustainable development and to reconfiguring social relations so as to help reduce the exclusion of historically marginal groups does in fact resonate more at this level of governance, as the Government of Wales Act (1998) has obliged the National Assembly since its inception to promote sustainable development and equality of opportunity in all its activities. The ability of *AF* to work within governance networks which operate beyond the local community (and immediate local authority area) is well illustrated by the fact that the National Assembly launched its Sustainable Development Strategy in 2000, precisely from *AF*'s renovated Trerhondda Chapel building. *AF* has also been featured in various media with a UK audience as an example of good practice, which suggests that setbacks forced upon it will have an equally high profile – and this, perhaps, can be used as a lever to its advantage.

Main dynamics of social exclusion, inclusion and innovation

The Rhondda Fach valley, which is where *AF* originated, is a typical area of the South Wales coalfield where the economic base has been precarious since the 1920s, with precipitous losses of manual (male) employment since 1945, only partly offset by new (female) manual jobs in light manufacturing sectors such as the consumer electronics sector and more generally in the service sector (Adamson, 1999; Dicks, 2000). New investment in infrastructure has been undertaken with the aim of attracting employers who use road-based freight, but public transport remains poor. Consequently there is a network of relatively isolated linear settlements, with high levels of deprivation, whereas those with resources are increasingly economically and socio-culturally oriented towards Cardiff, the dominant regional centre and capital of Wales.

It is clear that these are areas where social and economic networks are likely to be under considerable strain. There are serious problems of alcohol and substance abuse with related health problems, under-achievement in school, racism (against a very small minority ethnic population). In addition, there is the continuous rather messy process of renegotiating gender relations in relation to the increasing female participation in the workforce, against a background of established male dominance. Yet the ideal of the community providing support, identity and discipline for individuals appears to retain widespread appeal and to mark the distinctiveness of the valleys for many of its residents. This ideal has enormous political potency throughout Wales, but community is an ambiguous ideal (Young, 1990) and for many people a central social policy issue for places like the Rhondda Fach is how to reconstruct community in terms which do not simply mirror the imperatives of capitalism by privileging those who are active in the labour market, traditionally men (Rees, 1997). The activity of *AF* contributes very directly to this struggle, which is about reconfiguring social relations within as well as outside the local area. However, *AF* does not lose sight of the importance of training, which allows people to access jobs.

The tradition of governance in the Rhondda Fach, as in South Wales generally, in some (crude) ways prefigures the changes in local governance discussed so much in recent literature. South Wales has long been 'Quangoland', or the 'Costa Bureaucratica', its governance having elected local authorities at its core, but buttressing these with a plethora of agencies and ad hoc committees that draw in private and (to a lesser extent) voluntary sector organisations. Central to the coherence of this network has been a shared diagnosis of the area's problems and the necessary solutions – that only a narrow stratum of active individuals is involved and a hierarchical mode of operation that is ruthless in stifling dissent or questioning. This form of governance largely reflects the hegemony of cohesive, organised (male) labour in these settlements during the early decades of the twentieth century, yet it has persisted as a governance style, partly causing – and partly resulting from – the widespread alienation of the population from governance in all its forms (from elected councils through to residents' forums) (Cowell and Thomas, 2002). It is a style which requires, and encourages, passivity on the part of the population at large, so that appropriate agencies (usually the local council) can deliver services to address problems they define and in ways they see fit (Mungham and Morgan, 2000). *AF* has challenged this in more than one way – notably, in its own attempts to be a member-led organisation, and in its mobilisation of popular support (mass petitions and the like) in countering the local authority's opposition to its wind farm proposal.

The factors described above contribute to creating a situation of multiple needs that go unmet, partly material and partly related to the configuration of social and governance relations and the ideals subscribed to. In providing very low-cost, inclusive access to facilities and activities, *AF* has started to tackle many of these needs head on, opening the door to numerous people who are thus enabled to express such latent desires. *AF* offers opportunities for self-development – challenging labelling and self-concepts, increasing social contact, and, more simply, providing the platform to try out new and different things. Local involvement has been immediately attractive, as soon as people were made aware of the opportunities it presents, whether by word of mouth, public events or by referral through various agencies. It seems to have 'gelled' around the campaign to save the Trerhondda Chapel and subsequently sustained by ongoing openness to ideas and regular review, ensuring continued viability and local interest.

Many of the needs that *AF* seeks to address have historically not been well understood by local government agencies (e.g. that respect be accorded to disabled people and that local residents of deprived communities have a desire, as well as a right, to participate in their own regeneration) (Amin *et al.*, 2002). It has helped introduce new ideas into local political debates, ideas which go beyond the narrow concern of the traditional social agenda to re-create community by achieving full employment and seeks to encourage a rethinking of community as active citizen engagement together with just social and environmental relations. Significantly, it has avoided dependency relations with the local council, or any other agency in the regional web of governance. Its recent initiative in partnership with non-governmental development agencies elsewhere in South Wales is a clear example of how it avoids over-dependence on any one agency. This both provides space for the new ideas to develop and creates further value in proving the potential for self-determination and reliance through collaborative effort.

In these ways *AF* demonstrates an alternative – something that is making a difference where other agencies have not, both due to their lack of action and the way in which they conceive the 'problems' and 'solutions' (Amin *et al.*, 2002). It also, however, creates an implicit challenge to the established 'system' and this has often resulted in defensive reactions, particularly when *AF* has had to make actual contact and negotiate. *AF* is, for example, accused by local councillors of not respecting the local democratic process, which is deemed to have given them a popular mandate to speak on behalf of their local communities (despite the fact that this 'popular mandate' is based on fewer and fewer votes because of ever lower voter turn-out in local council elections). This local political criticism conveniently misses the point of what *AF* is actually trying to achieve. Such narrow-minded thinking may obstruct the implementation of *AF*'s ideals, but this and other difficulties (e.g. funding) do not seem to lead inevitably to deadlock: *AF*'s leaders have exhibited considerable determination and resource in achieving the organisation's goals, even if the means have required flexible thinking (e.g. considering an alternative industrial estate for Parc 21; and – more recently – looking for alternative commercial partners for the wind farm project). However, ultimate independence from the 'system' as currently conceived is also contingent upon its gaining planning permission and gifted buildings from the local authority. Constructive co-operation with the authority, beyond contractual relations, moves forward only slowly.

Beyond this engagement with the 'system' and attempts to gain consensus for *AF* ways of thinking, the other challenge is to ensure that *AF*'s members (and wider circles) take on board its vision as well as what it offers at the individual level. *AF* produces newsletters, organises activities and has organisational structures which are intended to achieve this. Yet, many observers suggest (with a degree of *Schadenfreude*) that there is a trend for *AF* to work in ways that are not dissimilar from the centralised approach taken by the agencies of governance that it deals with. This may derive from the need to acquire sufficient leadership drive to negotiate difficult territories, as well as from the habitual deference to those who are perceived to be better educated with 'system-savvy'. Overcoming these hurdles would seem to be a prerequisite to really changing the direction and nature of local institutions, formal and informal.

Conclusion

In summary, *AF* began as a way of recasting social relations involving a narrow group (those with learning disabilities) in a context of local political culture that had become increasingly paternalistic over the last 100 years. *AF* is now, de facto, challenging that broader culture. Through the influence of key individuals the project has drawn upon the experiences and inspiration of social movements, such as the disability movement, from the 1970s onwards. However, in the towns of the South Wales valleys, which remain essentially one-class settlements, a concern for inequalities related to disability or age has not been at the expense of a continued awareness of the significance of solidarity based on the lived experience of class in a specific place. *AF* has avoided over-reliance on the political elite and structures of its immediate locality, by engaging with networks of governance at regional (Welsh) level – which link it into UK and European priorities – and by cultivating a strong local base of support, through providing valued facilities/services and by offering opportunities for involvement.

In the South Wales context, *AF* is an attempt to reconnect with a tradition of grass-roots activism which is revered as a memory (in trade unions, chapels and welfare institutes) but has withered as a living reality for most residents. In doing so, it attends to human needs that are social rather than necessarily material, although they may be provided for through the provision of things such as community education facilities, and the plans for a wind farm to provide for local electricity needs. These human needs, in other words, are the need to participate in social activities, decision-making and actions for change, to feel able to create positive change in one's own life and in the general quality of life of the community, and to feel 'of value' in various dimensions. It therefore challenges hierarchical social relations, including passivity and feelings of powerlessness among 'ordinary people', both directly through particular 'battles' and indirectly through proving new capabilities.

AF is regarded with suspicion by mainstream politicians in the locality. It is difficult to know whether this is because they fear that, in fact, it is a new power base for the principal actors in *AF*, or whether they fear the implications of a renewed interest and confidence in civic affairs among the population at large. Within *AF* the challenge is to encourage genuine power-sharing and democracy; there remains a sense that the dynamism and vision of the founders still leaves others in their wake. One of the features of *AF* has been its readiness to undertake new ventures, while retaining a commitment to the principles of volunteer involvement and control. It is currently attempting to link traditional concerns about distributive justice and social inclusion with a concern to promote sustainable development in a very practical way. If this project is successful, it may well stabilise *AF*'s identity – thus countering a concern in some circles that the enthusiasm and readiness for new ventures has sometimes blunted its focus.

The *AF* case study is particularly interesting in relation to social innovation for the way it (1) illustrates a sustained attempt to bring some of the principles of empowerment and equality associated with new social movements to activism in an area with a history of narrow class-based activism; (2) provides a practical example of linking the politics of environmentalism with the countering of social exclusion and meeting basic needs (for energy, for example); (3) allows us to investigate the risks associated with energetic social entrepreneurialism in a project where there is a genuine desire not to concentrate power within the organisation; (4) illustrates the ways in which shifts in governance have opened up opportunities for such entrepreneurialism.

References

Adamson, D. (1999) 'Poverty and social exclusion in Wales today', in D. Dunkerley and A. Thompson (eds) *Wales Today*, Cardiff: Cardiff University Press.

Amin, A., Cameron, A. and Hudson, R. (2002) *Placing the Social Economy*, London: Routledge.

Christiaens, E., Moulaert, F. and Bosman, B. (2007) 'The end of social innovation in urban development strategies? The case of Antwerp and the neighbourhood development association "BOM"', *European Urban and Regional Studies*, 14(3): 238–51.

Clavel, P. (1983) *Opposition Planning in Wales and Appalachia*, Cardiff: University of Wales Press.

Cochrane, A. (1993) *Whatever Happened to Local Government?* Buckingham: Open University Press.

Cowell, R. and Thomas, H. (2002) 'Managing nature and narratives of dispossession: reclaiming territory in Cardiff Bay', *Urban Studies*, 39(7): 1241–60.

Dicks, B. (2000) *Heritage, Place and Community*, Cardiff: University of Wales Press.

Government of Wales Act (1998) Chapter 38, London, Stationary Office. Online. Available: www.opsi.gov.uk/acts/acts1998/ukpga_19980038_en_1 (Accessed 1 June 2009).

Hastings, J and Thomas, H. (2005) 'Accessing the nation: disability, political inclusion and built form', *Urban Studies*, 42(3): 527–44.

Means, R., Richards, S. and Smith, R. (2003) *Community Care: Policy and Practice* (3rd edn), Basingstoke: Palgrave Macmillan.

Mungham, G. and Morgan, K. (2000) *Redesigning Democracy: The Making of the Welsh Assembly*, Bridgend: Seren.

Rees, G. (1997) 'The politics of regional development strategy: the programme for the valleys', in R. Macdonald and H. Thomas (eds) *Nationality and Planning in Scotland and Wales*, Cardiff: University of Wales Press, pp. 98–110.

Sandercock, L. (2003) *Cosmopolis II: Mongrel Cities*, London: Continuum.

Young, Iris M. (1990) *Justice and the Politics of Difference*, Princeton: Princeton University Press.

9 The *Ouseburn Trust* in Newcastle

A struggle to innovate in the context of a weak local state

Sara González and Geoff Vigar

Introduction

This case tells the story of a community group, the *Ouseburn Trust*, who continue to play a key role in the development of an inner urban valley of Newcastle upon Tyne in northern England. The group has been very successful in revalidating the Valley from a marginal area in the city to a vibrant and culturally rich place for visitors, workers and companies. This has been possible due to their strong commitment to the place and key strategic linkages with the formal government arenas in Newcastle. However, the 'scaling up' of the Valley that the *Ouseburn Trust* made possible has made innovation difficult as other actors, such as local government and developers, have become interested in the area.

This case shows the intricate relationship between community action, local government and private developers. In the Ouseburn, this relationship has changed over time, depending on the internal dynamics of the community group, national urban regeneration policy, local politics, neoliberal entrepreneurial city discourses adopted by the city council, property market trends and informal linkages between people.

This paper deals with the question of how a community group can find space to innovate in an institutionally rigid environment, where local governance practices are to a large extent structured by pressures from national and international scales to be more 'economically' innovative.

Our research was based on qualitative methods. We conducted thirteen semi-structured interviews with key informants from the community sector, local council and market developers. We also attended regularly the monthly committee for the regeneration of the Ouseburn and other events organised by the *Ouseburn Trust* or other actors in the Valley.

The Ouseburn Valley: a laboratory for social innovation

The Ouseburn Valley has for decades been a place of rich social interaction and creativity. The area was home to the industrial revolution on Tyneside in the late eighteenth century and up until the 1960s it had a significant residential population of workers, which declined due to clearance programmes. By the late 1970s, the whole north-east region had become a 'redundant space' as mining and manufacturing employment declined. As part of this wider picture, the Ouseburn Valley became a leftover or a phased-out space, mostly marginalised from capital accumulation strategies. Into this space came many activities: a business community that ranges from car repairers, to martial arts trainers and pub staff; a community summer festival; several leisure uses, mostly pubs; music bands who rehearse in cheap studios; a large artist studio warehouse; a centre for Children's Books; a stabling facility dedicated to young people with personal, social or educational needs; the Star and Shadow autonomous social centre with an independent cinema; the Ouseburn Boat Club and the Homing Society, who specialise in breeding pigeons. The Valley is also home to a diversity of flora and fauna and has a stunning topography of steep valley sides passed over by a series of architecturally interesting bridges. In short, it is the sort of urban area, rich in industrial heritage that has become subject to intense gentrification pressure.

From the late 1980s until the 2008 financial crisis, Newcastle, like many other British cities, witnessed a waterfront property development boom. As in many cities, locally this was public sector-led, in this case through the Tyne and Wear Development Corporation (TWDC). Early TWDC plans were perceived by a group of local community leaders and church representatives as having the potential to endanger the built and natural heritage of the local area (see Figure 9.1 for an 'institutional history' of the area). This group of activists and volunteers, the East Quayside Group, contested not only TWDC's vision for the area but also the governance processes that excluded participation from the community. This was the start of the *Ouseburn Trust*, who finally formalised itself into a Charitable Trust in 1995. This signalled the start of a process of 'institutionalisation' for the group of activists, increasingly sucked into state structures and disciplinary practices as we will see.

In 1997, the *Trust*, together with Newcastle City Council and various other groups from the Valley, succeeded in attracting £2.5 million (€3 million) of central government funding to spend over a period of five years to improve the employment prospects, skills and education of local people, encourage a sustainable development of the local economy and promote an inclusive, well-designed environment. For five years, between 1997 and 2002, the so-called Ouseburn Partnership worked as a real devolved power steered by the *Trust* (see Table 9.1 for the different governance structures in the Ouseburn). With the end of partnership funding in 2002, the future of the development of the Ouseburn shifted back more centrally into the city council's hands. But building on the relatively smooth relationship with the *Trust* over the past years and in line with the city-wide and New Labour trend to devolve power to communities, the city council decided to keep a level of partnership and from April 2002, the Ouseburn Advisory Committee was set up, a half councillor-/half community-composed committee that directly advised the

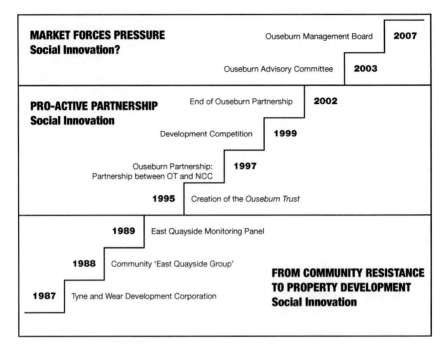

Figure 9.1 The institutional history of the Ouseburn 1987–2007
Source: Authors.

leader of the council plus a number of selected councillors. Effectively, they did not have to follow the Advisory Committee's decisions but a tradition was established in negotiations so that consensus was generally achieved. From 2007, however this structure has expired and a new Ouseburn Management Board has been established. The *Trust* is the single largest group on the Board but has only three members of the total of eleven.

Main dynamics of social exclusion, inclusion and innovation

Although all three dimensions of social innovation considered in ALMOLIN (see Chapter 3) are present in this case study, it is mainly on the second and third meanings – empowerment and changes in governance relations that we will dwell in our discussion of how the Ouseburn community made its voice heard and made innovative changes in the governance practices around the Valley. In this regard, we have identified three main dynamics that have either fostered or constrained social innovation in the Ouseburn Valley: the scaling-up of areas through state–industry nexuses; the sense of place and the importance of leadership in steering a progressive course; and the potentials,

Table 9.1 Different governance structures in the Ouseburn

Name	Ouseburn Trust (1995–)	Ouseburn Partnership (1997–2002)	Ouseburn Advisory Committee (2003–07)	Ouseburn Management Board (2007–)
Organisational form	Registered charity, not-for-profit development company.	A partnership to manage regeneration funding from central government.	City council committee.	City council committee.
Members	Local activists, nearby residents.	Ouseburn Trust (as the lead organisation) + eighteen partners (Newcastle City Council, TWDC, English Partnership, Home Housing Association).	Half councillors (5) half community members (5) (mainly from the Ouseburn Trust).	Two councillors, three from the Trust, two residents, two from the Arts and Culture Group, two business representatives.[a]
Function	Safeguard the interests of and develop or assist the development of the Ouseburn Valley.	Deliver a regeneration programme and manage the central government regeneration money.	Advise the Council on the implementation of the Lower Ouseburn Valley regeneration strategy.	Monitor development proposals, engage communities and market the area.

[a] The Arts and Culture group and business representation has been encouraged by the City Council to broaden the voice from the Valley; a response to a perceived narrowness in the Trust's constituency.

Source: Authors

difficulties and dangers of maintaining momentum in governing a place from outside the traditional state apparatus.

The scaling-up of the Ouseburn Valley community empowerment and development pressure

In the last ten years, the *Ouseburn Trust* first, and the Ouseburn Partnership later, have worked to make the Valley a 'visible' area, attracting policy interest and funding to improve the Valley's physical infrastructure while preserving its unique features. The main consequence of these activities has been the 'scaling-up' of the Valley and its emergence as an attractive location for property developers and for the council as a consequence.

From marginal area to 'urban village'

For the council, the Ouseburn is a key strategic site in the plans for the definitive re-imagination of Newcastle as a 'modern European city-region [that] acts as a key driver for the North East economy' (Newcastle City Council, 2008). It has been quoted as one of the 'competitive environments' in a Newcastle City Council strategy which suggests that 'the city's success depends on its degree of specialisation, entrepreneurship and innovation in globally focused, knowledge-based and cultural activities such as technology, finance, education and tourism' (ibid.).

The Council wants to achieve a 'Competitive Newcastle' in partnership with communities, encouraging participation and promoting cohesive and sustainable communities. The Ouseburn symbolises a paradox as the council regards it as a strategic economic space while, at least in principle, agreeing on the *Ouseburn Trust*'s vision of sustainable development, social mix and inclusiveness. In this paradox, the concept of 'urban village', attached to the Ouseburn Valley, seems to act as a superficial conciliation. The 'urban village' idea has been incorporated into the main discourse of urban planning in the UK in the last decade (Franklin and Tait, 2002) and is typically based on a mix of land uses at high densities on brownfield sites. It also meets a new emphasis in local economic development of creating assets that appeal to entrepreneurs in key industries in the 'knowledge economy'. The council itself owns four big sites and sees the Ouseburn as an opportunity to retain wealthy residents who may otherwise leave the city and its tax base and as a way of capturing capital revenue by selling the land to developers. By contrast, the *Trust* sees the urban village as denoting a smaller-scale set of developments centred on principles of social justice and asset preservation.

From the developer's point of view, the area now offers a unique combination of closeness to the city centre and the Quayside, but with green areas, a spectacular built heritage and a river. The first scheme built in the area has been sold in the marketing material as 'just minutes away from the vibrant life of Newcastle's Quayside' yet a historically rich area with 'fascinating old buildings' and a 'unique mix of historic riverside' (Metier, 2004). This offers possibilities for regeneration, but also risks a particular form of gentrification in a model common in heritage-rich areas.

A debate thus ensued as to what sort of development should be accommodated in the Valley. Although the *Ouseburn Trust* and some councillors have always been pushing for a social mix kind of housing, with affordable housing and possibilities for cheap working space, there is a danger of gentrification in the area. Attempts to ameliorate exclusionary tendencies in such development through cross-subsidisation of housing development from valuable riverside sites to others proved difficult due to local government accounting legislation. Latterly, as the market diminished for the sort of high density flatted development proposed by developers and sanctioned by the city council, schemes were being resubmitted as student halls of residence. These were seen by the *Trust* as failing to reflect the 'village' scale of the area and would lead to the over-dominance of a particular group in a still relatively unpopulated area.

Partnership and community disciplining

In the past two decades, British urban policy has been slowly moving towards a more participatory agenda involving more diverse stakeholders and opening government structures to alternative processes (Atkinson and Moon, 1994; Hill, 2000). This is part of the New Labour 'Third Way' agenda to encourage citizens to take part in decision-making processes and take up responsibilities (Hoban and Beresford, 2001). This move has crystallised in the establishment of partnerships between government agencies and community groups.

The Ouseburn Advisory Committee (OAC) and the subsequent Ouseburn Management Board (OMB) are examples of these partnerships. Given the development pressures unleashed from the late 1990s onwards, their meetings largely revolved around planning applications where two groups could be observed with differing views, frames of knowledge and rules of performance. On the one hand, some members of the *Ouseburn Trust*, community representatives and councillors adopted a defensive attitude, maintaining a generally critical view of all the planning applications. The group looked especially for how development impacted on traffic flows and pollution, at the density of population, the heights of buildings, respect for the heritage, design, the price of residential units and the mix of uses. On the other hand, the planning and economic development officers adopted a more 'professional' attitude, 'educating' the committee about existing regulations and policies that frame how applications must be considered. The meetings can, in some sense, be viewed as a process of translation between the more utopian and socially innovative language of the community, to the more official and formal language of local government professions. It can be seen as a process of 'disciplining' in Foucauldian terms where the community was disciplined within the rules and formal mechanisms of the state (Tooke, 2003; Raco and Imrie, 2000).

As part of this process, the *Ouseburn Trust* refined their vision for the Valley to fit with the formal language of planning, in the context of having to adapt to fast-changing market circumstances. The *Trust* wrote a 'development template' to act as a 'useful tool for assessing proposed developments, providing a framework of questions for all aspects of such development and the impact it may have on a local area' (OAC, 2004: 3). This template is interesting as it tries to assess the impact of proposed development in terms of its contribution to the local area, environmental impact and the benefit for the community, while effectively 'de-professionalising' the knowledge that resides in the planning officers. This report was welcomed by planning officers 'as a useful tool for officers in their dealings with developers' but they 'urged caution that the Advisory Committee should not prejudge or predetermine city council policy (which was a matter for the Development Control Committee)' (Ibid.: 4).

However, despite these efforts, developers do not consider the *Ouseburn Trust* or the community of workers and users of the valley as an interlocutor and negotiate directly with planning officers who inform them of the formal and informal policies in the Ouseburn. OAC and OMB meetings, as with other public hearings to discuss development, remain relatively irrelevant events where the community is left no other role than to behave in a defensive way and complain. Developers and planning officers fulfil their commitment to 'consult' the community and reinforce their idea that participation is a long, expensive and inefficient process.

Thus, one of the main dynamics that constrains the development of socially innovative ideas in UK neighbourhoods is the existence of a weak local state trying to regulate development in sensitive ways but within a system of rules that is structured nationally. This is coupled with the existence of nationally applied standards and practices, such as the promotion of brownfield regeneration. In addition, the council is under pressure to realise its land assets, with central government audit and inspection again heavily structuring their room for manoeuvre. Finally, the whiff of neoliberal, entrepreneurial city discourse – where Newcastle must compete in a globalised market of cities for jobs and investments – is the main policy frame under which the city council approaches regeneration and community participation (González and Vigar, 2008). These multi-scalar dynamics make the community and third sector groups relatively powerless.

Making space for innovation through sense of place and networks

Despite the difficulties of innovating in governance relations, the community has been successful in making some space for innovation and influencing the future of the Ouseburn Valley. This fissure in the traditional and tight governance system has been based mostly on a strong sense of 'place' and the active 'liaising' by key individuals across arenas, cultures and frames, often bypassing formal structures. The networks across different governance cultures and settings have sustained, through their commitment, a constant flow of transformative power but, as we have seen, with the approach of the realities of physical development, the low level of this power compared with that ascribed through the formal settings of the planning system and of wider structural conditions, has become clear.

The power of a sense of place

Attachment to the Valley as a place has been critical in raising and maintaining the interests of the actors. Chatting around a table in a local pub, the first members of the *Ouseburn Trust*, confronted with insensitive property develop-ment, were prompted to resist it. They then became more proactive, conceiving the transformation of the Valley itself. The Valley was imagined as an 'urban village' that would make 'use of existing good buildings which are part of the history of the Valley, and . . . creat[e] the kind of mixed use, housing, leisure, within one coherent design which is a reflection of the *Trust*'s vision for the valley as a whole' (The Ouseburn Partnership, 1996: 13). This integrative area imaginary was also complemented with a concern for social inclusion, manifested in the *Trust*'s desire to promote affordable or social housing, develop activities with underprivileged groups of society and activate an inclusive form of governance. Here marginal and leftover 'bits' (an urban farm, stables, the historic pubs, the artists) were brought together with new developments, notably social housing, to reimagine the Ouseburn.

The key symbolic element that connected people, and linked existing social networks transforming them into such a collective, was an emotional link with the place and the environment. One interviewee mentioned that he wanted to 'take care of the valley' and elsewhere he referred to a planning officer who was concerned for the 'well-being of the valley'. This emotional connection brought people together to act against the preconceived value that this was a largely 'derelict' or 'empty' area, and demonstrated that actually this place was full of social life and social networks and indeed provided a vital space for certain types of commerce. The sense of place acted as a mobilising, coordin-ative and integrative force.

Leadership and 'structural holes'

The capacity of some individuals to link across established groups that share enclosed information and codes has been identified as a key resource to foster innovation. Established communities such as city council planning officers or voluntary groups share different norms of behaviour and circulate in differ-ent flows of information with gaps or 'structural holes' (Burt, 2002) between them.

In the Ouseburn, socially creative resources have come from actors able to link across these gaps, particularly from one of the officers from the Newcastle City Council. This officer started to work in the Ouseburn when he belonged to the planning department in the 1980s and has performed somewhat different formal roles in different departments as the wider agendas of the council changed. He described his work, very much in Burt's terminology, as liaising with groups and businesses in the area and basically 'fill[ing] the gaps that other people have left' (Interviewee no. 12). According to a member of the *Ouseburn Trust* he 'is the guy that for several years would manage to wing small amounts of money from budgets that had not been spent which allowed us to fund [other projects]' (Interviewee no. 4).

Throughout the years he maintained a network of contacts with interests in the Valley from the *Ouseburn Trust*, business community and arts and culture community, which he skilfully and with great commitment linked together and plugged into the city council's formal and informal flows of money and influence. He successfully generated trust among key actors in the community by being able to trespass formal rules and regulations in the interest of the Ouseburn. He has stood, according to Burt (2004), near the hole that separates the city council from the community groups. Being on the edge of and closer to the holes has meant, in turn, that he is sometimes not trusted in the city council and he is regarded as having 'gone native'.

Similarly, another key figure in the development of the Valley demonstrated an extraordinary capacity to link different arenas and work across cultures. A vicar of the Anglican Church of England, he increasingly gained trust and respect among policy-makers and community groups. His role was essential in the early moments of the group when there was a confrontation with the Urban Development Corporation. In a moment of hostility, this vicar was able to confront the corporation with a confident and strong response, exposing in the local media their unfulfilled promises about a community training strategy. This initial conflict in a context of distrust and suspicion gave way to a much more collaborative situation. In a later stage, when Newcastle City Council turned away from the Ouseburn, his linking and liaising skills proved essential for the re-establishment of the relationships. The *Trust* was able to regain the confidence and the interest of the council due to its involvement in other regeneration partnerships across the city.

The fact that this key actor is a highly respected member of the Church of England must be considered as a significant dynamic of social innovation. The Church and faith communities have played an important role in urban regeneration in the last two decades (Smith, 2002; Lawless *et al.*, 1998). In Newcastle, local vicars have often proved to be powerful community leaders. They have been able to act as channels between formal politics and working-class communities. Their position as 'honest brokers' who can translate between the formal languages and practices of professionals and often distrusted officials and politicians and the community cannot be understated. That said, this particular actor has shown capacities and abilities that helped him move beyond the above role, leading the development of an alternative vision for the place.

Sustaining social innovation: the problem of strong ties

The *Ouseburn Trust* and the wider community of users and workers who are committed to the Valley make up a relatively small group. Although the Ouseburn Valley has in the past years become an important node for all kinds of activities, such as community festivals, live music, public art or horse riding, and more people have been drawn to it, the core of people who are involved in developing the activities and projects remains very small. This, in turn, slims down the chances of engaging more people in linking across arenas and connecting with further networks and struggles. It is what in Granovetter's (1983) terminology could be called a problem of too strong ties, where people in closed groups share often redundant information and do not reach out for fresh ideas and challenges.

The *Ouseburn Trust* has had particular difficulties in engaging more people and expanding their constituency. Since its foundation in 1995 it has grown to have between 80 and 100 members but only fourteen are active board members and almost all activity is initiated by four or five people despite the efforts of the *Trust* to engage more people in its activities. That said, there seems to be a problem connected with the character of some people involved in the *Trust* itself. The core people have been engaged with the *Trust* for over ten years now, developing their own particular culture, mode of communication and philosophy that are as difficult to penetrate as those they initially sought to challenge.

Since the early days, the *Trust* has developed a very strong vision for the Valley based on the preservation of the heritage, the landscape and its basic physical features. The basic arguments of this vision have not changed over the last ten years even though the area is now subject to many different pressures, the city council's attitude has shifted and the market conditions have also evolved. This 'immobility' or rigid approach to the changing context in which they act has become a stronger issue recently as the prospects of new developments and therefore new residents in the Valley are becoming more plausible. The *Trust* has been accused of being introverted and not opening up to new people. There have been suggestions that it is anxious about the possibility of new residents taking over who have very different visions and expectations. The *Trust* has indeed found it difficult to connect with the existing business community or the arts and culture community, which established itself as an alternative voice, in part prompted by the city council to do so. Thus, the relatively introverted nature of the *Trust* and its difficulties in linking to other groups to form a broad and diverse network has ended up posing difficulties for the further development of an innovative governance capacity:

> there is a potential conflict because it is a little bit incestuous down there, it is a small area and a relatively small number involved which is probably one of the weaknesses. [. . .] people sit on lots of different bodies and they

have their own subgroups, and it is always the same people and I am not quite sure . . . that's the flaw, everyone knows everyone else, always the same faces.

(Interviewee no. 7)

Conclusion

In a first phase, the Ouseburn community group adopted a resistance strategy and questioned the added value of physical regeneration processes for local communities. Progressively, the *Ouseburn Trust* developed a more focused future vision for the Valley and entered into partnership with local government to lead a regeneration project. During this period, the *Trust* designed, led and implemented a socially innovative local development strategy. As time passed by, property developers became more interested in the area and this was coupled with local and national government interest in inner city renewal. The community's vision for the Valley as an environmentally friendly, socially mixed and inclusive urban village did not connect with broader hegemonic discourses held either by the city council or with developers. The *Trust* thus found itself somewhat on the back foot, edged out, and so failed to develop a new pro-active vision in the face of the speed and scale of change coming forward from the professional planning and development sector – both public, in the form of design briefs and regeneration strategies, and private, in the form of development proposals.

That said, the *Trust* maintains a useful corrective voice and does much to promote heritage and community concerns on a day-to-day basis. In relation to the future of the place itself, debates about the innovative content of the *Trust* initiative can be appreciated if we ask ourselves how the Valley might have looked had this organisation never existed. Two hypotheses can be envisioned: it could still be a 'redundant space' where relatively insular alternative communities thrived with little external participation; or it could have been a continuation of the 'Quayside' model with luxury apartments, corporatised nightlife (Chatterton and Hollands, 2003) and the destruction of much of the environment and sense of place. Instead, the area is slowly being transformed. Slowness is important. The *Trust* has done much, often inadvert-ently, to hold up development, forcing a consideration of the implications of short term developments. This has resulted in a better built environment. The large-scale development that looked inevitable at one stage has been mostly resisted and new developments have often been sensitive to the need to provide cheap rents for artists, live-work units and a mix of housing types and prices.

Thus, the Ouseburn case can definitely be considered – certainly in its early phases – a story of community success, which is all the more significant given the structural weaknesses inherent in the local administration under the twin pressures of global neoliberalism and English state hyper-centrism (Loughlin, 2001). On the other hand, it now faces new challenges precisely because of those pressures in the face of its inherent 'inward' orientation that may hamper the sustainability of the innovative process.

References

Atkinson, R. and Moon, G. (1994) *Urban Policy in Britain*, London: Macmillan.

Burt, R.S. (2002) 'The social capital of structural holes', in M. Guillén, P. Randall, P. England and M. Meyer (eds) *New Directions in Economic Sociology*, New York: Russell Sage. Online. Available: faculty.chicagobooth.edu/ronald.burt/research/SCSH.pdf (Accessed 13 April 2010).

—— (2004) 'Structural holes and good ideas', *American Journal of Sociology*, 110(2): 349–99.

Chatterton, P. and Hollands, R. (2003) *Urban Nightscapes: Youth Cultures, Pleasure Spaces and Corporate Power*, London: Routledge

Franklin, B. and Tait, M. (2002) 'Constructing an image: the urban village concept in the UK', *Planning Theory*, 1(3): 250–72.

González, S. and Vigar, G. (2008) 'Community influence and the contemporary local state: potentials and contradictions in the neo-liberal city', *City*, 12(1): 64–78.

Granovetter, M. (1983) 'The strength of weak ties: A network theory revisited', *Sociological Theory*, 1: 201–33.

Hill, D.M. (2000) *Urban Policy and Politics in Britain*, Basingstoke: Macmillan.

Hoban, M. and Beresford, P. (2001) 'Regenerating regeneration', *Community Development Journal*, 36(4): 312–20.

Lawless, P., Else, P., Farnell, R., Furbey, R., Lund, S. and Wishart, B. (1998) 'Community based initiative and state urban policy: the Church Urban Fund', *Regional Studies*, 32(2): 161–74.

Loughlin, J. (2001) 'The United Kingdom: From hypercentralization to devolution', in J. Loughlin (ed.) *Subnational Democracy in the European Union: Challenges and Opportunities*, Oxford: Oxford University Press.

Metier (2004) Lime Square Property Development Brochure.

Newcastle City Council (2008) Executive Summary. Online. Available: www.newcastle.gov.uk/compnewc.nsf/a/executivesummary (Accessed 1 May 2009).

Ouseburn Advisory Committee (2004) 'Minutes of the 02/03/2004 meeting'. Online. Available: www.newcastle.gov.uk/cab2003.nsf/allbykey/96E0BF68BC0F635980256E3F00494448?opendocument (Accessed 1 May 2009).

Raco, M, and Imrie, R. (2000) 'Governmentality and rights and responsibilities in urban policy', *Environment and Planning A*, 32: 2187–204.

Smith, G. (2002) 'Religion and the rise of social capitalism: the faith communities in community development and urban regeneration in England', *Community and Development Journal*, 37(2): 167–77.

The Ouseburn Partnership (1996) 'The Ouseburn Valley: A sustainable future' Single Regeneration Fund Budget challenge fund submission to the Government Office for the North East, September 1996, Newcastle. Unpublished document.

Tooke, J. (2003) 'Spaces for community involvement: processes of disciplining and appropriation', *Space and Polity*, 7(3): 233–46.

Other sources

Attendance to various Ouseburn Advisory Committee meetings
Attendance to the 2004 *Ouseburn Trust*'s Annual General Meeting
Attendance to the 2004 Ouseburn Forum
Attendance to the launch of a real estate development scheme.

10 *New Deal for Communities,* Newcastle

Innovating neighbourhood regeneration policy in the context of a strong central government

Jon Coaffee

Introduction

Upon coming to power in 1997, the New Labour Government in the UK set in motion a host of different initiatives to renew the most disadvantaged neighbourhoods and to encourage community-led regeneration. *New Deal for Communities (NDC)* was seen as the flagship area-based regeneration initiative of this era, with an emphasis on addressing (individual) poverty or (geographical) deprivation. NDC drew on the Labour Government's early interest in this area, expressed initially through the inception of a new Social Exclusion Unit, reporting directly to the prime minister. In particular, concerns about the apparent ineffectiveness of prior urban policy informed the context into which the NDC programme was launched in 1998. NDC symbolised a shift in the direction of urban policy, moving away from the narrow land- and property-focused concerns of much of policy in the 1980s, and giving more emphasis to the wider social and distributional concerns (Coaffee and Deas, 2008).

The case study outlined in this chapter details the development of an NDC scheme in Newcastle upon Tyne in the north-east of England, seen as part of a wider neighbourhood renewal policy agenda by the national government. The NDC initiative was rolled out to thirty-nine different areas in the UK between 2000 and 2001 at a combined cost of £2 billion. NDC was seen as an innovative catalyst for turning around the multiple persistent problems experienced in some of the poorest neighbourhoods, while giving a clear leadership role to the local community. This case study highlights that, despite having a number of innovative features and a desire to facilitate active engagement with the community in an unprecedented way, the NDC scheme has, in part, become institutionalised and, in many ways, been 'taken over' by formal government modalities and practices. This has been made particularly stark by auditing practices, which forced the scheme to meet the rigorous evaluative criteria of central government. This, it will be argued, has diluted the creative and innovative practices that were envisaged as characterising this new approach to community-led regeneration.

On the other hand, some social innovation processes did occur. Newcastle's *NDC* highlights three main dimensions of social innovation, as conceived in ALMOLIN (see Chapter 3), albeit to different extents. Initially, it was developed to respond to unmet human needs and socio-economic exclusion, but also as a mandate to change and challenge top-down governance arrangements in the local state by increasingly involving the community. This consequently led to an increase in empowerment, that is, the socio-political capability and access to resources needed to enhance the rights to human needs satisfaction and participation in place-based decision-making.

The context

Newcastle's New Deal for Communities

The north-east region in the UK has undergone massive industrial change in recent years. The extensive decline in the region's traditional manufacturing industries (coal, steel, shipbuilding and engineering) has produced numerous policy interventions over the last thirty years aimed at dealing with the damaging economic and social consequences of industrial decline and the overdependence on a narrow industrial base. In particular, since 1997, comprehensive and multidimensional approaches to tackling social exclusion and neighbourhood disadvantage have been developed in the UK, which recognise that deprivation derives from a number of interrelated factors and requires a joined-up response from different agencies working in partnership (Regional Coordination Unit, 2002). This is the essence of *NDC*, of which the north-east region of the UK hosts four: Newcastle, Middlesbrough, Hartlepool and Sunderland.

Newcastle's West End neighbourhood, in which Newcastle *NDC* is located, is one of the most disadvantaged in Britain, suffering from large-scale population loss, high crime rates, poor education and health, high unemployment, fractured community relations and inadequate services. As such, a section of the area was chosen as an *NDC* scheme with the aim of achieving integrated or holistic regeneration through partnership between the community, the local state and other formal or informal stakeholders.

Historically, regeneration policy in this particular locality dates back to the 1960s with the slum clearance programmes, and to the 1970s with various redevelopment schemes and the Community Development Partnership (CDP), which sought similar goals to *NDC* today. After the CDP experience, regeneration efforts in Newcastle's West End have grown in time to cover the full range of state-led initiatives at neighbourhood level. There has been tremendous expenditure in this particular area prior to the £54 million (€80 million) given to Newcastle *NDC* to target particular regeneration dimensions: physical regeneration of housing, redevelopment of public spaces, vocational training, improved social services (particularly health and education) and enterprise creation (Coaffee, 2004). The creation and subsequent development of Newcastle NDC has also been strongly related to both national and local policy developments. These relationships will be explored in the remainder of the chapter. Table 10.1 summarises key national and local policy interventions, which have impacted upon the area where NDC now exists.

Issues and planning expectations

Newcastle NDC is situated in a predominantly residential belt to the west of Newcastle city centre. The disadvantages of this area starkly contrast with the nearby prosperity of the central shopping and office areas, which are undergoing significant economic renaissance (Cameron and Coaffee, 2005). At its inception, the total population of the NDC area was around 12,000 of which about 25 per cent belonged to Black and minority ethnic communities. The area (as part of Newcastle's West End) suffers from stigmatisation and in recent years has been viewed negatively by employers, service providers and residents of other areas. For example, as the regeneration initiative began, 'workless adults' comprised nearly 25 per cent and low-income households comprised nearly 40 per cent. The area also contained many houses that were earmarked for demolition.

In terms of administrative status, when Newcastle NDC was set up in 1999, it was run by an 'interim partnership board' which was to be in place until funding from central government was secured. The interim board consisted of representatives of the community (from a variety of backgrounds),

Table 10.1 Chronology of recent policy frameworks in the West End of Newcastle

1972	The Community Development Partnership in Newcastle's West End attempts to develop an integrated and community-focused approach to area-based regeneration.
1979–98	Nearly £500 million (€800 million) are spent on regeneration initiatives in Newcastle's West End.
1998	National Government launches Bringing Britain Together which sets out the framework for thirty-nine NDC schemes in the UK.
1999	Initial proposal is made by Newcastle City Council to have a NDC scheme – an interim steering group is established to develop a bid.
2000 (March)	A bid is made to national government for £54 million (€80 million). The bid is successful.
2000 (June)	NDC is affected by city council regeneration schemes to demolish a number of houses in the NDC area. These NDC schemes significantly impact upon the relationship between NDC and the local state.
2010	NDC ends.

Source: Author

professionals from a number of service providers (health, policing and education), local politicians and officials from the local city council. Although this interim board was chaired by a locally elected politician, funding and organisational responsibility came from the local city council. As will be highlighted later, this situation caused tensions between the local community and the local authority, as both felt they should be in control of the NDC process.

The task of the interim board was to draw up a ten-year plan for the area focusing on the core NDC themes of housing and the physical environment, education, health, worklessness, crime reduction, as well as methodologies for enhancing the capacity of the local community to contribute their views and skills to the regeneration of the area. Each of the prospective NDC areas were required to design such a plan, normally prepared by the local authority, setting out the evidence for the area's problems and potentials, specifying the ways in which these could be addressed, as well as the funding implications. The process was some distance removed from the discretionary funding regimes of previous regeneration initiatives where the emphasis was to a large degree a technocratic one and required competitive bidding for resources (Coaffee and Deas, 2008).

In Newcastle the indicative plan was accepted by national government, and in time, after funding was granted, the interim partnership became a fully established partnership board (mandated through locally held elections). Later the partnership changed its constitution and became a company limited by guarantee. This meant 'community representatives' became 'community directors' and assumed more power and responsibility, having first developed the skills to begin managing the project. This, at least in theory, gave NDC some independence from the local state, although it was acknowledged that NDC was not entirely autonomous and would be required to connect to the state and its service agencies in a variety of ways.

One of the serious criticisms of previous area-focused regeneration in the UK and in particular in Newcastle's West End was the 'short-termism' of intervention as well as questions posed about the applicability of area-scale regeneration when compared to larger and more strategic city-wide schemes. Those working for NDC were therefore determined that significant elements of long-term sustainability should be built into the life cycle of the programme (the ten-year cycle ends in 2010) to allow work to continue well past the official end of the scheme. Furthermore, NDC was seen not only as an area where innovative practice might be developed, but also as a mechanism that might help coordinate a diverse range of agencies, service providers and local community organisations. As NDC progressed, it was relatively successful at developing a rich network of linkages to all of the main planning and policy tools which connect to the area. Newcastle NDC was also innovative at joint-agency working, generating new governance and partnership relationships with service providers and agency staff in the police, health authority, educational establishments and employment services.

Conflicting scales of regeneration governance

In recent years national urban policy has been played out in Newcastle within a very particular historical and geographical setting. This is clearly observable through *NDC*. This local context framed the actions of governing authorities and community groups as attempts were made to deliver both area-based and city-wide regeneration simultaneously, as well as to alter the established relationships between the local state and citizens in regeneration practices. The focus of *NDC* has been on community empowerment, and not just participation, which is often seen as tokenistic. That said, it would be wrong to view *NDC* as autonomous, given the requirement to link to the local state in a partnership arrangement. Rather, it is perhaps best to characterise its connection with the state as semi-autonomous and interdependent.

While the newer *NDC* initiative has a much more bottom-up essence than previous neighbourhood regeneration approaches, at its inception it collided with a new top-down plan, the city-wide regeneration scheme Going for Growth launched in 1999 (Coaffee, 2004). This strategy was tied to wider concerns to reverse the population decline of the city (to stabilise the tax base), prevent the loss of more affluent residents to the commuter hinterland beyond the boundaries of the city and, within this, to directly address the specific problems posed by areas of unpopular housing in the city, the most acute problem being that of the West End (see Table 10.1).

A key concern for the local state was to achieve a balance between overarching strategy and local community involvement. The hope was that *NDC* and Going for Growth could become mutually compatible. The *NDC* partnership was seen as an opportunity to create new sets of relations between the city and its citizens in order to develop innovative ways of regenerating local neighbourhoods. However, a profound difficulty emerged as to how to forge new governance relationships between local communities and the city council against the fear of gentrification and displacement (often referred to as 'social cleansing' in local press coverage) which was brought about by the local authority's Going for Growth scheme (Coaffee, 2004).

It is this style of collaborative working, portrayed as the solution to intractable neighbourhood problems, that has led the Newcastle's *NDC* scheme and others in England, to experience a number of critical governance problems. In particular, these relate to the uneasy 'partnership' between local residents, local government and partner agencies in relation to 'the control of partnership agendas and decisions over how to spend the allocated funding appropriately, to schedule, and according to prescribed government guidance' (Coaffee, 2005: 31). At the start of the *NDC* programme at national level, Taylor (2000) had already highlighted concern about how 'community centred' *NDC* partnerships would actually be developed, given pre-existing governance styles and approaches with the local state as the primary actor. Equally there was concern that the innovative and creative elements that were supposed to characterise *NDC* working would be forced to take a back seat compared to strategies better fitting mainstream objectives and spending targets.

The managers of *NDC* in Newcastle faced all such difficulties when the partnership was established and formal arrangements and linkages were negotiated with the local state. Indeed, during the early *NDC* development process there were fears expressed by community representatives that the local state was 'taking control' in a process that was developed upon the rhetoric of 'equal partnership' and even community leadership. On the other hand, given the nature of the *NDC* process, the local state provided the only practical early leadership, as the community lacked the necessary skills, resources and technical abilities to undertake partnership management. This highlights an additional tension, common in many neighbourhood regeneration partnerships, between enhancing community involvement and delivering outcomes in the most efficient way. This is a particularly salient point given that the steep learning curve for those members of the community unfamiliar with the workings of regeneration partnerships is likely to slow down the speed of partnership working. It also highlights how such initiatives can have the innovation squeezed out of them by bureaucratic and professionalised demands of meeting targets and efficiency of working. As a regeneration worker in Newcastle noted:

> I had hoped *NDC* was going to be a fresh start but it is not. It is the same bureaucratic, tokenistic imposed set of criteria driven from the top-down. It's the same as the other regeneration programmes with a bigger pot of money and a longer running time. I find this highly disappointing.
>
> (Interview by the author, 2002)

As Newcastle *NDC* developed, it found it difficult to connect to the bureaucratic culture and procedures of the local state. In some cases, this served to isolate *NDC* from other regeneration providers, creating what was described as a separate 'island of regeneration'. Although organisational links between *NDC* and other actors have improved over time and some joint-working and innovative project developments have occurred, there is still a long way to go before a true partnership approach to integrated local area development is achieved. The next section will look at some of the key dynamics that sought to facilitate greater social inclusion and innovation.

Main dynamics of social inclusion and innovation

Newcastle *NDC* highlights all three main dimensions of social innovation identified in ALMOLIN, albeit to different extents. In terms of the satisfaction of human needs, high levels of social exclusion and multiple deprivations formed the rationale behind setting up the *NDC* scheme in the area, given its multiple socio-economic problems and high levels of stigmatisation. With regard to changes in social relations/governance, *NDC* was seen as an innovative scheme set up with the mandate of community-led regeneration, following a plethora of top-down schemes run by the local state or partner agencies. To this extent *NDC* has certainly helped destabilise, although not necessarily dislodge, existing and embedded governance relations in west Newcastle between the local city council, citizens and service providers. It has also helped to reduce the historical mistrust between the local state and citizens which had plagued previous regeneration attempts (Coaffee, 2005). Most importantly, NDC has succeeded in providing an arena where 'community voice' is valued and the regeneration of the local area has gained greater community control. As such, by increasing the socio-political capabilities and access to resources of community groups, evidence suggests that the NDC scheme has the potential to alter the power relationship between communities and the local state. This is particularly connected to the assertion that local people are best placed to highlight problems and devise innovative delivery mechanisms or solutions to assist in sustainable place-making.

In the case of the NDC programme, both nationally and in Newcastle, attempts to enhance social inclusion and embed innovative ways of working included efforts to reshape local service delivery policy to enhance the needs of the area and its community. This has involved shifting resources to respond to specific area needs and, in particular, improving the access of all groups and individuals within the area to facilities and services. More broadly this has led to attempts to change the culture of regeneration delivery by identifying and embedding innovation and creativity into service delivery, rather than relying on traditional top-down bureaucratic fixes.

The case study of Newcastle NDC has highlighted a number of specific processes that foster innovation from at least four points of view.

Community leadership

First, innovation has occurred through the establishment of community leadership. The concept of NDC is innovative in itself as it gives a clear leadership role to the community to deliver regeneration according to local needs and priorities. Although in the past the community had been encouraged to be involved in regeneration partnerships, NDC provided the local community with the opportunity to shape all aspects of how NDC functioned instead of just being token participants. Here it is clear that community involvement in local regeneration schemes is now seen in terms of effective empowerment rather than simplistic notions of participation and consultation.

The Newcastle NDC programme has concerned communities centrally in decision-making and through the development of some new and innovative solutions to entrenched neighbourhood problems. It stimulated resident leadership (through board membership) and involvement (through a broader array of mechanisms for canvassing resident needs and wants). Moreover, the NDC partnership is chaired by a local resident.

In Newcastle, with a long history of community activism, getting a dedicated and longstanding team of enthusiastic community representatives proved less of a problem than broadening engagement to the wider community. Indeed initial 'elections' to the *NDC* partnership board saw higher levels of voter-turnout than local state elections. In 2003, three years after *NDC* formation, a dedicated Community Regeneration Team (CRT) was established in order to facilitate the wider engagement of a much larger cohort of local residents in a more informal way, often through social events organised in community facilities. This was an important development as, prior to the establishment of the CRT, the partnership was seen to be focusing far too much on 'delivery' and not enough on 'engagement' issues.

Integrated action

Second, innovation has been noticeable through attempts at integrated regeneration. *NDC* was envisioned as an experimental scheme, which would offer joined-up solutions to the interconnected problems experienced in a small area to reduce multiple deprivations. In particular, social exclusion was conceived as an intractable and multifaceted entity that would require a sustained multi-agency response. In practice, Newcastle *NDC* has been partially successful in stimulating joint working between different area-focused regeneration initiatives, between the community and the local state, and between the local community and public services providers. *NDC* has also highlighted some of the difficulties of obtaining meaningful integration between service sectors and between different governance coalitions (for example different organisational cultures, evaluation systems and timescale of working). From the perspective of Newcastle *NDC*, facilitating joint-working practices led to a pressure to deliver measurable outputs. From a more negative perspective, this subsequently resulted in a reduction in the time available to contemplate innovative ways of delivering regeneration.

The activities of the *NDC* partnership are not only about funding specific projects but about creating a space for bringing different groups of people, agencies and organisations together in a constructive dialogue about the future of the area. Agencies involved in *NDC* have appreciated the opportunities to work more closely with other agencies and civil society organisations. *NDC* has also acted as a catalyst for agencies coming together to develop a more coordinated approach to working in the area, in order to avoid the duplication of effort.

Multi-scalar governance

The third way in which Newcastle *NDC* highlights efforts to foster social innovation is through attempts to link bottom-up and top-down initiatives. One of the reasons *NDC* was set up was to provide a link between communities and the more strategic decisions that were being taken at a higher government level. This linkage, however, has been fraught with tensions, given the historical mistrust of the local state by communities and the proposals for housing demolition in the *NDC* area under the city-wide regeneration scheme Going for Growth. On the other hand, over time, differences in process and approach between *NDC* and the local state are beginning to converge as the local state improves its community consultation mandate and *NDC* is 'forced' to undergo 'institutionalisation' as a result of a constant requirement to account for any money spent.

More critically, though, we might see Newcastle *NDC* as just another case of regeneration partnerships focusing too strongly on demonstrating outcomes, with less emphasis upon fostering more creative governance processes (Liddle and Smith, 2006). In its early days Newcastle *NDC* focused strongly upon delivery and at national level the partnership led the way in developing a performance management database by which spending against agreed targets could be monitored. The ability of the partnership to deliver projects did, however, give *NDC* increased confidence to reflect upon progress and then to begin to increasingly consider community engagement issues. On the other hand – and perhaps not surprisingly – despite the rhetoric of community-centred regeneration, there continues to be a high degree of focus upon economic and property-led initiatives to regenerating communities, as a way to enhance the marketability of a place, and upon meeting delivery targets.

Moreover, in Newcastle there is a strong suspicion that smaller area-focused initiatives, such as *NDC*, are not large or important enough to merit consideration within local state agendas of strategic city-wide intervention. This raises a critical point of concern regarding the compatibility of the outcomes of two distinct pathways to regeneration linked to city-wide and area-based concerns. The former often implies substantial displacement, often through plan-led demolition, of some existing communities. In contrast, redevelopment as exemplified through *NDC* is based on a strategy of bottom-up engagement of existing communities in the area and sustainable regeneration of their neighbourhoods. Likewise, there has been concern over the compatibility of the processes through which these two pathways to regeneration (top-down and bottom-up) have been approached. The rhetoric of *NDC* is about putting communities at the heart of regeneration. However, Newcastle *NDC*, like many similar schemes in England, has also been dogged by community infighting, an inability to make decisions (and hence spend money) and large-scale resentment about national and local government interference in the scheme.

Responding to needs

The fourth – and perhaps most significant – way in which *NDC* has been innovative is through project development and appraisal in the delivery of services. The *NDC* partnership has afforded statutory agencies and individual community groups the opportunity to be more innovative and more flexible in their approaches to dealing with problems in the area. In particular, this has been achieved by developing a new governance structure free from some of the constrictions of the organisations in which they normally work.

As *NDC* developed in Newcastle, partner agencies became increasingly positive about linkages made to *NDC*, seeing the partnership as an opportunity to add value and resources to their current services. Importantly, and in line with initial *NDC* objectives some partners also saw *NDC* as an arena where they might experiment with innovative approaches to longstanding problems. Other service providers felt *NDC* gave them an opportunity to better engage local communities of interests and identity and more effectively gain an understanding of local area conditions. For example, the *NDC* partnership group concerned with health has successfully promoted innovative schemes linked to 'complementary therapies' that are not normally available in the state health service. Similarly, Newcastle *NDC* has helped reshape and improve service delivery in the area by acting as a sounding board for ideas about service improvement and had a number of their projects 'rolled out' across the city of Newcastle in recognition of their success. For example, a project called the Arson Task Force was established between the *NDC* crime and community safety group and the fire services to tackle incidents of arson in the area. Another project called Heart Beat seeking to reduce the high incidence of coronary heart disease among Asian men was set up through joint working between the local health trust and the *NDC* health group.

All these developments have significantly altered the working practices of many formal organisations and has made them increasingly community and area-specific. This incorporation of innovative ways of working from special initiatives into the practice of standard service delivery is strongly encouraged by the national state; however, undermining such success is still a deep suspicion that *NDC* in some sectors is being used as a substitute for core service funding. In fact, the problem with diffusion of innovative practices is that they are funded almost entirely with *NDC* resources, and agencies have not dedicated significant amounts of their own monies to more experimental work. It will only be possible to test the commitment of agencies to new ways of working when they lose *NDC* funding in 2010, and will have to make use of their own resources.

That said, some projects are jointly funded and managed between *NDC* and service providers. This has led to additional money being 'levered' into the area. In short, *NDC* is often used as a conduit to develop roll-out innovative project ideas imported from other institutions, although paradoxically it is *NDC* (a bottom-up scheme) which has to develop innovative ideas for mainstream public service delivery (the responsibility of the local state).

Conclusions

With time, the *NDC* partnership has matured, learnt as an organisation and developed a positive organisational identity. At the end of 2008 it was reported that the Community Regeneration Team has helped thirty new community groups to become established and has given over 300 grants to local organisations for developing activities and events for residents. Likewise, it was reported that hundreds of local citizens have been active in neighbourhood improvement programmes where they played a part in selecting and prioritising the changes they wished to see. Moreover, it was announced that a new community organisation will be established as a successor organisation for NDC when it stops being centrally funded in 2010 (Newcastle NDC, 2008).

However, there has been, and continues to be, conflict over the balance between community capacity building and the effective delivery of projects. Arguably, the community leadership role entrusted to NDC has been weakened by the way in which the partnership was forced to operate in order to meet national government targets, in essence by being slowly institutionalised through integration into a prescriptive audit culture, which dictates how the partnership spends its money and how it establishes priorities. This raises the question of how success is measured for NDC. And, again, this depends on the perspective taken. Some would argue that success is measured through the depth of community involvement and capacity building, while others would argue success should be measured through the ability to deliver effective and efficient projects. Others further claim that the success of NDC can be determined by the linkages it made with strategic programmes, either 'rolled out' by the local state or by service providers.

Within the ALMOLIN theoretical framework, this boils down to three key questions which are often, but should not be, seen as mutually exclusive: Do local communities want better services? Do they want real and active participation in decisions that affect their place? Does this participation change governance relations? In the case of Newcastle answers are not clear-cut.

NDC finds itself situated at the frontier between constituting an 'alternative' approach to social and economic innovation and being part of mainstream public funding for service delivery. Despite being an 'imported' initiative which was artificially created by the local state in line with national government guidance, NDC has become somewhat of a niche, where innovative governance arrangements and project proposals have been explored. NDC also sits within a very confused and complex institutional landscape, which is in a constant state of flux (Lawless, 2006). Currently, and in the future, this poses a series of issues for the balancing of an overarching strategy and local community involvement in urban regeneration in Newcastle, and elsewhere.

The thirty-nine NDC schemes across England have acted as 'pioneer initiatives', which have attempted to construct socially innovative ways of working in local neighbourhoods through the collaboration of local people and the local state. This has not been an easy process and results are far from universally positive. Constructing coalitions of regeneration actors who span a variety of agencies, each with differing remits and performance targets, and often covering areas containing diverse communities, is a challenge that should not to be under-estimated. Developing suitable regeneration and governing mechanisms also sits uneasily alongside bureaucratic and electoral cycles, which demand more immediate evidence of results (Coaffee and Deas, 2008). The experience of Newcastle reiterates the enormity of the pressures typically placed on neighbourhood regeneration bodies to produce demonstrable outcomes at a relatively early stage, at the expense of the socially innovative elements that the scheme is also supposed to stimulate.

References

Cameron, S. and Coaffee, J. (2005) 'Art, gentrification and regeneration – from artist as pioneer to public arts', *European Journal of Housing Studies*, 5(1): 39–58.
Coaffee, J. (2004) 'Re-Scaling regeneration – experiences of merging area-based and city-wide partnerships in urban policy', *The International Journal of Public Sector Management*, 17(5): 443–61.
—— (2005) 'Shock of the new – complexity and emerging rationales for partnership working', *Public Policy and Administration*, 20(3): 23–41.
—— and Deas, I. (2008) 'The search for policy innovation in urban governance: lessons from community-led regeneration partnerships', *Public Policy and Administration*, 23(1): 167–88.
Lawless, P. (2006) 'Area based urban interventions: rationale and outcomes – the NDC Programme in England', *Urban Studies*, 43(11):1991–2011.
Liddle, J. and Smith S. (2006) 'Evaluation approaches', in J. Diamond, J. Liddle, A. Southern and A.Townsend (eds), *Managing the City*, London: Routledge, pp. 116–32.
Newcastle City Council (1999) *Going For Growth: A City-Wide Vision for Newcastle 2020*, Newcastle: Newcastle City Council.
Newcastle New Deal for Communities (2008) *New Deal News. Making It Happen in the West End*, Newcastle: Newcastle NDC.
Regional Co-Ordination Unit (2002) *Review of Area-Based Initiatives*, London: HMSO.
Social Exclusion Unit (1998) *Bringing Britain Together: A National Strategy for Neighbourhood Renewal*, London: HMSO.
Taylor, M. (2000) 'Communities in the lead: power, organisational capacity and social capital', *Urban Studies*, 37(5–6): 1019–35.

11 Autonomy and inclusive urban governance

A case of glocal action: *City Mine(d)* in Brussels

Johan Moyersoen

Introduction

City Mine(d) is a non-profit association founded in 1997 in Brussels by Flemish- and French-speaking urban activists that has evolved into a multi-local organisation with spin-off projects in London and Barcelona. The organisation's objective is to promote self-determined projects in public and semi-public urban spaces. Self-determined urban projects are projects that are self-governed and self-managed by those who initiate them.

City Mine(d) takes on projects initiated by actors (such as neighbourhood groups, youth groups, autonomous art collectives, urban activist groups, etc.) who, at the proposed project location, often lack the contacts necessary to realise their project. *City Mine(d)* assists the group of initiators by rallying a diverse, supportive coalition of city actors around the proposed intervention, thereby helping the initiators to conceptualise their project, to overcome different obstacles (authorisation requirements, the need for financial resources, etc.), and to implement the project. At the same time, the mobilisation of an inclusive support network of this type performs another function – countering the structural governance configurations that customarily prevent such actors from realising their initiatives. As such, the coalition introduces – at least during the realisation phase of the project – a new and more inclusive social power arrangement promoting local autonomy.

City Mine(d) employs five people (three in Brussels, one in London and one in Barcelona) and has a core group of fifty volunteers. The organisation has a support cell and a production cell. The 'support cell' seeks to provide logistical support, practical information, and legal and financial advice for groups aiming to realise self-determined urban projects. The groups that make use of this cell form a 'recruiting pool' from which projects are drawn. Members of the 'production cell' can initiate their own projects, though more often they select a project from the 'recruiting pool'. Projects are selected on the basis of feasibility in financial and legal terms, location and social potential to promote inclusive governance. They are mostly socio-cultural or socio-artistic in nature. Funding comes mainly from the Urban Fund (het Stedenfonds) of the Flemish

Regional Government and from the National Lottery. For individual projects, the organisation draws on funding from a diverse set of government and private bodies.[1]

During the thirteen years of its existence, *City Mine(d)* has supported the realisation of more than ninety self-determined projects, mainly in Brussels, Barcelona and London. Each project has mobilised a support network with links to state, market and civil society actors at the local, metropolitan and supra-urban levels. As the support network for each project is anchored in a different locality, the number and mix of projects have contributed to the establishment of a multi-locality network. For *City Mine(d)*, the 'thickness' of such a multi-local network should, eventually, contribute to a reshuffle of the power geometry in the city fabric towards a more inclusive urban governance.

By supporting the realisation of self-determined projects, *City Mine(d)* seeks to combine two normative objectives, at two different levels. At the individual level, it promotes positive freedom by facilitating the realisation of self-determined projects; at a broader level, it encourages inclusive governance. The by-product of this strategy is the creation of a new governance scale within the city, a multi-local (glocal) network. *City Mine(d)* perceives this network as a collective resource, and it is through the formation of this new glocal scale that local actors are able to acquire the necessary social contacts for their own projects and that institutions are able to reclaim local autonomy. Nevertheless, as we will see, this strategy creates many paradoxes – in terms of the role the organisation has to adopt and the locations in which it intervenes – that also hamper the organisation in attaining its objectives.

The Brussels conundrum

The underlying reasons why *City Mine(d)* juxtaposes positive freedom at the local level and inclusive governance at the overall urban level have to be understood in terms of the politico-institutional context within which the organisation originated. *City Mine(d)* emerged as part of the short-lived uprising of a new urban movement in Brussels in the early 1990s. This movement arose as a reaction against the structural impasse in the economic, political and institutional fabric of Brussels that made any spontaneous urban projects basically impossible (De Lannoy *et al.*, 2000; Kesteloot and Mistiaen, 2002). The predominant reasons for this impasse were a weak government, a fragmented civil society and an environment conducive to speculative private real estate development (Timmermans, 1991; Papadopoulos, 1996). A coalition between real estate entrepreneurs and parts of the Brussels political establishment had promoted large-scale infrastructural projects and speculation in vast areas of the city centre with little concern for the needs of local citizens. The speculative developments were so devastating in scale that they disrupted the social, cultural and architectural texture of the city. Examples of such projects, which wiped out entire popular, working-class neighbourhoods, are the 1990s extension of the Manhattan project at the Brussels North railway station, the European neighbourhood project in Leopoldswijk, and the TGV terminus at the Brussels South railway station (Papadopoulos, 1996; De Corte *et al.*, 1995).

In the early 1990s, VrijstadBXLVilleLibre, a direct action and multilingual urban movement, tried to turn the tide. The core of this movement was a bundling together of the forces of civil society associations across the politico-institutional divide.[2] In 1993, fifty urban activists with active support from the core group and under the collective name of Foundation Crowbar/Open-Door (Stichting/Fondation Pied de Biche/Open Deur), began a squat in a vacant block of houses in front of the Brussels stock exchange right in the centre of Brussels. The squat lasted for ten days, a protest against real estate speculation and urban planning procedures that did not take into account the needs of the inhabitants. A sequence of self-determined urban actions, initiated by the occupiers, temporarily regenerated the housing block. The projects were either 'situationist' (art projects, the creation of a model flat, the installation of plants at the windows of the occupied house), or social-cultural (the opening of a social restaurant, the organisation of debates and concerts). During the course of the squat, 5,000 people visited the occupied building, 120 organ-isations in Brussels and Belgium signed a manifesto and the campaign received local, national and international media attention. Although the action was focused on the 'micro' level – that is, on the specific housing block – it had an emblematic effect at a larger, extra-local scale, becoming the symbol of a new style of urban movement and reversing the dominant 'Bruxello-negativism' into a 'Bruxello-positivism'. Its success encouraged the campaigners to under-take other emblematic direct urban actions.

The ensuing sequence of emblematic direct actions led to the establishment of a member-based multilingual urban movement, named Freetown Brussels (VrijstadBXLVilleLibre). The movement's objective was to reclaim the city for the groups who actually live in and enjoy the city. Every six months the movement organised a general meeting, in which individuals could propose a project, engage in a deliberative process with other members present in order to enrich the proposal and mobilise people to support their initiative. It was hoped that the diverse perspectives of the members would empower individuals to envisage and realise their own self-determined projects.

The tactical innovation of direct urban action and Freetown Brussels associated the positive freedom to act and enjoy the city (through the realisation of self-determined urban interventions) with the issue of the overall governance culture of the metropolis. The radical 'deed' of realising self-determined projects that temporarily and symbolically regenerated public and semi-public spaces also became a tool used by *City Mine(d)* to confront those segments in the state, civil society and the market which stood in the way of the develop-ment and further nurture of the 'cosmopolitanisation' of the city.

The emergence and evoluton of *City Mine(d)* came about through cycles of tactical innovation by urban activists that challenged both the fragmentation of governance in the city and the subsequent adaptation of the dominant governance configurations to these innovative actions (McAdam, 1983; Tarrow, 1991; Myers, 2000; Meyer, 2004). As an example of the latter, the Flemish-speaking parts of the government created an opening for the insurgent movement by increasing the subsidies for Flemish institutionalised civil society associations that were part of the core group of the urban movement (Beursschouwburg and Brusselse Raad voor het Leefmilieu). In contrast, the French-speaking parts of the government (with the exception of Ecolo, the French-speaking Green Party) disassociated itself from the movement. However, both French and Flemish politics had a negative effect on the insurgent movements in civil society as they triggered the disintegration of the core group that had coordinated the urban movement itself. Thus, Flemish institutionalised civil society organisations returned to their traditional practices to capitalise on the new funding they received, while French institutionalized civil society organisations quietly withdrew their support. As a result, the whole movement disintegrated, leaving a vacant space that permitted the creation of the organisation *City Mine(d)*. The initiators were urban activists who had been involved in the direct action described above. The child of its time, *City Mine(d)* inherited the mission to support self-determined projects as its main *raison d'être.*[3]

Nevertheless, *City Mine(d)* should not be regarded as a mere continuation of the original urban social movement. Although its objectives were identical to those of the preceding movement, the institutionalisation of *City Mine(d)* was itself the product of a sectarian policy: the urban activists jumped on the bandwagon created by the Flemish civil society organisations that had been part of the core group and sought funding from the Flemish Regional Government. The fact that the organisation is still predominantly funded by the Flemish Regional Government makes collaboration with French-speaking (institutionalised) actors an uphill struggle.

The drivers of social innovation

The role of facilitator: empowerment and inclusion

City Mine(d) was strongly influenced by the alienation of Brussels inhabitants as a consequence of the real estate speculation in the 1980s and 1990s, which was perceived as a symptom of the detachment of the economy from the collective decision-making processes of the city. *City Mine(d)* regarded the real estate land developers as a mere fragment of the city, who were acting autonomously and taking over the city in a totalitarian way.

To discourage unilateral communication, *City Mine(d)* took on the role of facilitator and fostered direct communication between the groups involved in each of its projects. Around each self-determined project, *City Mine(d)* rallied a supportive 'transversal' network of actors from state, market and civil society institutions. Such direct communication allowed non-hierarchical reflective urban networks to be established and three main ones emerged. The first consists of the myriad of informal civil society organisations in the city and individuals with ideas for self-determined projects. The second involves actors from state, civil society and market institutions sympathetic to self-determined projects. The third network comprises peer organisations in Brussels and other cities and countries which exchange experiences and methods. I estimate that today these networks engage over 400 active participants annually and mobilise more than 8,000 visitors. By creating these networks of direct communication and creative production with ties to state, civic, and commercial organisations, *City Mine(d)* has sought to create a new form of 'public' arena, conceived as a space where traditional divides and hierarchies are blurred. Hence, *City Mine(d)* not only mobilised the neighbourhood actors, but also actors at all scales of the city.

Since 1997, the organisation has realised some sixty projects in Brussels (Serroen, 2004). Examples include PaleisVanSchoor (the conversion of a vacant plot into a well-designed park), PleinOPENair (a sequence of open-air film screenings in symbolic locations illustrating either the negative consequences of governance fragmentation in Brussels or the positive richness of the cosmo-politan city), LimiteLimite (the construction of a tower and meeting place in a deteriorated neighbourhood), Barake (the construction of an artists' dwell-ing on stilts) and MAPRAC (a month-long participatory project, in which the future use of the present site of the State Ministry of Finance was discussed).

The rise of the international elites: from social inclusion to co-optation

In 2001, the organisation's efforts to establish positive freedom for self-determined projects and to promote inclusive governance were threatened by a part of the establishment trying to cash in on the increasing presence of the European elite in Brussels. The strategies and activities of *City Mine(d)* and its predecessors had developed independently from the rapidly increasing inter-nationalisation of Brussels. While *City-Mine(d)* concentrated on the social fabric and the mobilisation of local/regional governmental institutions, the new international 'glocal' socio-economic elite was becoming increasingly preva-lent in Brussels (Elmhorn, 1998). These elite groups operated within Brussels, but separately from the social world of the local urban movements and *City Mine(d)*. Although *City Mine(d)* mobilised diverse actors – from state, market and civil society institutions – for its projects, it focused on the 'intra-urban' governance institutions (i.e. the nineteen municipalities, the French and Flemish Community Commissions and segments of the Regional Government of Brussels). The international elites remained outside its 'field of vision'. Thus, a disconnection between the local territorial governance bodies and the networked 'supra-urban' reality (the 'glocal' elite) soon became evident.

The growing presence of the 'glocal' elite had a fundamental impact on both the city and *City Mine(d)*. In addition to the disruptive changes already associated with the crawling proliferation of Euro-infrastructure and services, their presence put significant pressure on the Brussels real estate market, especially in the city centre. Furthermore, the government's fiscal deficit increased the pressure on the real estate market even more (Swyngedouw and Moyersoen, 2004). In an attempt to decrease the deficit, the various governments adopted a policy of attracting even more of the 'glocal' middle and upper classes to the city centre. As a result, a coalition of entrepreneurs in the service sector, with support from the local government, reinvented the centre of Brussels as an attractive place to live for the cosmopolitan middle and upper classes (Baeten, 2001b; Baeten, 2001a).

A paradox thus unfolded. The very self-determined urban initiatives that had developed as a way to reshuffle governance practices were 'appropriated' into the new urban 'myth'. The bohemian, experimental, vanguard downtown lifestyle of Brussels was celebrated by the new 'glocal' elites and mobilised as a marketing instrument to 'gentrify' the city (Zukin, 1993; Ley, 2003). A new generation of young, trendy, urban-minded middle class groups settled in the city centre. This newly formed gentrifying coalition co-opted the self-determined projects initiated by organisations such as *City Mine(d)* for their own purposes. *City Mine(d)*'s intention of facilitating interaction between diverse users of the city in order to further positive freedom was taken over by a meta-discourse put forward by the newly emerging urban regime that promoted the recapitalisation of the city centre by the middle class, a process that Neil Smith defines as the 'revanchist city' (Smith, 1996; Smith and Williams, 1986).

The awareness that *City Mine(d)* was losing its innovative drive forced the organisation to revise its strategy and to look out for other niches in the city. From 2001 onwards, it increasingly positioned itself in the 'glocal' (global/local) niche between the local/territorial governance configurations operating at the 'intra-urban' level on the one hand, and social actors operating at the 'supra-urban' level on the other. The loss of control experienced by institutions promoting positive freedom as a result of the nascent alliance between elite segments of the international 'market' and parts of the state made it clear that the role of facilitator was vulnerable to manipulation and dependency. In addition, the new-found 'glocal' niche enabled the organisation to assert its 'role as a broker' providing self-determined projects with the structural autonomy to self-direct and self-govern (Burt, 1992; McAdam *et al.*, 2001).

This perspective helps in understanding the tactical decision taken by *City Mine(d)* to expand its activities to other cities, such as Rotterdam, London, Belfast and Barcelona and to open spin-off branches in Barcelona and London. *City Mine(d)*'s multi-city repositioning was inspired not only by a desire to diffuse its tactics to other European cities, but also by the necessity of anticipating the loss of (local) control capacity over its projects.

From facilitator to power broker

The ability of *City Mine(d)* to drive social innovation lies in its dual role of facilitator and power broker. However, in adopting this dual role, *City Mine(d)* embarked on a course of action based on a paradoxical and often problematic model of project realisation. The two different roles emphasise two different approaches to the question of autonomy. The role of facilitator promotes relational autonomy, a position that enables participants to deliberate and exchange ideas with diverse groups in the city, whereas the role of power broker advances structural autonomy, taking on positions that enable participants to gain sufficient control to realise the project. These different forms of autonomy occur in different social spaces and in different places, and the discrepancy between them (social and physical) suggests the emergence of an 'urban crack theory'. We shall use the example of the Bubble, a project supported by *City Mine(d)*, to help identify the paradoxes inherent in our 'crack theory' (see also Table 11.1).

The Bubble is a vast transparent plastic bag (6 m x 12 m x 3 m) shaped like a pillow. The transparent bag can be inflated with a simple ventilator into a performance and meeting room for 100 people. Groups that are excluded from a specific public space can employ the Bubble as a means of (re)claiming space for their activities. The interior of the Bubble provides the excluded group with a stage on which to realise their self-determined project in a public space. Various groups have transformed the interior of the Bubble into a tearoom, a retail shop, a playground, a conference room, a gallery, a performance hall, a place to play *jeux de boules* and a party room.

The role of a facilitator: relational or embedded autonomy

City Mine(d)'s primary objective was to promote the ability of the inhabitant – the commuter, the worker or the passer-by – to imagine or conceptualise an urban project. This objective sets *City Mine(d)* in the role of a facilitator aiming for 'relational or embedded autonomy' (Christman, 2004; Mackenzie and Stoljar, 2000; Nussbaum and Sen, 1993). Relational or embedded autonomy emphasises the importance of the social networks in which an individual is embedded, and the way these networks and their mechanisms of socialisation impede or improve the ability to function (Brison, 2000). For example, when a group converted the interior of the Bubble into a tearoom, *City Mine(d)* assisted with contacting local shops to borrow tea sets; helped the group to invite people in the neighbourhood to bake cakes; assisted in inviting the Chinese community to give a demonstration of a tea ceremony; enabled them to invite an accordionist; supported them in contacting the director of an international firm to ask for funding; and guided them to the key people in government for authorisation and financial support. Thus, the role of *City Mine(d)* was to broaden the actor's capability for self-knowledge and self-

Table 11.1 Historical, socio-institutional analysis of the foundation and evolution of the non-profit association *City Mine(d)*

Time frame	STRUCTURAL CONTEXT		REACTION	OUTCOME	
	Configuration of market, state, civil society	*Political, economic, social and cultural factors*	*Reaction against structural context*	*Activities*	*Emerging concepts and visions*
1 Rise of an urban movement in Brussels (early 1990s)	Fragmented city: • Weak state • Fragmented civil society • Speculative market co-opting the state of Brussels	Overall negativism: • Alienation between citizens' everyday life and the politico-institutional reality between formal and informal civil society	• Alliance of formal civil society across the politico-institutional divides in Brussels • Rapprochement Freetown-Brussels	• Sequence of emblematic direct actions • Rise of multilingual member-based urban movement	Development vision: • Direct association of individual freedom to act and enjoy the city with overall governance culture of the metropolis
2 *City Mine(d)* (1997–2003)	Distorted co-optation of urban movement by the state • Limited reaction of the French-speaking component	• Openness of the Flemish-speaking components of government • Self-managed reflective network of self-determined initiatives • Connections between market, state and civil society in support of initiatives	• Re-fragmentation of civil society • Founding of *City Mine(d)* • Encouraging direct and non-hierarchical communication • Creation of public spheres • Location: public spaces	*City Mine(d):* • Sixty self-determined urban interventions	Role of facilitator: • Relational autonomy • Extension of people's capability sets
3 *City Mine(d)* (2003–present)	Glocal alliance between state and market: • Concurrent re-positioning of segments of state and market at the glocal scale	Internationalisation of Brussels: • Government's tax deficit	*City Mine(d)* jumps scales: • Curtailment of innovative capability of *City Mine(d)* • Expansion of *City Mine(d)* as multi-local urban organisation	Glocal organisation: • Establishment of *City Mine(d)* London and *City Mine(d)* Barcelona • Focus on inter-urban and intra-urban competition • Network of expertise for self-determined urban initiatives	Role of power broker: • Structural autonomy • Promotion of self-efficacy • Structural holes • Location: places that embody the lack of communication and/or the ongoing competition between civil society, market and state institutions

Source: Author

direction by embedding self-determined projects in reflexive, reciprocal social networks in the city.[4]

The best way for *City Mine(d)* to realise the objective of embedded autonomy was to locate its projects in public or semi-public spaces. Squares and streets are the natural exchange platforms in cities; people of diverse social and cultural origin meet there and share experiences of urban life. Bubble-projects have been organised in parks, right in the middle of symbolic crossroads, in neighbourhood squares, in front of schools, on sport grounds, etc. In each project *City Mine(d)* was able to rally an inclusive partnership of local and non-local actors, with diverse perspectives and areas of expertise. This glocal support network increased the initiator's ability to engage positively – in this case by realising self-determined projects – with the city-fabric.

The role of a power broker: structural autonomy

City Mine(d)'s second objective was to support empowerment or the freedom to realise a self-determined project. To achieve this objective, *City Mine(d)* adopted the role of power broker. While in the role of facilitator the aim was to extend the set of choices available to the actor, in the role of power broker the aim was to remove burdens and constraints preventing the initiator from making autonomous choices. As we have seen, the political deadlock and the subsequent establishment of Brussels as the EU coordination centre significantly reduced the control capacity available to project initiators. Therefore, *City Mine(d)* as a power broker aims strategically to position projects in locations (both social and physical spaces) which can ensure structural autonomy, that is, in spaces temporarily unused and unclaimed, and which then enable the initiator to take control and empower participants to realise their self-determined projects.

The most effective way to use the Bubble to assert 'structural autonomy' is indeed through the appropriation of 'structural holes', that is, positions in the social networks of the city where different governance configurations are in a state of ongoing competition or non-communication (Burt, 1992). Such settings are typically those strategic locations situated between 'localised spaces' (in the social spheres of the intra-urban governance institutions) and 'globalised spaces' (in the 'supra-urban' reality of the glocal elite). A good example of this strategy is the choice of location for a social art project, which was implemented in a social and physical space that embodied the fissure or frontier between gentrified and non-gentrified areas in the city. It is in these frictional 'glocal' locations that *City Mine(d)* can best take the tertius role – the position of the unique interlocutor between different groups in the city. This tertius position as single contact point for all allows *City Mine(d)* to gain 'monopoly rent' (Harvey, 2001a; Simmel, 1955; Simmel and Wolff, 1950).

Thus, while the Bubble when used by *City Mine(d)* in its role of facilitator functioned as a catalyst for inclusion and exchange, in the role of power broker it was deployed as a means to play a third party role. The two functions are located in different social spaces, which are also embodied in separate physical spaces.

Concluding remarks: 'glocal' urban action to sustain social innovation

City Mine(d) has inflated the Bubble on more than fifty occasions in different public and semi-public spaces in Brussels, Barcelona, Rotterdam, Belfast and London, and with various groups; with each intervention, it has mobilised a unique supportive network. The result of this multi-local strategy is a trans-national patchwork of supportive networks, each of which is anchored within a specific micro-space (Keck and Sikkink, 1998; Serroen, 2004). In fact, although oriented towards the local context, the various supportive networks share a common objective, which is to support local actors in conceptualising and realising their own self-determined projects (Olzak and Uhrig, 2001).

As a result, each additional project is complementary (in a modular sense) to the already existing multi-local network and extends the socio-political weight of the movement in counterbalancing exclusionary policies and, ultimately, in reshuffling the local power geometry for more inclusive govern-ance. In addition, the multi-local network re-enforces positive freedom at the micro-level, in such a way that the network represents the ideal of the city as a collective resource for *City Mine(d)*.

Examples of the empowerment promoted by *City Mine(d)* at the local level are: feeling part of social networks within the city; enjoying the freedom to be respected and treated with dignity; being able to participate in and having some influence over political decision-making; being able to play in one's own neighbourhood; being able to experience different ways of living; being able to work in the labour market or carry out artistic projects; being able to be sheltered and to live in a safe and pleasant environment; having freedom from exposure to violence of any sort; being creative; having the freedom to be mobile; being able to take part in the life of the community.

The political capital of each project contributing to the weight of the multi-local network is generated by several factors: the act undertaken to reclaim local autonomy through realisation of the project, the weight of the mobilised supportive network in terms of expertise and solidarity, the media coverage (newspapers, television, radio) and the tactical innovation involved in the organisation of the project.

But in addition to the recruitment of their own networks, each group of initiators mobilises members of the multi-local network to assist in the conceptualisation and realisation of their self-determined project. In turn, the multi-local network brings together diverse expertise and perspectives to create new ways of mobilising financial resources for projects, engineering more adequate organisational modes for self-determined projects, etc. (and this is where tactical innovation occurs).

In sum, each *City Mine(d)* project can be seen as a 'glocal' urban action which enables local actors to jump scales and reach the extra-local level, becoming part of a broader movement that aims for inclusive governance. At the same time, each project obliges the multi-local network to localise, to nurture and promote positive freedom and find innovative tactics for organising such projects in particular socio-political global/local contexts.

Yet, as revealed in this analysis, *City Mine(d)*'s two-pronged objective – to promote both positive freedom and inclusive governance – confronts the organisation with paradoxical demands. This approach obliges the organisation to adopt two social roles at the same time: while the 'facilitator' seeks to position the projects in embedded, reciprocal (non-hierarchical) networks, the 'broker' wishes to claim a unique bridging position among conflicting governance configurations and thus to occupy a power position within social spaces. Mediating this tension between fostering non-hierarchical reciprocal relations and occupying a pivotal power position within a particular socio-institutional space produces a series of contradictory tensions that are often difficult to manage, mediate, or control.

Notes

1   Examples of such funding sources are the Koning Boudewijn Stichting, the European Union, JP Morgan Bank, Ondex, Centre de Cultura Contemporània de Barcelona, the British Council, Brussels Capital Region and the French Regional Government.

2   The most important associations were Beursschouwburg (Contemporary Performing Art Centre), funded by the Flemish government, Brusselse Raad voor het Leefmilieu (Flemish federation of neighbourhood associations), Inter-Environnement Bruxelles (the French-speaking counterpart of the Brusselse Raad voor het Leefmilieu) and Atelier de Recherche et d'Action Urbaines (French-speaking urban think-tank).

3   The urban movement and its sequence of direct emblematic actions provided the impetus for a generation of artists engaged in the city. Examples are Nathalie Mertens, Tristan Wibault, Sabine De Coninck, Thierry Decuypere, Anoek De Smet, Eric Pringels, Demma, Arabi and Chris Rossaert.

4   This notion of empowerment owes much, in addition to the ideas of Friedmann (1992) and our own theory of social innovation, to the 'capability approach' of Amartya Sen and Martha Nussbaum. For these authors, 'capability' envisages a broader notion of well-being, focusing on the freedom of individuals to pursue their own lives (Nussbaum and Sen, 1993; Sen, 1999). Nussbaum and Sen employ the term 'functionings' to cover the various things that a person manages to do, or be, in the course of living. Capability reflects the alternative combinations of functionings that are individually achievable, and from which he or she can choose one set. Accordingly, capability is a set of functionings, reflecting the person's freedom to lead one type of life or another.

References

Amin, A. and N. Thrift (1992) 'Neo-Marshallian nodes in global networks', *International Journal of Urban and Regional Research*, 16(4): 571–87.

Anonymous (2004) 'Leegstand in Brusselse vijfhoek gedaald', *De Morgen*, 16 May.

Baeten, G. (2001a) 'Clichés of urban doom: the dystopian politics of metaphors for the unequal city – A view from Brussels', *International Journal of Urban and Regional Research*, 25(1): 55–69.

—— (2001b) 'The Europeanization of Brussels and the urbanization of "Europe" – Hybridizing the city, empowerment and disempowerment in the EU district', *European Urban and Regional Studies*, 8(2): 117–30.

Bandura, A. (1971) *Psychological Modeling: Conflicting Theories*, Chicago: Aldine Atherton.

—— and Wood, R. (1989) 'Effect of perceived controllability and performance standards on self-regulation of complex decision-making', *Journal of Personality and Social Psychology*, 56(5): 805–14.

Berlin, I. (2002) 'Two concepts on liberty', in H. Hardy (ed.) *Isaiah Berlin: Liberty*, Oxford: Oxford University Press.

Brenner, N. (1998) 'Between fixity and motion: accumulation, territorial organization and the historical geography of spatial scales', *Environment and Planning D: Society & Space*, 16(4): 459–81.

—— (2003) 'The formation of the global city and the re-scaling of the State's space in post-Fordist Western Europe', *Eure-Revista Latinoamericana de Estudios Urbano Regionales*, 29(86): 5–35.

Briffault, R. (1999) 'A government for our time? Business improvement districts and urban governance', *Columbia Law Review*, 99(2), 365–477.

Brison, S. (2000) 'Relational autonomy and freedom of expression', in C. Mackenzie and N. Stoljar (eds) *Relational Autonomy: Feminist Perspectives on Autonomy, Agency, and the Social Self*, New York and Oxford: Oxford University Press.

Bunker Souple (1997) *Repertorium*, Brussels: Bunker Souple.

—— (2000) *Repertorium*, Brussels: Bunker Souple.

Burt, R.S. (1992) *Structural Holes: The Social Structure of Competition*, Cambridge, MA and London: Harvard University Press.

—— (2000) 'The network structure of social capital', *Research in Organizational Behavior*, 22: 345–423.

Camagni, R. (1991) *Innovation Networks: Spatial Perspectives*, London: Belhaven.

Christman, J. (1999) 'Autonomous agents: from self-control to autonomy', *Journal of Philosophy*, 96(2): 95–99.

—— (2004) 'Relational autonomy, liberal individualism, and the social constitution of selves', *Philosophical Studies*, 117(1–2): 143–64.

Cox, K. (1995) 'Globalisation, competition and the politics of local economic development', *Urban Studies*, 32(2): 213–24.

De Corte, S., De Lannoy, W. and Rijdams, M. (1995) *Les immeubles à l'abandon et la spéculation à Bruxelles, Région de Bruxelles-Capitale*, Bruxelles: Vrije Universiteit Brussel.

De Filippis, J. (1999) 'Alternatives to the "New Urban Politics": finding locality and autonomy in local economic development', *Political Geography*, 18(8): 973–90.

De Lannoy, W., Lammens, M., Lesthaeghe, R. and Willaert, D. (2000) 'Brussel in de jaren negentig en na 2000: een demografische doorlichting', Geografisch Instituut en Steunpunt Demografie, Vrije Universiteit Brussel. Online. Available: http://aps.vlaanderen.be/statistiek/nieuws/brussel/brussel1.doc (Accessed 1 June 2009).

Dryzek, J. S. (1996) 'Political inclusion and the dynamics of democratization, *The American Political Science Review*, 90(3): 475–87.

Elmhorn, C. (1998) 'Brussels in the European economic space: the emergence of a world city? *Bulletin de la Société Belge d'Etudes Géographiques*, 1: 79–101.

Festinger, L., Schachter, S. and Back, K. W. (1950) *Social Pressures in Informal Groups: A Study of Human Factors in Housing*, New York: Harper.

Frankfurt, H. (1971) 'Freedom of the will and the concept of a person', *Journal of Philosophy*, 68(1): 5–20.

Friedman, J. (ed.) (1992) *Empowerment: The Politics of Alternative Development*, Cambridge, MA: Blackwell.

Goetz, E.G. and Clarke, S.E. (1993) *The New Localism: Comparative Urban Politics in a Global Era*, Newbury Park; London: SAGE.

Granovetter, M. (1985) 'Economic action and social structure: the problem of embeddedness', *American Journal of Sociology*, 91(3): 481–510.

Harvey, D. (2001a) 'The art of rent: globalization and the commodification of culture', in D. Harvey (ed.) *Spaces of Capital: Towards a Critical Geography*, Edinburgh: Edinburgh University Press, pp. 394–411.

—— (2001b) 'From managerialism to entrepreneurialsim: the transformation in urban governance in late capitalism', in D. Harvey (ed.) *Spaces of Capital: Towards a Critical Geography*, Edinburgh: Edinburgh University Press, pp. 345–68.

Healey, P. (2002) 'On creating the "city" as a collective resource', *Urban Studies*, 39(10): 1777–92.

Hogue, B. (2001) 'BIDs: business improvement districts', *Journal of the American Planning Association*, 67(1): 115–16.

Homans, G.C. (1951) *The Human Group*, London: Routledge and Kegan Paul.

Hooghe, L. (1991) *A Leap in the Dark: Nationalist Conflict and Federal Reform in Belgium*, Ithaca: Cornell University Press.

Jonas, A.E.G. and Wilson, D. (1999) *The Urban Growth Machine: Critical Perspectives Two Decades Later*, Albany: State of New York University Press.

Keck, M.E. and Sikkink, K. (1998) *Activists Beyond Borders: Advocacy Networks in International Politics*, Ithaca and London: Cornell University Press.

Kesteloot, C. and Mistiaen, P. (2002) 'The Brussels Case: Institutional Complexity', in C. Kesteloot (ed.) *The Spatial Dimensions of Urban Social Exclusion and Integration*, Amsterdam: Urbex.

Kipfer, S. (2005) 'Why the urban question still matters: reflections on rescaling and the promise of the urban', Paper presented at Conference *Towards a Political Economy of Scale*, Studies in Political Economy Annual Conference, February 3–5, 2005, 34 pp., York, Canada: Department of Environmental Sciences, York University.

Ley, D. (2003) 'Artists, aestheticisation and the field of gentrification', *Urban Studies*, 40(12): 2527–44.

Lichterman, P. (1996) *The Search for Political Community: American Activists Reinventing Commitment*, Cambridge: Cambridge University Press.

Lijphart, A. (1984) *Democracies: Patterns of Majoritarian and Consensus Government in Twenty-One Countries*, New Haven and London: Yale University Press.

Lundvall, B. (1992) *National Systems of Innovation: Towards a Theory of Innovation and Interactive Learning*, London: Pinter.

McAdam, D. (1983) 'Tactical innovation and the pace of insurgency', *American Sociological Review*, 48(6): 735–54.

McAdam, D., Tarrow, S.G. and Tilly, C. (2001) *Dynamics of Contention*, Cambridge and New York: Cambridge University Press.

Mackenzie, C. and Stoljar, N. (2000) *Relational Autonomy: Feminist Perspectives on Autonomy, Agency, and the Social Self*, New York and Oxford: Oxford University Press.

Macleod, G. (2000) 'The learning region in an age of austerity: capitalizing on knowledge, entrepreneurialism, and reflexive capitalism', *Geoforum*, 31(2): 219–36.

Mertens, S., Adam, S., Defourny, J., Marée, M., Pacolet, J. and Vandeputte, I. (1999) 'The nonprofit sector in Belgium', in L.M. Salamon, H.K. Anheier, R. List, S. Toepler, W. Sokolowski *et al.* (eds) *Global Civil Society: Dimensions of the Nonprofit Sector*, Baltimore: The Johns Hopkins Center for Civil Society Studies, pp. 43–62.

Meyer, D.S. (2004) 'Protest and political opportunities', *Annual Review of Sociology*, 30: 125–45.

Myers, D.J. (2000) 'The diffusion of collective violence: infectiousness, susceptibility, and mass media networks', *American Journal of Sociology*, 106(1): 173–208.

Nussbaum, M.C. and Sen, A.K. (1993) *The Quality of Life*, Oxford: Clarendon Press.

Olzak, S. and Uhrig, S.C.N. (2001) 'The ecology of tactical overlap', *American Sociological Review*, 66(5): 694–717.

Papadopoulos, A.G. (1996) *Urban Regimes and Strategies: Building Europe's Central Executive District in Brussels*, Chicago: University of Chicago Press.

Peterson, P.E. (1981) *City Limits*, Chicago and London: University of Chicago Press.

Ryan, A., Berlin, I. and Hardy, H. (1979) *The Idea of Freedom: Essays in Honour of Isaiah Berlin*, Oxford: Oxford University Press.

Scott, A.J. (1998) *Regions and the World Economy: The Coming Shape of Global Production, Competition, and Political Order*, Oxford: Oxford University Press.

Sen, A.K. (1992) *Inequality Reexamined*, New York and Oxford: Russell Sage Foundation, Clarendon Press.

—— (1997) *Choice, Welfare and Measurement*, Cambridge, MA and London: Harvard University Press.

—— (1999) *Development as Freedom*, Oxford: Oxford University Press.

Sennett, R. (1977) *The Fall of Public Man*, Cambridge: Cambridge University Press.

Serroen, F. (2004) *Glocal Urban Interventions: Brussels – Barcelona – London*, Brussels: Vrije Universiteit Brussel.

Simmel, G. (1955) *Conflict*, Glencoe: Free Press.

—— and Wolff, K.H. (1950) *The Sociology of Georg Simmel*, Glencoe: Free Press.

Smith, N. (1996) *The New Urban Frontier : Gentrification and the Revanchist City*, London: Routledge.

—— and Williams, P. (1986) *Gentrification of the City*, Boston and London: Allen & Unwin.

Soja, E.W. (1996) *Thirdspace: Journeys to Los Angeles and Other Real-and-imagined Places*, Cambridge, MA and Oxford: Blackwell.

Stoker, G. (1998) 'Public-private partnerships and urban governance', in J. Pierre (ed.) *Partnerships in Urban Governance: European and American Experience*, Basingstoke: Macmillan, pp. 34–51.

Storper, M. (1997) *The Regional World: Territorial Development in a Global Economy*, New York and London: Guilford Press.

Swyngedouw, E. (1997) 'Neither global nor local: "glocalisation" and the politics of scale', in K.R. Cox (ed.) *Spaces of Globalization: Reasserting the Power of the Local*, New York and London: Guilford Press, pp. 137–66.

—— and Baeten, G. (2001) 'Scaling the city: the political economy of "glocal development – Brussels" conundrum', *European Planning Studies*, 9(7): 827–49.

—— and J. Moyersoen (2004) 'Reluctant globalisers: the paradoxes of "glocal" development in Brussels', in K. Archer (ed.) *World City Formation on the Periphery*, London: Routledge, pp. 157–77.

Tarrow, S. (1991) 'Collective action and political opportunity structure in waves of mobilization. Some theoretical perspectives', *Kölner Zeitschrift für Soziologie und Sozialpsychologie*, 43(4), 647–70.

Timmermans, A.I. (2003) *High Politics in the Low Countries: An Empirical Study of Coalition Agreements in Belgium and the Netherlands*, Aldershot: Ashgate.

Timmermans, G. (1991) *In Brussel Mag Alles: Geld, Macht en Beton*, Antwerpen: EPO.

Watson, G. (1997) 'Free action and free will', *Mind*, 96(382): 145–72.

Witte, E. and Van Velthoven, H. (1999) *Language and Politics: The Belgian Case Study in a Historical Perspective*, Brussels: VUB University Press.

Young, I.M. (1990) *Justice and the Politics of Difference*, Princeton: Princeton University Press.

—— (2000) *Inclusion and Democracy*, Oxford: Oxford University Press

Zukin, S. (1993) *The Cultures of Cities*, Oxford: Blackwell.

12 The end of social innovation in urban development strategies?

The case of *BOM* in Antwerp[1]

Frank Moulaert and Etienne Christiaens

Introduction

For about two decades, the city of Antwerp has been the stage for creative co-operation between civil society and local authorities in the field of urban development (see Loopmans, 2008). In 1990, the Neighbourhood Development Corporation *BOM-Buurtontwikkelingsmaatschappij* launched an innovative Integrated Area Development (IAD) strategy to abate social exclusion, first in the North-East Antwerp neighbourhood and, later, in the South Edge and Canal Zone, where it acted as local project developer and facilitator of relationships between different actors, projects and funding institutions. *BOM* also prepared one of the first Neighbourhood Development Plans in Flanders and, towards the end of its trajectory as an independent development agency, designed and began to implement a socio-economic renewal strategy for the Northern Canal Zone. Through its initiatives, *BOM* succeeded in putting deprived neighbourhoods on the political agenda and having the quality of its socially innovative approach recognised by institutions at various spatial levels (EU, region and city).

However, over the last few years, powerful political and economic forces in Antwerp have urged local authorities to make a U-turn in urban policy, which endangers the continuity of social innovation planning and actions. Today, after fourteen years of successful application, the concept of 'social' neighbourhood development seems politically incorrect, as it does not fit the logic of city marketing and real estate-based urban development.

In the following pages we will reconstruct the particular socio-economic, territorial and institutional context of Antwerp during the last thirty years. We will especially dwell on how *BOM* developed its socially innovative strategies over a period of almost two decades and contributed to beating social exclusion through the empowerment of neighbourhood residents. Finally, we will briefly assess the present outlook for social innovation in neighbourhood development in Antwerp.

The rise and decline of *BOM* in the context of Antwerp's urban policy evolution

Urban renewal and community development in the 'merger' metropolis (1983–90)

In the course of the 1980s, in the context of an urban policy mostly focused on urban renewal and in the presence of a strong grass-roots movement that resonated with the social transformation spirit of the post-1968 period, the Antwerp regional and city authorities explored feasible institutional structures which would improve the connection of their own policy views and practices with those of bottom-up organisations active in deprived neighbourhoods.

In June 1982, with its first Decree on Urban Renewal, the Flemish Regional Government began to provide financial support to cities with the aim of improving their housing stock and reconstructing the public domain in deprived neighbourhoods or 'urban revalorisation areas' (*stedelijke herwaarderingsgebieden*). The decree was also meant to promote participatory decision-making by establishing citizen 'steering committees'. In the same year a major local administrative reorganisation occurred with the merger of the various municipalities of the Antwerp Metropolitan Area into one 'merger city'. A year later, with the 1983 Decree, the Flemish Minister of Culture terminated the subsidies supporting grass-roots-oriented neighbourhood initiatives[2] and replaced the existing system with the Regional Institutes for Community Development (RISO-*Regionaal Instituut voor Samenlevingsopbouw*). These new institutions were officially recognised as 'project works focused on the direct solution of the collective problems of neighbourhoods, districts and regions with the participation of the inhabitants [. . .], but with a special attention to the most vulnerable groups'. They were supposed to 'give voice to the inhabitants, [and] mobilise their capabilities in order to resolve their problems in partnership with other instances' (RISO Antwerp, 1986). In this new approach, neighbourhood development was no longer to be considered as mere urban renewal, but had to also include improvement in the quality of life, housing, job creation, diversity and education, while the city was no longer to be considered as an adversary but rather an ally of community workers (Moulaert *et al.*, 1997).

Thanks to the vision developed in the Global Structure Plan of Antwerp and adopted by the political coalition of the 'merger city' in 1982,[3] neighbourhoods outside the historical inner city and belonging to the nineteenth-century industrial belt were recognised as 'urban revalorisation areas' for the first time (Antwerp City *et al.*, 1990). Fifteen such areas were selected and a programme was launched that included over 100 projects targeting the improvement of the public domain and forty (small-scale) social housing projects (Wittocx *et al.*, 1994; Willems and Vandenbroucke, 2007).

The Antwerp RISO, established in 1983 to support citizen participation, became one of the most vocal critics of the city's neighbourhood development policy. It immediately pointed out, among other things, the absence of immigrants in the steering committees, the insufficient resources for participation, the lack of objective criteria for delimiting the urban renewal areas, the largely techn(ocrat)ic approach adopted by civil servants and, finally, the lack of motivation, collaboration and coordination among public partners. RISO also criticised the fragmented, purely physical and project-oriented approach, together with the absence of a socio-economic vision of neighbourhood development policy, and the danger of both real estate speculation and gentrification (Verhetsel and Ceulemans, 1994). Finally, RISO emphasised the difficulties experienced by neighbourhood projects in getting off the ground and achieving visible results (Van Maele, 1994; Baelus, 1996). In short, RISO exposed the fact that the valorisation of deprived neighbourhoods and the participation of their inhabitants were not a real political priority for Antwerp City Hall (RISO Antwerp, 1984, 1986).

This situation, coupled with the progressive political disempowerment of remote neighbourhoods within the large 'merger city', led to extreme distrust among the neighbourhoods' inhabitants vis-à-vis local politicians. By the end of the 1980s, awareness of the enduring deprivation of particular areas, growing discontent with local state practices (also expressed by the rise of the extreme right), lack of pro-activity in traditional community development organisations, together with new opportunities offered by the EC's Third Poverty programme, provided fertile ground for the creation of the neighbourhood development corporation *BOM*.

BOM: an emblematic neighbourhood development corporation (1990–99)

The EU's Third Anti-Poverty Programme (1989–94) offered a unique opportunity to test a more integrated approach to neighbourhood development. The programme was actively exploited by *BOM* – *Buurtontwikkelingsmaatschappij*, a public–private partnership founded in 1990 and initially operating in North-East Antwerp (Van Hove, 2001; Koning Boudewijnstichting, 1995). Born of distrust between civil society and local politicians about urban development policy and assuming that RISO's purported bottom–up approach would not produce tangible results, *BOM* promoted so-called 'impulse' projects, selected on the basis of development potential, expected multiplier effects for the neighbourhood, and opportunities for partnership and funding.

Instead of the physical renewal projects supported by the city hall, *BOM* launched specific economic projects as engines of development, such as the NOA Business Centre, a neighbourhood enterprise incubator. These projects were connected to other initiatives involving training, participation, housing and the improvement of public space. It was an essential element of *BOM*'s strategy to bring these initiatives together in an integrated Neighbourhood Development Plan (Moulaert, 2000).

Thanks to funding by the Third Anti-Poverty Programme (DGV 1989–94) and the setting-up of an Urban Pilot Project (UPP 1994–96), *BOM* developed an integrated programme for the revitalisation of North-East Antwerp – the most deprived zone of Antwerp, consisting of the neighbourhoods of Stuivenberg, Dam and the north-east of Oud Borgerhout. In 1994, *BOM* perfected its action-oriented approach in a fully fledged Neighbourhood Development Plan, the first in Flanders,[4] by integrating different sectoral strategies and involving different actors from the public and private sector (Nieuwinckel, 1996; BOM and SOMA, 1995). See Figure 12.1.

The 1994 municipal elections resulted in a new blatant political victory for the far-right party, Vlaams Blok.[5] With 28 per cent of the vote it supplanted the traditional democratic parties, became the major single political power in Antwerp and the largest party in the new city council (eighteen seats out of fifty-five). A new, and difficult, local government coalition was formed among four democratic parties, forced to collaborate in order to exclude the Blok. The new majority became aware of the availability of substantial EU funds for neighbourhood development and recognised the success of the *BOM* approach. In fact, although *BOM* enjoyed great freedom and autonomy in launching its innovative initiatives in the neighbourhood, it had succeeded in attracting wider attention from city hall itself, as well as from other economic partners. Recognised as a 'model alliance' and cited as 'one of the most inspiring multi-dimensional and socially innovative neighbourhood development projects', the *BOM* approach certainly influenced the philosophy of two other major urban programmes in the period 1995–99: the EU-funded URBAN I programme and the Flemish region's Social Impulse Fund SIF 1 (Flemish Community and Antwerp City, 1996).

Thus, at the beginning of the 1995–97 legislatures the city, *BOM* and other organisations collaborated in drafting new Neighbourhood Development Plans and programmes fitting the logic of SIF 1 or URBAN I, all with a clear integrated neighbourhood development approach and focused on target groups within deprived neighbourhoods. Furthermore, the city sought to integrate into this approach the variety of existing and forthcoming projects, human resources and financial funds involved in urban development. To this end, in 1995 the alderman of social affairs reactivated a small, dormant, urban non-profit organisation called SOMA – Stedelijke Ontwikkelingsmaatschappij (Urban Development Corporation) and made it responsible for the planning, funding and implementation of the various projects in the North Antwerp area (SOMA, 1994; Wittocx *et al.*, 1994; Van Maele, 1994). SOMA then became responsible for the management of URBAN I funds and some of those from SIF.[6]

At the end of 1997, having completed the majority of its projects in the North East, *BOM* received financial resources (especially SIF) to spread its approach further and moved to the South Edge, a neighbourhood with a high diversity of development challenges (social housing, improvement of public space fragmented by the physical forms of the transportation network, local socio-

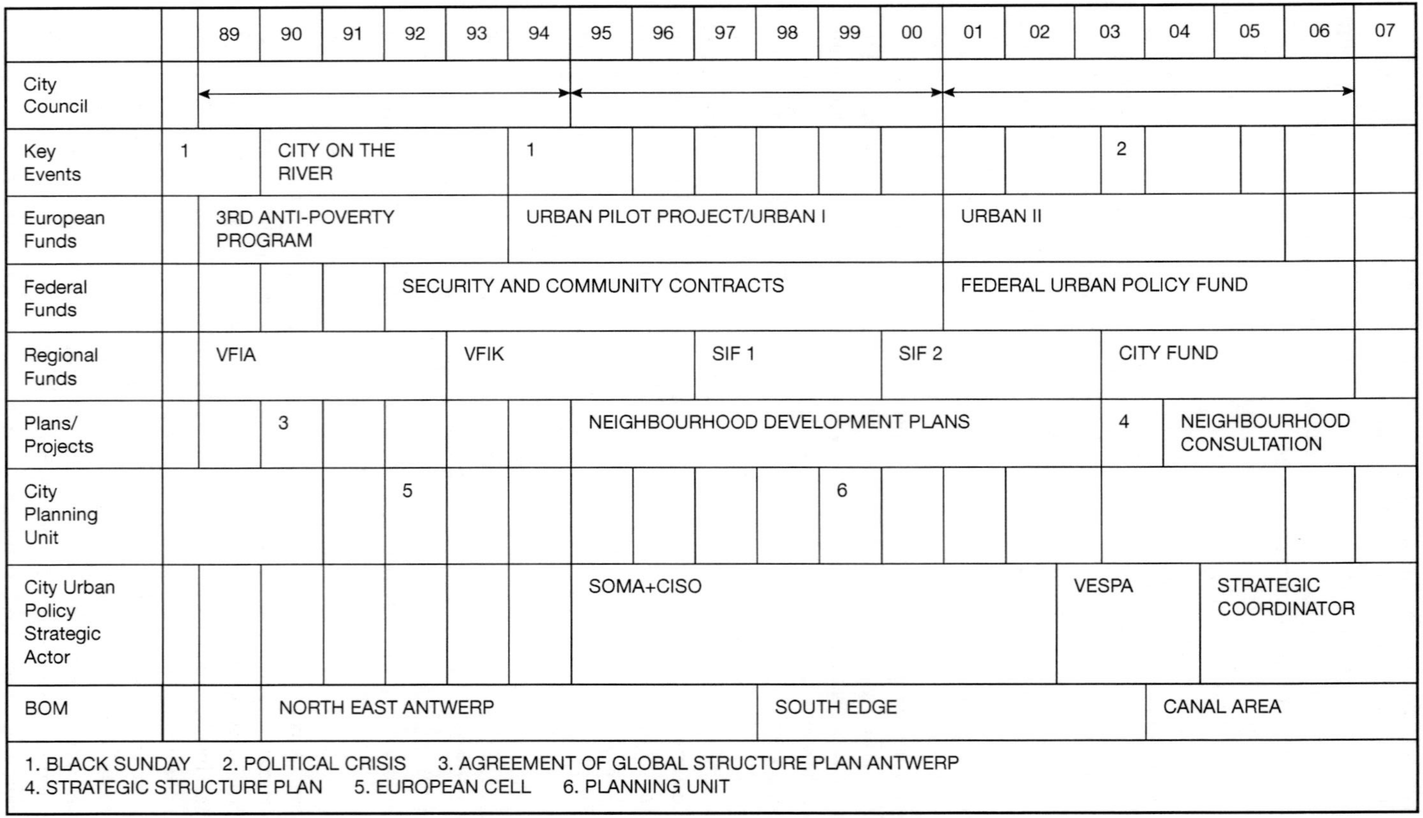

	89	90	91	92	93	94	95	96	97	98	99	00	01	02	03	04	05	06	07
City Council		←———————————————————————→				←—————————————————————————————→													
Key Events	1	CITY ON THE RIVER				1									2				
European Funds	3RD ANTI-POVERTY PROGRAM				URBAN PILOT PROJECT/URBAN I							URBAN II							
Federal Funds				SECURITY AND COMMUNITY CONTRACTS								FEDERAL URBAN POLICY FUND							
Regional Funds	VFIA				VFIK			SIF 1				SIF 2			CITY FUND				
Plans/Projects		3				NEIGHBOURHOOD DEVELOPMENT PLANS									4	NEIGHBOURHOOD CONSULTATION			
City Planning Unit				5							6								
City Urban Policy Strategic Actor							SOMA+CISO								VESPA		STRATEGIC COORDINATOR		
BOM	NORTH EAST ANTWERP						SOUTH EDGE						CANAL AREA						

1. BLACK SUNDAY   2. POLITICAL CRISIS   3. AGREEMENT OF GLOBAL STRUCTURE PLAN ANTWERP
4. STRATEGIC STRUCTURE PLAN   5. EUROPEAN CELL   6. PLANNING UNIT

Figure 12.1 Evolution of the political, financial and organisational dimensions of urban development in Antwerp

Source: Authors.

cultural service provision, cleaning up of insalubrious areas such as industrial sites located outside the first city belt). It is not clear whether this move was a conscious choice by *BOM* or the result of political pressures to limit its influence on the political agenda. Three other Neighbourhood Development Plans[7] were worked out by SOMA and the city services, but without the involvement of *BOM*. The Integrated Planning Unit (Geïntegreerde Planningscel) created in 1999 within SOMA played an instrumental role in this. Probably, the sidetracking of *BOM* was symptomatic of the incumbent organisational changes within the city's administration, the growing perspective on urban development of the 'city-as-a-whole' – rather than the neighbourhood – as well as a firmer focus on security issues.

The return of urban renewal sectoral programmes

In the 2000 municipal elections, the Vlaams Blok confirmed its position as first party in the city council and in 2001 the former majority was renewed – still isolating the extreme right party from the city government.[8] A major institutional change also occurred. For the first time, the city government decided to assign the competences (and financial resources) of urban development, previously held by the alderman for social affairs, to the alderman for spatial planning and public works. In this capacity the latter succeeded in attracting most city development funds to his service (the Business Unit for Civil Affairs) and to non-profit organisations (such as SOMA and CISO). But in the new political situation the four aldermen (spatial planning and public works; city patrimony and human resources; city development; community building and social affairs) all claimed more control over these growing funds. Together they formed the Council Team for City Development (Collegeteam Stadsontwikkeling), responsible for making political and strategic choices in the field of urban development (Christiaens *et al.*, 2007). To this end they could count on the Urban Development Unit (Cel Stadsontwikkeling), also created in 2000, to prepare and support the team's work. 'The unit was, among other things, responsible for developing a global vision on spatial planning, urban development, social-economic policy, the drawing up of coherent memos regarding spatial planning, urban development and social cohesion' (Willems and Vandenbroucke, 2007, p. 165).

The four aldermen team continued to involve civil society organisations in its strategy, but it also developed a growing ambition to be the 'managing director' and sole implementing actor for urban development projects. It argued that there were now enough skills and services available inside the city's own administration to achieve what *BOM* had undertaken in the 1990s. In so doing, the local government played down the constructive collaboration developed so far with the civil society, which – it was argued – was better suited to narrower community development projects because of the local knowledge and integrated action experience acquired in specific neighbourhoods and for specific target groups.

Another major change was the clear-cut strategic shift from 'integrated' neighbourhood development focused on socio-economic disparities *à la BOM*, to 'sectoral' urban development programmes across all neighbourhoods within the city districts, with a particular focus on real estate operations. The tendency towards more visible and physical interventions and the pursuit of greater security and well-being for the city as a whole was significantly influenced by the new political context. The dark shadow of the far right with its political focus on the exploitation and control of fear and the restoration of urban order was reflected in the changed funding criteria for the programmes and eventually led to a turnaround in urban development policy – from the socio-economically oriented URBAN I to the physically oriented URBAN II and from the 'impulse' policy against exclusion in the SIF to programmes against urban decline favoured by the new City Fund (De Decker and Loopmans, 2003; Loopmans, 2002; 2003; Boudry and Vanattenhoven, 2003). Defending the view that regional urban funds should not be used to fund the operation of NGOs, the new Flemish City Fund was reduced by 25 per cent compared to previous SIF funds. Greater security (e.g. against juvenile crime) and hard physical investments were also at the forefront of the new federal urban policy (Chancellerie du Premier Ministre, 2003; Antwerp City, 2002).

The new priorities involved the progressive disappearance of an urban development policy stressing the social dimension through the integrated-project-based approach *à la BOM* in favour of a repressive and preventive safety approach. A new discourse wormed its way into political and economic circles, arguing that 'since [for] fifteen years the city had made enormous investments in many social projects, the "social boys" had had enough opportunities, while in the meantime economic development was neglected and Antwerp had lost its position on the world map'. In short, according to this economic accumulation logic 'it was time to build, to score with prestigious projects and to communicate about these new achievements,[9] while the rest would follow'.[10] Therefore, large-scale 'hard' projects for the redevelopment of abandoned manufacturing and infrastructure sites – such as Petroleum South, New South or Railway North – into new urban spaces interwoven with the surrounding neighbourhoods became the new drivers of city development and captured most of the new funds.

The end of integrated neighbourhood policy

In March 2003, because of financial scandals and at the instigation of the far right opposition, first the city secretary, the local tax officer and the police chief, and later the whole city government, resigned. Most of the non-profit organisations (especially SOMA) were criticised for their lack of democratic control and fell into disrepute, although it is believed that they served as scapegoats to impart a last big blow to the social planning tradition. The Council Team for Urban Development and the Urban Development Unit were both dissolved.

In 2003, the city established the autonomous municipal corporation (*autonoom gemeentebedrijf*)[11] VESPA, which became responsible for the management of any of the city's real estate involved in urban renewal projects. VESPA took on board some of the tasks of the Urban Development Unit and became responsible for the management of regional, national and European funds. But the disclosure of further malpractice in 2004 led to another new administrative restructuring.

The city administration is now based on two pillars (ANTenne, 2003): day-to-day activities are carried out by the city secretary's office, whereas more strategic programmes are led by the coordinator for integrated city development projects. Acquisition of funds and management of projects are no longer VESPA's responsibility, but fall within the competence of a 'strategic cell' within the city administration under the sole responsibility of a strategic coordinator. Appointed for the period of the legislature, the strategic coordinator has the overriding authority to claim, from the various departments in the city administration, all the human and financial resources needed to accomplish the targets on the 'mayor's short list'. SOMA, as the last remaining independent non-profit organisation, was integrated into the regular city administration in 2006.

Pressured by the Flemish government and aware of the lack of coordination among the 114 urban projects of various scales in progress within the city (Antwerp City, 2003), the new political team has sought a 'harmonised' vision of city development through a new Strategic Spatial Structure Plan for Antwerp, which uses a city-wide spatial approach and has no links with the integrated approach of the Neighbourhood Development Plans launched by *BOM* or elaborated by SOMA.

The Strategic Spatial Plan of Antwerp, commissioned by the city in 2003,[12] was approved by the Flemish authorities in 2006 (Antwerp City, 2006). Although the Plan has a clear-cut 'action-oriented part' which targets strategic spaces and projects, it is not only generic ('rules to be applied to everybody, and to the city's entire territory' – as rephrased by Willems and Vandenbroucke, 2007), but also applies a spatial logic that is explicitly supra-local. Thus, the new spatial planning approach downplays both neighbourhood and social dimensions – the major drivers of the urban development approach of the 1990s.

In this context, *BOM* was forced to restructure and merged with Vitamine W, grouping its management tasks into a new holding structure called Groep B&W (*Buurt & Werk*) – Group for Neighbourhood and Work. In 2006 Levanto was created, an organisation that integrated the activities of *BOM*, B&W, Vitamine W and a few other not-for-profit organisations.

The social innovation trajectory of *BOM*

The trajectory of *BOM*, as retraced in the previous section, provides a very good illustration of how social innovation interacts with the institutional dynamics of the places where it occurs.

We have stressed how *BOM* sprang up in the 1990s in reaction to the economic, socio-cultural and physical decay in one of the most deprived Antwerp neighbourhoods, characterised by high unemployment (especially of young and poorly educated people) and housing and community (coexistence) problems involving minority groups (immigrants, elderly, marginalised youths, asylum seekers, homeless). It reacted to the reluctance of private capital to invest in these neighbourhoods, but also to a sectoral and fragmented urban policy that focused almost exclusively on physical interventions. In contrast also to the overly sectoral approach of community development organisations in the 1980s, *BOM* launched a truly integrated project-based area approach.

BOM's resources, institutional entrepreneurship and networking

The strong culture of independence of *BOM* made it attractive to young motivated professionals 'who wanted to work for the city, but not in the city (administration)'.

From 1990 to 1994, while *BOM* was based in the North-East neighbourhood, its staff grew to forty-five employees, and it possessed a budget of about €1.5 million a year, 0.2 million of which came from the EU and the rest from *BOM*'s institutional partners and other public authorities. In the 2000–03 period, when based in the South Edge, its employment level reached eighty (half on full-time work contracts and half subsidised through Work Experience Projects), and funding amounted to about €1.25 million a year, largely coming from SIF. Always successful at pooling resources, *BOM* managed to triple this amount by capturing EU URBAN II funds.[13]

However, in 2003 resources from SIF – now controlled by the City Fund – were halved. As a consequence, *BOM* had to lay off some of its staff and its dependence on public funding emerged as a serious weakness, leading eventually to merger with Vitamine W and incorporation into Levanto.

The determination to maintain its autonomy with respect to the political world as well as its role of social incubator and pragmatic neighbourhood project developer distinguished *BOM* from the typical social work organisation. Its mode of working was also radically different from such sectoral approaches as those applied by VITAMINE W, a social enterprise promoting integration of low-skilled workers into the labour market on a city-wide scale. Compared to the RISO approach of the 1980s, *BOM*'s participation model was more project- than process-oriented (Van Pottelsberghe, 1997) and focused on short-term visible results in order to regain trust from the population (Koning Boudewijnstichting, 1995).

Revealing and satisfying basic needs through integrated local development

For *BOM*, this integrated action against poverty, as synthesised in the 'Three Ps' slogan – project development, partnership, participation – had a clear territorial dimension, with the neighbourhood playing a central role both as a *social network* and as an *action space* for vulnerable groups (Meert and Peleman, 2001; Soenen, 2003; Baelus, 1996). *BOM* promoted the concept of IAD by grouping and integrating resources, actors, sectors of intervention and projects into one neighbourhood programme or development plan, with the objectives of improving the living conditions of the most deprived (mainly the long-term unemployed, people living on welfare and young people with learning difficulties), reintegrating them into society and the economy through custom-ised training and individual counselling, as well as revitalising the economic base of the neighbourhood (Nieuwinckel, 1996; Moulaert, 2000).

In the North-East neighbourhood, long considered an economic desert, *BOM* succeeded in launching a number of economic pilot projects, which offered solutions to its core problems. From 1990 until 1997 *BOM* worked on the 'Four Ws' dimensions of basic needs: *wonen, werken, weten, welzijn* (housing, work, knowledge and well-being) and implemented multidimensional projects in line with the IAD strategy, combining three action spaces: economic activity, housing and the socio-cultural life of the neighbourhood (Demazière, 1997; Moulaert, 2000). The emphasis on actions to improve the socio-economic base of the area represented a clear break with the inner city policies of the 1980s, which focused almost exclusively on environmental and housing improvements.

For the first time in Flanders the business community (the group Leysen via Anbema, VKW, Centea, Mercator, the local Chamber of Commerce) was directly involved in an urban redevelopment initiative of this kind. The NOA Business Centre, *BOM*'s flagship project, was the first in Flanders to be set in a deprived inner-city context, rather than a growth area or business district (Eurocities, 1994). The Centre stimulated small businesses and encouraged labour market integration measures in North-East Antwerp. Among its side effects can be mentioned a labour market scheme (*werkwijzer*) that is now widely applied across Flanders by the regional employment agency (VDAB) in its *werkwinkels*.[14]

However, when in 1998 *BOM* moved to the South Edge of Antwerp, it was only moderately successful in starting up neighbourhood and social econ-omy activities, generating multiplier effects for neighbourhood employment, or involving private partners. The Cosmolocal project was short-lived and did not survive the making of its business plan. The Outfort initiative was transmuted into a co-operative association working on the revalorisation site of Fort 8 in Hoboken and was mainly involved in organising outdoor training, professional training, seminars and also festivities. The CEON project, which focused on sustainable entrepreneurship, was integrated into Vitamine W until URBAN II funding came to an end.

More successful was the BBBZuidrand initiative (Neighbourhood Manage-ment Enterprise of the South Edge), which promoted a number of work experience ('learn-as-you work') projects such as selective domestic waste col-lection in high-rise social housing, ecological construction, remover logistics, restoration and refurbishment works. Also interesting were several 'communi-cation' initiatives, such as a periodic neighbourhood report (*BOM*, 1997, 2000,

2001, 2002) and the Zuidrand op Band videos (South Edge on Tape) concerning specific neighbourhood issues. *BOM* also organised City Dreams, a
large-scale cultural event, the '4x4' socio-cultural initiatives at the crossroads
of the four parts of the neighbourhood, and the posting of positive messages
and drawings from the South Edge area on trams travelling to the city centre.
Seeking to meet the social specificities of the South Edge, *BOM* also created
a youth meeting place ('backspace') with a cyberspace and a dog-walking service
(*stadsbeest* or 'urban animal') for disabled and/or single people.

With regard to housing, however, while the *woonwijzer* (housing consulting)
initiative had constituted a real answer to the housing problems of the North-
East neighbourhood, in the South Edge *BOM* was not really effective, as the
social housing domain was quasi monopolised by co-operatives whose
partnership with *BOM* remained limited to technical and logistical support
(see Figure 12.2).

Changing social relations and empowerment: strengths and limitations

Among the most important socially innovative features of the *BOM* approach
is, undoubtedly, its determination to initiate a *dialogue* between actors *within*
the neighbourhoods through new governance dynamics. Thus, besides providing opportunities for revealing needs ('pioneer' function) and investing in
the neighbourhood ('impulse' function), *BOM* supported interaction between
diverse groups ('catalyst' function) and evolved new ways of co-operation
('empowering' function) through interdependent projects which developed
progressively into independent entities ('engine' function). To make these
projects autonomous, *BOM* created new organisations (e.g. the social restaurant,
ATEL, NOA) in which it retained only the role of administrator and the
provision of logistical support. Some functions were actually handed over to
the city hall (e.g. *woonwijzer*) or shared with friendly associations, such as
werkwijzer with the regional employment agency, or work experience projects
with Vitamine W in the building sector.

As a pioneer organisation it was relatively easy for *BOM* to implement its
IAD approach and to make the initiated projects self-sufficient in North-East
Antwerp; it was much more difficult to replicate the approach later in the
physically and socio-economically more fragmented South Edge. Progressively
in the North East, but more especially in the South Edge, *BOM* had to reckon
with both divergent external institutional dynamics and important internal
tensions within its original objectives. On the one hand, *BOM* was successful
in promoting integrated development of economic and socio-cultural (so
called 'hard' and 'soft') initiatives in specific neighbourhoods and for specific
target groups (a positive discrimination approach), and in providing new
impulses for action – its so-called IAD approach. On the other hand, *BOM*'s
emphatic non-paternalistic and bottom-up development approach, which
involved making its innovative projects self-sufficient, also hampered the

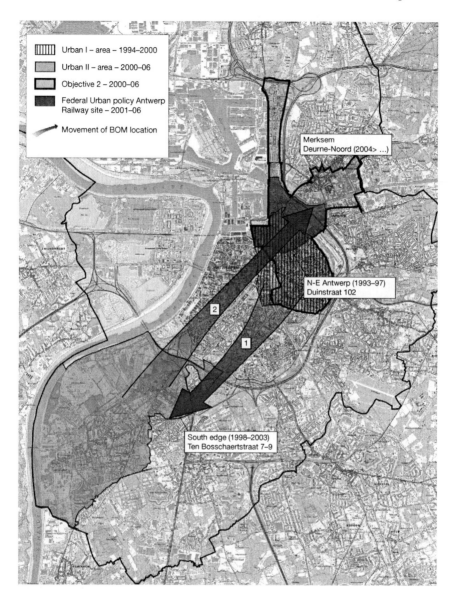

Figure 12.2 The errant ways of *BOM*
Source: Authors on city map.

ambitions of the IAD model. For example, by its choice to centralise all economic projects in the NOA Business Centre as a separate non-profit enterprise, *BOM* weakened its potential for steering interaction among the economic, social and physical domains of neighbourhood development, which is an essential component of the integrated approach. In the same way, by handing over some initiatives to friendly non-profit organisations or by allowing them to become integrated into the city administration, *BOM* engendered both a shift away from the original (social) objectives and a loss of the neighbourhood dimension.

In time, the growing scale of the *BOM* organisation, together with the increased efforts needed to sustain its development, to ensure its logistical and financial support, as well as to guarantee the quality control of the diverse initiatives became constraints in themselves and threatened its very innovative capacity. In the end, *BOM* decided to return to its core 'impulse' activities: the launching of pump-priming projects on the one hand, and project management and development consulting on the other. The merger with Vitamine W to form Groep B&W, and the initiatives launched in 2005 in the Canal Zone with the harbour and the Canal Authority, as well as the final integration into Levanto in 2007, all obey this logic. Today's activities – within Levanto – are limited to facilitating the integration of older and poorly skilled workers into the regular labour market. The neighbourhood focus is much reduced, although there is still some follow-up to some of the activities developed by *BOM* in the South Edge and in the Canal Zone (e.g. Wireless Dok).

The end of social innovation in Antwerp?

Our analysis has revealed how the evolution of *BOM* was related to the socio-economic and institutional dynamics of the city's politics and, especially, to its urban policies. After the merger of the Antwerp municipalities in 1983 into one greater 'merger city' and under the pressures coming from neighbourhood groups and community development professionals, urban policy had turned its focus onto renewal programmes in areas of the nineteenth-century belt. By 1990, attention had shifted to the most deprived areas in that same belt – those particularly affected by the restructuring of the urban economy and its harbour. Throughout this decade, driven by these very groups and professionals and with the financial support of mainly regional and European programmes, the local government had eventually adopted the integrated neighbourhood development and positive discrimination approach as conceived by the newly born civil society agent *BOM*. During this period, community development, neighbourhood and work placement organisations had thus received increasing recognition.

However, starting in 2000, confronted with negative socio-economic scores, increasing public debt and growing dissatisfaction among a population cleverly manipulated by the right-wing party Vlaams Blok, the city hall reverted to a sectoral, undifferentiated urban policy, focusing mainly on real estate projects and 'priority' actions. The advent of the new regional and federal City Funds in Antwerp, managed by VESPA and, later, by the strategic cell in the city administration, has meant a return to real estate-led urban development, very much concerned with security and attracting the middle class. The socially innovative neighbourhood focus of the city's urban development approach of the 1990s has thus given way to a city-wide, project-based development approach. This evolution is quite clearly expressed in the new Strategic Spatial Structure Plan.

On the other hand, it must also be stressed that after fourteen years of *BOM* activity, first strongly rooted in North-East Antwerp, then un-rooted (or loosely rooted) in the South Edge, and ambiguously re-geared towards the Canal Zone, the city authorities do seem to acknowledge the innovative capacity and the developmental role of its civil society organisations in coping with urban challenges from a strategic point of view. The criticisms of this approach – that it was too area-focused and insufficiently concerned about the well-being of the urban fabric as a whole – were partly well founded. But the conclusions that were drawn are awkward, to say the least: an integrated local planning system with a social logic was replaced by a strategic spatial structure planning with an explicit hierarchy in agency, and in which economic and real estate interests, but also security concerns, prevail.

Hopefully, the current situation is not the sad end of the story. A vibrant urban society has disempowered its most active social agents by applying principles of new public management both in its city administration and its planning procedures. But the antithesis of this is a political process in which a new synthesis between the values of social, bottom-up planning and social innovation will soon need to be found.

Notes

1 The authors thank Bie Bosmans, former coordinator of *BOM* Antwerp, and Griet Geerinck, coordinator of 'Spatial Planning Antwerp' for their useful comments on a previous version of this chapter. Obviously, all responsibility for its content remains the authors'.

2 Because in his opinion they were run by radical groups of intellectuals rooted in the 1968 student revolts and urban movements.

3 Originally Antwerp City Hall wanted only the inner city to be considered as a 'renewal area' and would have preferred to abstain from public participation in its operation.

4 These plans provided a global framework for the projects and combined territorial with community perspectives. The objective was to plan, organise and coordinate the different initiatives and interventions within an area and for a certain period of time.

5 Renamed Vlaams Belang in 2004.

6 In 2001 – and until 2003 – it actually became responsible for the management of all supra-local resources for urban development (Willems and Vandenbroucke, 2007). The Social Impulse Fund (SIF) was organised through two three-year programmes – SIF 1 for the period 1997–99 and SIF 2 for the period 2000–02 – each inspired by two different regional majorities. The SIF 2 programme was clearly focused on the return of the middle class to the cities, abandoning the neighbourhood and poverty approach, that had formed the essence of the SIF 1 programme.

7 From 1995 to 2000 Neighbourhood Development Plans were implemented for North Antwerp (1995), Oud-Borgerhout (1997), Oud-Berchem/Groenenhoek (1998) and Deurne-Noord (2000).

8   In the 2000 elections the far-right wing obtained the largest number of seats. The democratic parties constituted a *cordon sanitaire* around the Vlaams Blok and refused to form any government coalition with this party. Aldermen in the new city government included three Socialists, two Christian Democrats, two Greens, three Liberals plus the socialist mayor.

9   'Toespreken' instead of 'inspreken', meaning talking 'to' rather than 'with' the people about projects.

10 Opinions such as the above were expressed, e.g. in interviews on TV by the president of the Chamber of Commerce of Antwerp.

11 An autonomous municipal corporation is an enterprise in which the majority of the board of directors is constituted by city councillors, thereby guaranteeing democratic control, although the enterprise can carry out commercial and economic activities, free from the encumbrance of municipal regulations.

12 As a consequence of the Flemish government decision of 1999, by which all Flemish municipalities had to generate a spatial structure plan.

13 The city would have lost these funds if *BOM* had not successfully applied for them.

14 By engaging in activities with a local partner, the VDAB discovered that its services could be made more accessible to the local population and to groups that it had previously failed to reach.

References

ANTenne (2003) 'Hoe ziet de Stad er straks uit?' *Personeelsblad voor de Stad Antwerpen*, 1(10) November 2003.

Antwerp City (2002) *Federaal Programma Grootstedenbeleid Antwerpen*, Antwerp: City Hall.

—— (2003) *Ruimtelijk Structuurplan Antwerpen stroomlijnen*, Informatiebrochure, Antwerp: City Hall.

—— (2006) *Strategisch Ruimtelijk Structuurplan, Antwerpen Ontwerpen*, Antwerp.

Antwerp City and Atelier Stramien (1990) *Antwerpen, herwonnen Stad. Synthesenota Globaal Structuurplan Antwerpen*, Antwerp.

Baelus, J. (1996) 'De wijk, ruimte bij uitstek voor (stads)ontwikkeling', in P. Dedecker, B. Hubeau and S. Nieuwinckel (eds), *In de ban van stad en wijk*, Berchem: EPO vzw., pp. 63–78.

BOM (1997) *Wijkontwikkelingsplan Oud-Borgerhout, Wijkontwikkelingsplan voor Stuivenberg-Dam en Borgerhout intramuros, Synthese*, Antwerp.

—— –Buurtontwikkelingsmaatschappij Zuidrand (1997) *Startrapport Zuidrand*, Antwerp.

—— (1997) *Startrapport Zuidrand, Syntheserapport*, Antwerp.

—— (2000) *Aanzetten voor een impulsprogramma voor de ZuidRand, 2000–2003, Planning 2000*, Antwerp.

—— (2001) *Jaarverslag 2001*, Antwerp.

—— (2002) *Jaarverslag 2002*, Antwerp.

—— (2002) *Voorstel Kanaalzone: Een nieuwe uitdaging voor de BOM. Bedrijven leren wonen*, Tekst voor de algemene vergadering van de BOM op 1 oktober 2002, Antwerp.

BOM – Buurtontwikkelingsmaatschappij and SOMA – Stedelijke Ontwikkelingsmaatschappij Antwerpen (1993) *Wijkontwikkelingsplan Antwerpen-Noord, Wijkontwikkelingsplan voor Stuivenberg-Dam en Borgerhout intramuros*, Antwerp.

—— and —— (1995) *Wijkontwikkelingsplan Antwerpen-Noord, Synthese oktober 1995*, Antwerp.

Boudry, L. and Vanattenhoven, G. (2003) 'Het Vlaams Stedenfonds. Instrument voor een globaal en geïntegreerd stedenbeleid', *Terzake: cahier* 2003/1, 35–37.

Chancellerie du Premier Ministre, Direction Générale de la Communication Externe (2003) *Une Belgique creative et solidaire. Du souffle pour le pays. Déclaration gouvernementale et accord du gouvernement.*

Christiaens, E., Moulaert, F. and Bosmans, B. (2007) 'The end of social innovation in urban development strategies? The case of Antwerp and the neighbourhood corporation BOM', *European Urban and Regional Studies*, 14(3): 238–51.

De Decker, P. and Loopmans, M. (2003) 'Nieuw Vlaams stedenbeleid verergert de armoede. Sociale rechtvaardigheid bij de verdeling van middelen naar de achtergrond verdrongen', *Agoria*, 19(1): 27–29.

Demazière, C. (1997) *L'espace urbain face au développement économique. Approche de la croissance et du déclin d'un quartier ouvrier d'Anvers*, Note de recherche n°61, Centre de Recherche sur l'Industrie et l'Aménagement (CRIA), Institut de Géographie, Paris.

De Rynck, F. and Vallet, N. (2003) 'Stedelijke netwerksturing, Bestuurlijk beleid van stadsbesturen', in F. De Rynck and L. Boudry *et al.* (eds) *De eeuw van de stad, Over stadsrepublieken en rastersteden, Voorstudies*, Brussels, pp. 365–92.

Eurocities (1994) *Bedrijvencentrum NOA als speerpunt voor economische ontwikkeling*, Antwerp.

Europees Centrum voor Werk en Samenleving (2000) *Sociaal Impulsfonds Antwerpen 1997–1999, Evaluatierapport, Regiefunctie lokale besturen*, Maastricht, Brussels.

Flemish Community and Antwerp City (1996) *Urban Renewal and Social Integration*, A leaflet for the Triennal of Milan.

Kesteloot, C. and Vandenbroecke, H. (1997) 'Achtergestelde buurten en stedelijk beleid in Vlaanderen' (Deprived Neighbourhoods and Urban Policy in Flanders). *Planologisch Nieuws*, 17(2): 100–23.

Koning Boudewijnstichting (1995) *Solidariteit met de armsten. Europese armoedeprojecten in België*, Brussels: Koning Boudewijnstichting.

Loopmans, M. (2002) 'From hero to zero, Armen en stedelijk beleid in Vlaanderen', *Ruimte en Planning*, 22(1): 39–49.

—— (2003) 'Het Stedenfonds, Interview met Linda Boudry', *Ruimte & Planning*, 23(2): 124–31.

—— (2008) 'Relevance, gentrification and the development of a new hegemony on urban policies in Antwerp, Belgium', *Urban Studies*, 45(12): 2499–519.

Meert, H. and Peleman, K. (2001) *Cultuur en migratie, omtrent ruimte, migranten en sociale relaties.* Unpublished document.

Moulaert, F. (2000) *Globalisation and Integrated Area Development in European Cities*, Oxford: Oxford University Press.

——, Delvainquiere, J.C. and Delladetsimas, P. (1997) 'Les rapports sociaux dans le développement local: les rôles des mouvement sociaux', in J.L Klein, P.A.Tremblay and H. Dionne (eds) *Au-delà du néoliberalisme. Quel rôle pour les mouvements sociaux?* Sainte-Foye: Presses Universitaires du Québec, pp. 77–97.

Nieuwinckel, S. (1996) 'De wonderjaren voorbij? Wijkontwikkeling in Antwerpen', in P. Dedecker, B. Hubeau and S. Nieuwinckel (eds), *In de ban van stad en wijk*, Berchem: EPO, pp. 229–48.

RISO Antwerp (1984) *Met een baksteen in de maag. Een beoordeling van één jaar werken aan herwaarderingsgebieden in Antwerpen door de bewonersgroepen die er actief zijn*, Antwerp: RISO.

—— (1986) *Een kat een kat noemen of 't wordt een kater . . . voor iedereen. Drie jaar herwaarderingsgebieden in Antwerpen*, Antwerp: RISO.

Soenen, R. (2003) 'Diversiteit in verbondenheid' in *De eeuw van de stad, Over stadsrepublieken en rastersteden, Voorstudies*, Brussels, pp. 179–207.

SOMA – Stedelijke Ontwikkelingsmaatschappij Antwerpen (1994) *Perspektiefnota 19de eeuwse gordel*, Antwerp: RISO.

SOMA – Stedelijke Ontwikkelingsmaatschappij Antwerpen (2000) *In Antwerpen doen we dat zo, Sociaal impulsfonds Antwerpen, Actie-evaluatierapport, SIF-programma 1997–1999*, In opdracht van Stad Antwerpen en OCMW Antwerpen.

Van Hove, E. (1995) 'Social Engineering', in I. Loots and D. Mortelmans (eds), *Drie letters. . . . één seconde, Bloemlezing uit het werk van prof. Dr. Erik Van Hove*, Antwerpen, Apeldoorn: uitg. Garant, pp. 95–109.

—— (2001) *Networking Neighbourhoods*, South Carolina, Columbia: University of South Carolina Press.

—— and Nieuwinckel, S. (1996) *Het BOM boek. Het verhaal van de buurtontwikkelings-maatschappij Noord-Oost Antwerpen*, Brussels: Koning Boudewijnstichting.

Van Maele, L. (1994) 'De Antwerpse gordel van de 19de naar de 21ste eeuw', *Planologisch Nieuws*, 14(4): 386–400.

Van Pottelsberge, E. (1997) 'Voorbij . . . de inspraak in Oud-Berchem', in G. Hautekeur (ed.), *Naar een levende stad, Congresboek Europees Forum Stedelijk Beleid*, Een uitgave van Terzake en De Wakkere Burger. Brugge: uitg. Die Keure.

Verhetsel, A. and Ceulemans, S. (1994) 'Stadsvernieuwing en speculatie op vastgoed. Een gevalstudie: Sint-Andrieskwartier – Antwerpen', *Planologisch Nieuws*, 14(2): 111–28.

Willems, D. and Vandenbroucke, T. (2007) 'The spatial policy quest in Antwerp', *Urban Trialogues*, 3: 147–71.

Wittocx, P., Hubeau, B. and De Pauw, H. (1994) 'De uitdaging van gisteren, Stadsontwikkeling binnen de Antwerpse 19e eeuwse gordel', Planologisch Nieuws, 14(4): 378–85.

Interviewees and date of interviews

- Goorden Jan, project coordinator of SOMA (01/04/2003)
- Bosmans Bie, director of *BOM* (14/04/2003)
- Van Trier Walter, administrator of Vitamine W (14/04/2003)
- Nieuwinckel Stefan, coordinator of the Neighbourhood Work Division in the Business Unit Civil Affairs and Willems Dries, coordinator of the Planning Division in the Business Unit Urban Enterprise (22/07/2003)
- Cop Eddy, administrative director and De Wit Paul, advisor of the City administration (18/12/2003)
- Goossens Jos director and Geerinck Griet coordinator City Development of AG VESPA (18/12/2003)
- Coppietters Bruno general coordinator and Van Hoof Els coordinator shopping street management of SPRA (03/03/2004)
- Groffy Luk coordinator of RISO and Busschots Walter coordinator community work in Antwerp North (22/03/2004)

13 The limits of 'controlled modernisation'

The *Grätzelmanagement* experience in Vienna

Andreas Novy, Elisabeth Hammer and Bernhard Leubolt

Introduction

This chapter focuses on recent attempts at modernising the existing tradition of 'gentle urban renewal' policies in Vienna, exemplified by the implementation of two pilot projects of *Grätzelmanagement*, that is, 'neighbourhood management' in 2002. The institutional setting of these two projects, their aims and scope of action were highly structured by the interaction between local and EU governance dynamics, the latter emerging as the dominant force in moderating these new arrangements of governance at the local scale. The projects serve as a clear example of 'controlled modernisation' from above, which severely limited the potential for social innovation both in scale and scope. The importance of moving from traditional neighbourhood initiatives to more bottom-linked and multi-scalar coordination, together with the lack of democratic involvement in administrative modernisation, will be highlighted. On the other hand, the case will be made that the socially innovative potential of the pilot projects should not be underestimated, as they did experiment with new forms of inclusive local practices.

The institutional context of the *Grätzelmanagement* experiences is an evolving one. Urban renewal policy in Vienna has, in fact, undergone significant transformations over the last two decades, owing to Austria's entry into the EU, international socio-economic restructuring and Central European integration (Lengauer, 2004; Mayerhofer, 2007). A 'scale-sensitive' approach to local governance is thus needed in order to grasp change at the neighbourhood level as part of broader urban, European and global dynamics, as well as the interplay of actors and institutions at different spatial scales. In our case this refers to the interplay between the districts of the Viennese municipal government – within the Austrian nation state – and the European Union (Becker and Novy, 1999). In line with the governance approach, we will also stress the interplay between the state and non-state actors who also took part in the process (Brenner, 2004; Leubolt, 2007).

The focus will be on the evolution of the Viennese strategies of 'Sanfte Stadterneuerung' ('gentle urban renewal') (see Förster, 2002), which attempted to promote alternative models of local innovation via programmes of Integrated Area Development (Moulaert, 2000; Moulaert *et al.*, 2005). Within this approach, special attention will be given to two recent pilot projects of *Grätzelmanagement*,[1] which were established to improve the economic, environmental and living conditions of residents in two of the poorest areas of the city. The two neighbourhoods, situated near each other in the second and twentieth districts, were entitled to EU Objective 2 funding, which was a major financial incentive to implement the projects.

The 'gentle urban renewal' approach

Social innovation in urban planning and governance – as defined in Chapter 3 (see also Friedmann, 1987; 1992) – should open up new spaces, modernise existing modes of agency and experiment with new institutions, applying a power-sensitive approach to governance. It should link bottom-up and top-down dynamics and lead policy-making towards institutional settings adequate to deal with tensions between the two.

In line with Viennese history and a conservative political culture, the local social democratic apparatus, in control of the city administration during all democratic periods of the twentieth century, consciously opted for a strategy of modernisation that could smoothly transform institutions of clientelism and hierarchy without abdicating control and top-down decision-making. We have labelled this form of conservative reform 'controlled modernisation', as it implements modernising procedures without touching on the hierarchical, centralised and opaque structure of decision-making. This strategy led to tensions, which have been overcome without open escalation of conflict. However, it also resulted in latent discontent, which did undermine the broad consensus to the social-democratic welfare regime. The electoral success of the extreme right, especially in depressed areas, has been a clear expression of this discontent.

Vienna is a municipality as well as a province of the Austrian federal state. The municipality of Vienna has a strong, centralised administration with 60,000 employees. Based on the Austrian way of neo-corporatism, the social democrats have engaged in a limited form of administrative decentralisation, which has opened – among other things – political space first for the oppositional conservative party, and later for the greens. The municipality is divided into twenty-three districts, each headed by a district chairman and a district council, which are elected in a separate process during municipal elections. They represent a countervailing power to the municipal government, as they decide on local infrastructure and they also control – after the municipal decentralisation reform of 1987 – their own budget.

This form of government gives strong, nearly autocratic prerogatives to the district chairman, who is supported by the district council, composed of elected representatives of the parties. Thus, district chairmen are nodal points in the local power network (Sickinger, 2003; Sickinger, 2006; Toth, 2004) and the local power structure has its cornerstone in the capacity of political parties to mediate between civil society and the central state. Local initiatives, social movements, as well as more conventional and conservative segments of civil society such as the church or school councils, all try to obtain their support. In brief, due to the specific Austrian form of neo-corporatism, the relationship between government and civil society is a mixture of benevolence and co-optation, generating a civil society that is heavily under state influence. This results in the lack of a political culture of participation (Novy *et al.*, 2001).

Nevertheless, historically Vienna has also been the site for several socially innovative experiments, often with links to other scales of government. During 'Red Vienna' after the First World War, socially innovative experiments flourished in Vienna, in opposition to the conservative national state (see Chapter 2, Becker and Novy, 1999; Novy *et al.*, 2009). After the Second World War, a more consensus-oriented style of governance came up, mainstreaming policies and co-opting radical deviance. In the late 1970s, socially creative strategies were promoted as an answer to the crisis of Fordism, which especially shook the central state-centred Austrian regulation and its reliance on top-down engineering. In those years the national state encouraged and supported an emerging alternative policy culture which aimed at reducing unemployment at the regional and local level (Novy *et al.*, 2009).

At the neighbourhood level the above changes were reflected in progressive efforts towards an Integrated Area Development approach (Moulaert, 2000). In 1974 a pilot programme was initiated in line with community development strategies (see Table 13.1). It was called 'Sanfte Stadterneuerung' – 'gentle urban renewal' – stressing neighbourhood upgrading without gentrification, in contrast to creating 'islands of renewal in seas of decay' (Hamnett, 2000: 332), often the result of 'hard' urban renewal policies. From 1978 to 1999 the pilot programme was institutionalised with the establishment of several urban renewal offices and resulted in an improvement of the housing stock in many of the most densely populated parts of the city.

In the 1990s, however, geopolitical transformations and the renewed focus on business-friendly urban policies led to a reappraisal of urban development strategies in Vienna (Palme and Feldkircher, 2005). In 1999, the 'gentle urban renewal' programme was subjected to an evaluation and in 2001 a new type of urban renewal office was established (see Table 13.1).

The more recent phase of urban renewal policies in Vienna began in 1999 with the twenty-fifth birthday of urban renewal offices in Vienna. The City Planning Bureau commissioned an evaluation report on the activities of the urban renewal offices. The result was a ten-point programme serving as a guideline for the strategic reorientation of urban renewal policy. The new programme confirmed urban renewal offices as one instrument of the ongoing 'new public management' reform within the overall city administration. The suggestions of the programme ranged from 'taking over management tasks' to 'improvement in information flows and co-operation with politicians, municipal authorities

Table 13.1 Chronology of Integrated Area Development initiatives in Vienna

1974–78	Pilot phase of 'gentle urban renewal' in the district of Ottakring; controlled experience of Integrated Area Development, inspired by the tradition of community work and aiming at direct involvement of citizens in planning procedures; experiment of low-impact urban restoration.
1978–99	Institutionalisation and extension of 'gentle urban renewal'; establishment of urban renewal offices, operating in densely built quarters of Vienna; focus on the coordination and promotion of rehabilitation programmes; cooperation with planners and construction firms; empowerment from below, but only within the limits imposed from above.
From 1999 onwards	Strategic reorientation of urban renewal policies in Vienna; urban renewal offices become major vehicles of the ongoing public management reform; first ideas of genuine *Grätzelmanagement* ('neighbourhood management') projects.
2001	Establishment of a new type of urban renewal office for council–owned residential housing; stress on community work; support of 'conflict-free cohabitation'.
2002–06	Implementation of two pilot projects of *Grätzelmanagement*; 'controlled modernisation' with restricted empowerment of citizens; potential forums to transform city administration and local policy-making; experiments with new forms of inclusive local policies; multi-scalar arrangements: EU-funding – local administrative staff.
From 2007 onwards	As EU-funding expired, the pilot projects were cancelled; return to 'gentle urban renewal' mainly based on housing; business start–up initiatives (Mingo, Business and Research Centre Hochstädtplatz).

Source: Authors

and funds'. The authorities acknowledged the wide range of demands in the field of urban renewal, and this suggested a higher status for non-technical expertise and community work. Moreover, the improved access for urban renewal personnel to training courses relating to communication methods and techniques was identified as crucial (König, 1994; Feigelfeld, 2000).

Following this reorientation process, in 2001, a new type of urban renewal office was set up for council-owned residential housing. The overall objective was to support a so-called 'conflict-free cohabitation' between Austrian, neo-Austrian and foreign inhabitants, in close co-operation with the municipal Integration Fund. Bit by bit, urban renewal offices transformed themselves into interface points for local inhabitants – or, in the official terminology, 'on-site sensors of the city of Vienna' – thereby showing the flexibility of this instrument. Nearly 400,000 inhabitants – a quarter of the entire Viennese population – live today in quarters covered by an urban renewal office, either of the traditional or the redesigned type. In these areas, the share of those without

Austrian citizenship amounts to about 29 per cent. Thus, migrants represent an important target group for urban renewal offices (Municipal Government, 2001).

Grätzelmanagement in Vienna as social innovation

In this section we trace in greater detail the institutional setting and development of two *Grätzelmanagement* pilot projects that are very good examples of what we have characterised as 'controlled modernisation' of Austrian 'gentle urban renewal' policies, stressing their socially innovative potential and corresponding contradictory dynamics.

With regard to the latter, a major source of tension was the EU co-financed character of the projects. Although in line with the established municipal programme of urban renewal, the projects widened the municipal objectives and scope in order to accommodate Objective 2 funding criteria, that is, integrating the local population and especially migrants more systematically. The projects finished in 2006, but they significantly influenced the reform of urban renewal offices, which continue to shape neighbourhood development in Vienna to this day (see Table 13.2).

Table 13.2 Features of the social innovation dynamics of *Grätzelmanagement* projects

Why? *In reaction to what?*	Ongoing extension and modification of 'gentle urban renewal' programmes as a local necessity; possibility of linking these projects to EU Objective 2 funding; also a strategy for modernising the administration.
How? *Inspired by what?*	Linking strategies of new public management with integrative and horizontal forms of governance; new stakeholders; creation of a neighbourhood advisory council and business incubators to foster direct representation of local residents and business.
Socially innovative content	Widening the goals of 'gentle urban renewal' (pro-participation and pro-business); integrating migrant communities; promoting active citizenship and entrepreneurship; potential for social innovation emerges where contradictions become apparent.
Empowerment struggle	Persisting inclination of district politics towards controlled modernisation, reinforced by access to EU funding; constant struggle of citizens for transparent decision-making and open and more democratic ways of allocating resources; tensions in combining top-down and bottom-up strategies.
How long was the 'new' new?	The pilot projects did not survive the closure of EU funding in 2006; improved strategies of 'gentle urban renewal' continue to be cornerstones of integrated neighbourhood development; renewed focus on conflict resolution in social housing; business start-up initiatives.

Source: Authors

Grätzelmanagement *as modernisation from above*

The implementation of the pilot project of 'neighbourhood management' in Vienna was based on a combination of local and European dynamics. On the one hand, the ongoing extension and modification of the 'gentle urban renewal' approach followed the local necessity to respond to socio-economic challenges due to the crisis of Fordism. On the other hand, the European Regional Policy framework and EU co-funding have powerfully shaped the concrete form of the Viennese urban renewal programme of the last few years.

In 2000, Andrea Breitfuss and Jens Dangschat from the Vienna University of Technology, in co-operation with the City Planning Bureau, which was in charge of 'gentle urban renewal' projects, started to develop a concept to comprehensively modernise Viennese urban renewal policies, drawing on other European, and particularly German, experiences. Such policies were more explicitly linked to labour market, training and social programmes via an integrated policy approach, which aimed at strengthening existing human resources as 'endogenous potential' by developing and supporting sustainable social cohesion of disadvantaged neighbourhoods. In contrast with traditional 'gentle urban renewal' strategies in Vienna, local mobilisation, self-organisation and participation were identified as priorities. Consequently, initiatives to involve the local residential and business communities were encouraged, with the aim of enabling modernisation from below. Thus, the new concept of *Grätzelmanagement* (neighbourhood management) was first elaborated as a strategy for modernising the administration – 'managing new problems in new ways' (Breitfuss and Dangschat, 2001; Dangschat and Breitfuss, 2001: 1). Over the last few years, in line with global trends, the city administration decided to implement a new public management strategy (Theimer, 2004), which aims at improving efficiency without abdicating control of the city bureaucracy. The implementation of this strategy reoriented the governance approach of the municipality of Vienna. Tools such as contract management and decentralised budget management were introduced to transform the centralised–hierarchical structure of public administration into a more horizontal system. As a new form of decentralised and flexible administration, *Grätzelmanagement* was based on an organisational design that clearly identified procedural steps for the imple-mentation, completion and evaluation of the projects.

A major influence in the *Grätzelmanagement* experience came from the possibility of linking these projects to Objective 2 EU funding. Irrespective of their process-oriented objectives, *Grätzelmanagement* projects gained consid-erable appeal for district politics because of the possibility of receiving co-financing from the European Union. Therefore, the link between planning dynamics at the local level and stimulation by supranational bodies such as the EU via structural funds (Moulaert *et al.*, 2002: 56) was a major trait in Viennese experimentation, opening up possibilities for social innovation both in terms of changes in social (power) relations among different (institutional) actors and in terms of residents' empowerment (see Chapter 3). In fact, while the inhabitants were deemed to be taking part in decision-making processes concerning the use of resources for small projects, the financial resources for these projects were actually provided by the European Union (EU) and the administrative staff by the Viennese city government. It must also be stressed, however, that the very regulations of EU funding complicated the involvement of grass-roots initiatives.

Tensions between a top-down and a bottom-up approach

The combination of the top-down oriented new public management strategies with the bottom-up approach sought by the new *Grätzelmanagement* projects led to contradictory dynamics of social innovation. Such contradictions were further reinforced by the linking of the pilot projects with the Objective 2 EU-funded programme for Vienna. These tensions constrained the scope for social innovation and, thereby, the impact of the pilot projects.

The chosen neighbourhoods in the second (Leopoldstadt) and twentieth (Brigittenau) districts were classified as urban problem areas and as such were both eligible for EU funding under the 2000–2006 Objective 2 programme. Both districts – which form sort of urban 'islands' because encircled on all sides by the Danube and the Danube Canal – were characterised by high population densities (over 750 inhabitants per hectare) and high unemployment rates. Moreover, the number of Austrian residents had significantly decreased (minus 11,000 between 1984 and 1998), whereas the number of foreigners had more than compensated (plus 14,000), bringing the foreign population up to 38 per cent (and in certain quarters above 45 per cent). The social democratic party had the majority – as well as the district chairman – in both districts, whereas the extreme right was the second strongest party.

Power and discursive brokers worked together. Breitfuss and Dangschat were the discursive brokers who translated the social-liberal discourse of the European Commission into local planning strategies. They produced a discourse that served the interests of the local as well as the European power holders. In line with European discourse they justified the need for a modernisation of the administration and an opening up of corporatist networks that were compatible with local power interests. The main local power broker had always been the social democratic party, which had acquired the ability to reconcile systemic necessities with the exigencies of local political and economic powers and had managed to remain in power because of its constant efforts to modernise.

The *Grätzelmanagement* projects attempted to attract broad support and multiple project partners. The ambition was to link strategies of new public management with the integrative approach of 'gentle urban renewal', as well as with horizontal forms of governance (Breitfuss and Dangschat, 2001; Dangschat and Breitfuss, 2001). But the institutional architecture of the pilot projects was significantly influenced by the effort to gain EU financial support. The reorganisation of the existing rather bureaucratic urban renewal offices was not pursued, on the presumption that these branches of the municipal bureaucracy possessed neither the skills nor the organisational flexibility needed to manage EU projects. Instead, the Vienna Business Agency (WWFF – Wiener Wirtschaftsförderungsfonds), an organisation owned by the municipality and targeted towards business and location promotion, was persuaded to manage and implement the projects, thereby strengthening an urban development philosophy biased towards business promotion. The Vienna Science Centre (WZW – Wissenschaftszentrum Wien) and Municipial Department 25, in charge of 'gentle urban renewal', pooled their responsibilities in urban renewal and became project partners. Other public actors, competent in vocational training and social cohesion, such as the Vienna Employee Promotion Fund (WAFF – Wiener ArbeitnehmerInnen Fonds) or the Vienna Integration Fund (WIF – Wiener Integrationsfonds), did not participate, an indication of the swift shift in concern from social cohesion to business entrepreneurship and competitiveness. It is remarkable that the promotion of local business survived the exhaustion of EU resources – the Vienna Business Agency in fact created Mingo and BRC (Business and Research Center) Hochstädtplatz, to support local start-ups, micro and migrant enterprises.

A neighbourhood advisory council was created to foster direct representation of local residents. It was an important element in the organisational structure of the pilot projects and functioned as a supervisory board. Next to the project partners, the district chairmen, Municipal Department 27 (responsible for the handling of EU funding), the City Planning Bureau, the neighbourhood managers, as well as elected representatives of the residents were full members of the council.

Thus, the institutional and organisational structure of *Grätzelmanagement* in Vienna displayed continuity as well as change compared to the established management of 'gentle urban renewal' programmes. The continuity refers to the inclusion of Municipal Department 25 and the City Planning Bureau, and was partly reinforced by the double function of neighbourhood managers, who were not only responsible for 'gentle urban renewal' but also for the new *Grätzelmanagement* projects. On the one hand, the integration of the Vienna Business Agency and Municipal Department 27 represented an innovation that was necessary for the local bureaucracy to handle the project. On the other hand, the district chairmen became members of the neighbourhood advisory council, which meant that the former informal power structures of 'gentle urban renewal' policies were now increasingly formalised into the *Grätzelmanagement* projects. The true innovation in the institutional structure of the latter consisted in the integration of citizens, who made up to 50 per cent of the full members of the neighbourhood advisory council.

In conclusion, the institutional structure of *Grätzelmanagement* displayed different elements, some supporting, others hindering social innovation. While the initial goal was to comprehensively reform 'gentle urban renewal' programmes, the organisational structures that came to be established showed considerable continuities and incremental adaptations to the requirements of EU regional policy on the one hand, and to local power politics, on the other.

As already discussed, this preference for what we have called 'controlled modernisation' seems to remain the *leitmotiv* of social democracy in Vienna (Redak *et al.*, 2003). Even in this new phase of urban renewal policies the traditional political and bureaucratic practices of the social democratic apparatus were perpetuated.

Experimentation, empowerment and social struggle

In principle, *Grätzelmanagement* should have integrated both the process-oriented and the content dimensions of social innovation as explained in Chapter 3 of this book. With respect to the process dimension, it did widen the scope of 'gentle urban renewal'. According to the initial proposals of the projects, *Grätzelmanagement* efforts had to focus on promoting and shaping active co-operation between the city administration, decentralised socio-political institutions, private firms, households and the social economy. The overall objective was to improve the living, economic and environmental conditions in the area in order to maintain the social viability of the neighbourhood. Compared to established forms of local urban renewal, for example, the pilot projects for *Grätzelmanagement* explicitly integrated immigrant communities. This was indirectly due to EU co-funding, as the proportion of migrants was a major indicator in the selection of Objective 2 projects. In terms of content, among the relevant aims of the *Grätzelmanagement* projects can be mentioned the revitalisation of an old market place, programmes in support of businesses run by the immigrant population in the neighbourhood, and language courses (ABIF, 2003a; 2003b). A district journal and a community TV programme – financed by a separate project – created channels for public communication and information, in print and via the web.

But the attempt to reconcile top-down-oriented funding criteria with the development of project ideas from below substantially restricted the potential for true process-oriented social innovation. The aim of enhancing endogenous development in degraded areas with the participation of residents and local business people was adjusted, in one way or another, to fit predefined quantitative evaluation criteria. Although a number of project ideas developed by residents and local business corresponded to the aim of fostering neighbour-hood and community communication, other projects such as organising a flea market or diverse social and cultural events in the neighbourhood did not match the criteria of EU-funding. The pro-business bias was stronger than the pro-participation commitment. As the city of Vienna did not contribute extra financial resources to carry out such ideas, the integrative impact of *Grätzel-management* was substantially reduced.

On the other hand, compared with previous forms of local urban renewal, *Grätzelmanagement* did promote active citizenship and did experiment with new modes of articulated co-operation with the public sector. In both neighbour-hoods a journal was founded, which seemed to be of prime importance in fostering a culture of integration and tolerance, and the respect of diversity.

The institutional structure of the neighbourhood advisory councils provided a framework for district politics to become more transparent and a wider public was involved in decision-making. And yet, the institutional structure of the project also helped the inclination of power holders to control the ongoing changes and squeeze out participatory democracy. Although the pilot projects were to be managed by so-called neighbourhood managers, these did not have a vote in the advisory council. Thus, their room for manoeuvre was rather limited and their main task was restricted to administrative handling of the projects. The inclination of district politics towards controlled modernisation was reinforced by the way EU-funding was organised, while the main institutional actors of the project, the Vienna Business Agency and the district chairpersons, tended to ignore the established participatory governance structures of the project. Thus, there was a constant struggle by citizens for transparency of political interests and greater visibility of resource allocation. As was the case in 'gentle urban renewal', professionals played a crucial role, acting as intermediaries, lobbying for democratic governance procedures and politicising the local communities.

It is a recurring characteristic of Integrated Area Development projects in Vienna that the potential for social innovation emerges exactly where the contradictions of the project become apparent. This was evident in the case of Local Agenda 21, another participatory process taking place at the local level in Vienna (Novy and Hammer, 2007). Here, participation gained momentum in 2002, exactly in a phase of confrontation with public authorities – when activists fought against a large-scale real estate project driven by a federal government agency, in charge of developing former public property and welcomed by local and district politics. During and after the pacification of the protest, the pilot project was extended from the initial district throughout the city as a whole, supported by a special branch of the city administration (Binder-Zehetner, 2004). In this case, the small-scale initiatives mainly attracted middle-class citizens, who obtained more deliberative power than was offered within the *Grätzelmanagement* pilot projects. The LA 21 process, indeed, still exists, even though it has lost creativity and dynamism, as deviant, more political and interest-based agency is made increasingly difficult.

The different evolution of Integrated Area Development experiences in Vienna shows the difficulty of combining top-down and bottom-up strategies. In *Grätzelmanagement* bottom-up methods for mobilisation and self-organisation of citizens were more limited than in LA 21 and tended to be instrumentalised for implementing top-down goals. An open budgetary process may have helped to reconcile the aspirations of the local population with the norms imposed by the European Commission. Yet, it was impossible to solve the conflicts between a population interested in cultural initiatives and basic needs, and EU-funding norms that focused on economic development and job provision – especially as the municipal administration was not inclined to invest in the former type of citizen initiative.

The limits of Grätzelmanagement in Vienna

Neighbourhoods in a city are not self-contained islands and neighbourhood initiatives take place as part of broader urban development trends. In other words, neighbourhoods are places, embedded in complex politics of scale, which shape the potential for social innovation. *Grätzelmanagement* was an innovative form of modernising the Vienna Municipal Administration and empowering its inhabitants, but it was implemented and financed from above, by the city council together with the EU. The institutional structure was a clear example of a restricted form of empowerment. EU funding strengthened the procedural rules imposed from above and limited the emerging space for citizen involvement and grass-roots initiatives. The unwillingness to broaden participation by discussing the rules of the game with the local population was imposed by the local administration and facilitated by EU norms.

On the other hand, even if more immediate effects of social innovation may have been limited, the potential of the *Grätzelmanagement* and LA21 experiences in transforming local policy-making must not be underestimated, as both programmes fostered discussions on how to organise social change and mobilisation. These bottom-up, small-scale and decentralised initiatives of modernisation definitely differ from urban flagship projects based on partnerships with real estate capital, which have contributed to the fragmentation of the city (Redak *et al.*, 2003).

It remains to be seen how much the described projects contributed to the co-optation of committed citizens and initiatives. In one field or another, these discourses and practices may actually result in transformative agency, as is timidly occurring with the renewed urban renewal offices. Nonetheless, the importance of spaces of experimentation and public participation, even within such contradictory processes, cannot be overstressed. These initiatives are strongly ingrained in the community, but also linked to urban dynamics. The potential of neighbourhood development lies precisely in these bottom-linked strategies, which are able to tackle the challenges of a politics of scale.

Note

1 *Grätzelmanagement*, i.e. 'neighbourhood management' has similar characteristics to the German *Quartiers-Management* (Krummacher *et al.* 2003). *Grätzel* is a Viennese term for a local area that is generally larger than a neighbourhood but smaller than a quarter.

References

ABIF, A. B. u. i. F. (ed.) (2003a) *Evaluierung des Pilotprojektes 'Grätzelmanagement Volkert- und Alliertenviertel'* im 2. Bezirk, Vienna: ABIF.

—— (2003b) *Evaluierung des Pilotprojekts 'Grätzelmanagement rund um den Wallensteinplatz'* im 20. Bezirk, Vienna: ABIF.

Becker, J. and Novy, A. (1999) 'Divergence and convergence of national and local regulation: the case of Austria and Vienna', *European Urban and Regional Studies*, 6(2), 1999: 127–43.

Binder-Zehetner, A. (ed.) (2004) *Lokale Agenda 21 Wien*, Vienna: Association Local Agenda 21 in Vienna.

Breitfuss, A. and Dangschat, J. (2001) 'Pilotprogramm "Grätzel-Management Wien". Konzeptpapier B – Projektebene – Projekte in Wien – Leopoldstadt "Nordbahnviertel" und "Stuwerviertel"', in *Pilotprogramm 'Grätzel-Management Wien'*, Vienna.

Brenner, N. (2004) *New State Spaces, Urban Governance and the Rescaling of Statehood*, Oxford: Oxford University Press.

Dangschat, J.S. and Breitfuss, A. (2001) 'Pilotprogramm "Grätzel-Management Wien". Konzeptpapier A – Programmebene. Das Grätzelmanagement – eine Idee zur Verwaltungsmodernisierung und zu einer großstädtischen Sozialpolitik', in *Pilotprogramm 'Grätzel-Management Wien'*, Vienna.

Feigelfeld, H. (2000) *25 Jahre Gebietsbetreuung in Wien: Bilanz, Perspektive, Strategie*, Wien: Municipal Department 50.

Förster, W. (2002) *80 Years of Social Housing in Vienna*, Wien: MA 25. Online. Available: http://gebietsbetreuungen.wien.at/htdocs/socialhousing.html (Accessed 27 August 2008).

Friedmann, J. (1987) *Planning in the Public Domain*, Princeton, NJ: Princeton University Press.

—— (1992) *Empowerment. The Politics of Alternative Development*, Cambridge: Blackwell.

Hamnett, C. (2000) 'Gentrification, post industrialism, and industrial and occupational restructuring in global cities', in G. Bridge and S. Watson (eds) *A Companion to the City*, Oxford: Blackwell, pp. 331–41.

König, I. (1994) 'Noch ein "Wiener Modell". Gebietsbetreuung und partizipative Stadterneuerung', in E. Antalovsy (ed.) *Planung initiativ. Bürgerbeteiligung in Wien*, Wien, pp. 38–42.

Krummacher, M., Kulbach, R., Walz, V. and Wohlfahrt, N. (2003)' Soziale Stadt – Sozialraumentwicklung – Quartiersmanagement', Herausforderungen für Politik, Raumplanung und Soziale Arbeit, Wiesbaden: VS Verlag für Sozialwissenschaften.

Lengauer, L. (2004) 'Sozioökonomische Veränderungen in der Vienna Region 1971–2001 – Ausgewählte Ergebnisse', in *SRE-DISC.2004/06*, Wien: Wirtschaftsuniversität Wien.

Leubolt, B. (2007) 'On the different facets of the debate on governance', *Journal für Entwicklungspolitik*, XXII(1): 4–25.

Mayerhofer, P. (2007) 'Städtische Ökonomien unter neuen Rahmenbedingungen: Strukturelle Wandlungsprozesse am Beispiel der Wiener Stadtwirtschaft'. Online. Available: www.gbw-wien.at/documents/Stadtentwicklung-Modul2-Mayerhofer.pdf (Accessed 25 June 2009).

Moulaert, F. (2000) *Globalization and Integrated Area Development in European Cities*, Oxford: Oxford University Press.

——, Martinelli, F., Swyngedouw, E. and González, S. (2005) 'Towards alternative model(s) of local innovation', *Urban Studies*, 42(11): 1969–90.

——, Rodriguez, A. and Swyngedouw, E. (2002) 'Large-scale urban development projects, urban dynamics, and social polarization: a methodological reflection', in F. Moulaert, A. Rodriguez and E. Swyngedouw (eds) *The Globalized City: Economic Restructuring and Social Polarization in European Cities*, Oxford: Oxford University Press, pp. 47–64.

Municipal Government (2001) *Einheitliches Programmplanungsdokument (EPPD) für Ziel 2 Wien 2000 bis 2006*, Wien: Municipal Department 27.

Novy, A. and Hammer, E. (2007) 'Radical innovation in the era of liberal governance: the case of Vienna', *European Urban and Regional Studies*, 14(3): 210–22.

—— —— and Leubolt, B. (2009) 'Social innovation and governance of scale in Austria', in J. Hillier, F. Moulaert, S. Vicari-Haddock and D. MacCallum (eds) *Social Innovation and Territorial Development*, Aldershot: Ashgate, pp. 131–48.

—— Redak, V., Jäger, J. and Hamedinger, A. (2001) 'The end of Red Vienna: recent ruptures and continuities in urban governance', *European Urban and Regional Studies*, 8(2): 131–44.

Palme, G. and Feldkircher, M. (2005) 'Centrope – Europa Region Mitte: eine Bestandsaufnahme', *WIFO*. Online. Available: www.oenb.at/de/img/wifo_arbeitspaket_tcm14–38413.pdf (Accessed 1 July 2006).

Redak, V., Novy, A. and Becker, J. (2003) 'Modernizing or polarizing Vienna?', in F. Moulaert, A. Rodriguez and E. Swyngedouw (eds) *The Globalized City: Economic Restructuring and Social Polarisation in European Cities*, Oxford: Oxford University Press, pp. 167–80.

Sickinger, H. (2003) *BezirksvorsteherInnen in Wien*, Vienna: University of Natural Resources and Applied Life Sciences.

—— (2006) *Bezirkspolitik in Wien*, Wien: Studienverlag.

Theimer, E. (2004) 'Der Weg zum Bürger – Verwaltungsmodernisierung in Wien. Der Stand der Dinge', in M. d. S. Wien (ed.) *Handbuch der Stadt Wien*, Vienna: City of Vienna, pp. 111–16.

Toth, A. (2004) *Dezentralisierung und Governance in Wien. Das Beispiel des Grätzelmanagements in der Brigittenau*, Vienna: Department of City and Regional Development, University of Economics and Business Administration.

14 Creatively designing urban futures

A transversal analysis of socially innovative initiatives

Flavia Martinelli, Frank Moulaert and Sara González

Introduction

In this chapter we present a *transversal* analysis of the socially innovative initiatives studied in this book. In the first section we explain and compare the features and achievements of the socially innovative experiences across case studies in light of the three dimensions of social innovation considered in Chapters 1 through 3. In the second section we compare the territorial setting, spatial reach and inter-scalar relations of our case studies, paying particular attention to the way neighbourhood-initiated innovative experiences can have a broader spatial impact. In the third section we address the reproductive dynamics of social innovation: we analyse the philosophical roots, the historical trajectory and the cultural conditions of socially innovative initiatives; we also reflect on the role of resources, especially human and financial. We end our analysis by returning to the tension already addressed in Chapter 1, about the role of 'community' versus 'society' in socially transformative dynamics. This tension can only be overcome by giving a proper status to scalar socio-politics. In this perspective, society becomes an ensemble of multi-scalar social relations, in which communities, despite their natural affinity with the local (the 'neighbourhood' in this book), remain privileged places of human initiative, co-operation, deployment of resources, etc., all contributing to the building of society.

This Chapter 14 devotes less attention to governance dynamics and its relation with socio-political transformations and urban policy options. These are specifically addressed in Chapter 15.

Features and dimensions of social innovation

In presenting our analytical approach in Chapter 3, we stressed the three main dimensions of our conception of social innovation: a) the satisfaction of human needs, b) the empowerment of marginalised groups and communities, and

c) the change in social/power relations. We also stressed how these dimensions are strongly interconnected. In our case studies, in fact, one occurred rarely without another. In the majority of cases, the urgent need to satisfy alienated basic needs was the initiating motive and proved a means to empower local groups and/or change relations within the community and/or between the community and other actors and scales; but in several instances the triggering motive was changing governance relations, that is, fighting against top-down politico-institutional systems, mainstream urban policy and policy delivery systems. It is, therefore, imperative to discuss these dimensions in their dynamic relationships.

Nonetheless, in Table 14.1 we have 'deconstructed' these dynamics and tabulated the main features of social innovation, as we observed them in our case studies, loosely grouping them according to the three dimensions. It should be stressed at the onset that entries in the table only refer to actual change 'outcomes', whether intentional or not. The table, in fact, does not seek to measure the 'success' of innovative experiences in relation to intentions, but only the articulation of 'actual' social innovation features, in a static way. The risk of this approach is that we may become a bit enumerative, losing the coherence of the analysis. But the advantage is to show the particularity of many cases against the background of the shared social innovation agencies and processes.

Satisfaction of human needs

The satisfaction of basic human needs was indeed a central dimension of social innovation in the majority of our cases. They were not just material needs, such as housing, work or social services, although these were acutely felt in most cases (*Arts Factory, NDC, AQS, Leoncavallo, Olinda, BOM, Alentour*), but also needs involving more 'existential' fields, such as artistic self-expression and cultural events (*Arts Factory, Ouseburn Trust, AQS, Leoncavallo, Olinda, BOM, City Mine(d)*). In fact, the role of arts and culture in socially innovative initiatives was critical in many of our case studies: artistic and cultural activities as an expression of identity, or cultural heritage; as use values, but also as marketable services; as means of communication and socialisation; as vehicles of political expression, resistance, re-appropriation.

Among the many cases, a particularly emblematic one is *Leoncavallo*, which gave a prominent place to meeting socio-cultural needs in addition to more basic ones: besides offering free meals, short term hospitality, protection and legal assistance, job information and job opportunities to immigrants and the homeless, psychologically impaired and generally poor people, the social centre also responds to the demand for autonomous and not commercialised culture, in collectively defined forms. Also in the *City Mine(d)* case culture and creative self-expression are at the core of social innovation, leading to the re-appropriation of alienated urban public spaces, through artistic and cultural events.

Table 14.1 Features and dimensions of social innovation in the case studies

Socially innovative initiatives

Dimensions/features of social innovation	Arts Factory, UK	Ousebum Trust, UK	NDC Newcastle, UK	AQS, Italy	Leoncavallo, Italy	Olinda, Italy	BOM, Belgium	City Mine(d), Belgium	Alentour, France	Grätzelmanagement, Austria
Satisfaction of needs										
Providing/improving quality of welfare and social services	X		X	X	X	X	X		X	
Integrating needs (housing, work and training, public space, social services)	X		X	X		X	X		X	
Embedding endogenous development at neighbourhood level	X						X			X
Incorporating arts and culture into local development	X	X								
Creating space and opportunities for free culture and sociality	X	X		X	X	X	X	X	X	
Preservation of heritage	X	X								
Change in relations										
Combining satisfaction of human needs with innovation in social relations	X	X	X	X	X	X	X			X
Improving governance relations	X	X	X	X	X	X	X	X		X
Bringing government dynamics from city hall to neighbourhood				X	X		X			
Improving 'local urban management'	X	X	X		X	X	X	X	X	X
Linking different governance scales/creating partnerships	X	X		X		X	X	X		X
Using the city as a collective resource								X		X
Changing (external) perception of cultural attitudes concerning community	X		X		X	X				
Empowerment										
Reinforcing social bonds at neighbourhood level	X	X		X		X	X		X	
Creating/recognising community identity	X	X		X		X			X	
Creating/reinforcing shared community learning	X			X		X	X	X	X	
Overcoming politico-institutional alienation of citizens				X	X	X	X	X	X	
Empowerment starting from condition of exclusion and alienation	X	X	X	X	X	X	X	X	X	X
Integration of migrants into governance/government dynamics	X		X						X	

Source: Authors

Changing social relations within the neighbourhood, local communities and beyond

The satisfaction of basic needs was in several experiences a means to change, improve (re)create social relationships *within* the community (*Arts Factory, AQS, Leoncavallo, Olinda, BOM, Alentour*) and empower previously marginalised groups (*Arts Factory, AQS, Leoncavallo, Olinda, Alentour*), a case in point of the strong interconnection between our three dimensions of social innovation. This interconnection is strongest in the cases that work according to an Integrated Area Approach (Chapter 1) such as *BOM* in the first place, but also *Olinda, Leoncavallo, AQS* and *Arts Factory*. *BOM* is a leading example, as the basic needs of the neighbourhoods (the '4 Ws' in German, i.e. housing, work, knowledge, well-being) were satisfied through multidimensional projects – social, cultural, economic – within *integrated actions at the neighbourhood scale*, in line with the IAD approach.

Another emblematic case is the *Arts Factory* experience, where needs were considered as 'opportunities'. Responding to the diverse community needs became a strategy to renegotiate relations within the community and empower marginalised groups, such as the elderly and the disabled, through their participation in decision-making. Also in the *Alentour* case, the satisfaction of basic 'material' needs was a vehicle for (re)developing 'social' links and building 'trust' within the fragmented neighbourhood and improving the socio-political capabilities of the weakest groups. In other words, the 'co-production' of social services for the neighbourhood was carried out by the very users, who thus found simultaneously employment and social integration, within an area-wide, more or less integrated approach.

The *Leoncavallo* case should be mentioned as well. The centre provides opportunities for socialisation, communitarian relationships and human recognition to people who are daily treated as non-persons. Not just services, thus, but also opportunities for social exchange in a non-exploitative environment. Here the link between satisfaction of basic needs and empowerment is very clear: 'citizenship' is an output of the services produced, but also an input for social change. Similarly, the *Olinda* experience shows how the satisfaction of basic needs (services to the inpatients) through self-help and the production of services for the market (the neighbourhood and the city at large), simultaneously contribute to change social relations between the inpatients, the community and the city, and to empower the inpatients.

Over time, however, we have observed a moving away from this integrated approach, towards the satisfaction of needs in specific social services, certainly reflecting a 'new realism' in the face of increasingly neoliberal urban policies and the privatisation of collective services, but also reflecting – in some cases – the institutional–political question about which government level can best deliver particular services. We will return to the territoriality and inter-scalarity of our case studies in a later section.

Among changes in social relations, a very important form of social innovation concerned changes in culture and, more precisely, changes in the 'perception' of particular social groups or issues, whether by the involved people (how they perceive themselves) or by the public at large (how they perceive the marginalised groups or specific issues). This type of change was particularly relevant in the cases of *Arts Factory*, *Leoncavallo* and *Olinda*. Changes in the way the community viewed itself and its problems were also relevant for creating and/or recognising a shared community identity in the experiences of *Arts Factory*, *Olinda* and *Alentour*.

Changing governance relations and empowerment . . .

Changing governance relations and giving greater voice to local communities in decision-making processes was another ambition in most of our case studies (especially *Arts Factory*, *Ouseburn*, *AQS*, *Leoncavallo*, *Olinda*, *BOM*, *NDC*, *Grätzelmanagement*). Changing governance relations involves changing social power relations both *within* the community and *between* the local community and civil society, institutional and private actors, such as city hall, the regional or national government, and/or private businesses. In most cases, the process was initiated from below, either to satisfy unmet needs or in reaction to authoritarian planning decisions or private redevelopment pressures, but in two cases (*NDC*, *Grätzelmanagement*) it was a more or less successful 'top-down' experiment.

An interesting illustration of changes in the social power relationships between the neighbourhood and city hall, is the case of the *Ouseburn Trust*. Born in reaction to developers' pressures in the late 1990s, this organisation has managed to temper public redevelopment schemes and to establish a temporary and fruitful partnership with local government for the regeneration of the area within the limits set by the community (i.e. promoting inclusive, well-designed environments, sustainable development, employment and education for local people, etc.). Despite their different approaches (the one more economic-oriented and the other more social-oriented) the two parties managed to exchange knowledge and establish a common language, 'educating' each other. Also in the *AQS* experience, the initiative contributed significantly to changing governance relations from below, making it clear that welfare provisions could not be conceived in terms of undifferentiated services or money transfers, but had to be tailored to the specific needs of the neighbourhood with participation from below. To implement this approach, the association became a veritable development agency, channelling the neighbourhood's previously unexpressed needs into structured projects and interacting with city hall.

BOM is another example of an initiative that ushered in important changes in governance relations. Acting as a development broker, it was able to change relations at different government levels and between the different actors. Besides dialogue among residents, an explicit strategy of this organisation was the establishment of partnerships with private business and other non-profit enterprises and the co-operation with government institutions (at different scales) to implement integrated projects. And in Roubaix, negotiations between the neighbourhood *Association Alentour* and the municipal government succeeded in 'mediating' among the residents and the state (at its various scales) in addition to re-creating internal social bonds. *City Mine(d)*, then, achieved changes in power relationships in terms of communication between government, civil society and business interests, breaking established unidirectional governance patterns, through the organisation of cultural events.

Among the cases of top-down initiated experiments to promote greater local governance, a partially successful one was *NDC* in Newcastle. Here, joint work and partnerships between community groups, between projects, and between residents, the local state and public service providers were effectively stimulated. There were also significant processes of mutual 'learning', that is, the city council listening to the community and the community learning institutional capabilities. On the other hand, as we shall discuss later and in Chapter 15, pressures from national policies and the unsolved tensions between the economic performance-oriented and the social needs-oriented approaches have undermined the sustainability of such changes in the power relationships at the local level.

. . . Empowering communities

The creation of shared community identities and learning, together with changes in governance relations, also triggered, in most of our cases, the successful empowerment of marginalised groups and communities and their relative integration into governance dynamics. Empowerment catalyses the creation of capabilities and the formation, strengthening or even bridging of social capital at the community level. Citizens living in depressed neighbourhoods (*Arts Factory, NDC, AQS*), communities of immigrants (*BOM, Alentour, Grätzelmanagement*) and marginalised groups (*Olinda, Leoncavallo*) all became to some extent capable of expressing their 'voice', of being politically and economically 'visible', of challenging more powerful agents, and/or of engaging local governments in more community-focused strategies and programmes. In most of these cases empowerment stemmed from conditions of social, economic or political exclusion. But the growing appropriation of public spaces by private developers and the increasingly authoritarian style of many local/central governments also triggered resistance among less deprived groups and communities (*City Mine(d), Ouseburn Trust*).

The extent of the socially innovative impact of empowerment is place-sensitive and often path-dependent – both in the sense of deploying sociopolitical resources from the past, or radically breaking with them. In the case of *Arts Factory*, for example, the empowerment of previously excluded groups – through their participation in decision-making about actions and their own transformation – represented a radical break with established community development schemes and public service provision, on the one hand, and traditional working-class politics, on the other hand. In Antwerp, by creating interaction at the neighbourhood level and giving voice to residents about concrete actions at that level, *BOM* contributed to empowering marginalised groups who never had a voice and gave them access to wider socio-political networks. In the case of *AQS*, organising basic support and welfare services for women, children and poorly educated young people with few skills was instrumental in creating 'capabilities', that is, making people traditionally excluded, drop-outs or passive recipients of welfare feel they could 'make a difference' for themselves and their neighbourhood. And well beyond participation or consultation of residents only, *NDC* succeeded in generating a robust 'community leadership', by institutionalising the notion that the community had a voice and a space where this voice could be exercised. For *City Mine(d)*, empowerment was achieved by providing structured financial and organisational support and by facilitating networking for different civil society groups.

Territorial setting and spatial reach

Throughout the whole book we have been very sensitive to the geography of our case studies and in particular to their local embeddedness, as well as their scalar articulations. As we explained in Chapter 3, we were able to identity three different ways in which the initiatives embedded themselves in the territory: i) neighbourhood-centred initiatives, ii) neighbourhood initiatives with a wider geographical outlook and iii) city-wide initiatives. Obviously this is an oversimplified typology as most initiatives were *relationally* connected to a variety of networks with their specific geographical imprints and, therefore, show a more complex geography than their 'type' of embeddedness suggests. We will discuss this in greater detail below.

Among the *neighbourhood-centred* initiatives, a straightforward case is that of *AQS*. Located in a very dense area in the 'wombs' of Naples, it needed to territorially root itself at the heart of the neighbourhood in order to reach its residents. It thus based its premises in one of the *bassi*, typical ground floor spaces in Naples, to set up a neighbourhood-based social network. Although with time the association opened up to form partnerships with local and regional institutions, the focus has always been on the creation of an alternative culture, on the empowerment and on the satisfaction of the needs of the most fragile residents of the Quartieri Spagnoli themselves.

In a completely different context, the *Ouseburn Trust*, in northern England, is also an initiative deeply embedded in its territory. In fact, it could be said that it was the landscape and the rich texture of the area that brought people together in an organised group to preserve and maintain the cultural and social heritage of the neighbourhood. Interestingly, this very territorial focus has meant that the *Ouseburn Trust* was not always successful at opening up and linking with other groups in the city and has remained a relatively introverted initiative. Many people from the wider area and in Newcastle do not even know about the existence of this neighbourhood and the trust has not succeeded in broadening its membership base, thereby limiting the socially innovative potential of the initiative.

Among the *neighbourhood initiatives with a wider reach*, Olinda is worth mentioning as its explicit scalar strategy was to break away from the shell of the psychiatric hospital (which used to be a rather hermetic institution – an asylum), to link up with the neighbourhood around the hospital (which used to be hostile) and reach the whole city and beyond, through its cultural activities and also the resources and expertise coming from its involvement in the European movement for the 'deinstitutionalisation' of psychiatric services. Its triple slogan – (1) 'never alone', (2) 'never with the usual', (3) 'be interactive' – speaks of its drive to networking.

BOM is another interesting case of wider spatial reach because it managed to root and uproot itself from three locations. This speaks of the ability of its organisers to empathise with different contexts and of their strongly held convictions, but also of the methodological strength of the IAD approach, which could reproduce itself through the articulation of neighbourhood-based, city-wide and regional networks.

Among the *city-wide cases*, that is, the initiatives that combined a strong attachment to a particular territorial setting with an explicit broader urban and trans-scalar strategy, are *Leoncavallo* and more significantly *City Mine(d)*. *Leoncavallo*, like *BOM*, had to change locations, as the initially squatted building was repossessed by the local authorities. But the creation of a self-managed space, supplying socio-cultural services to the neighbourhood and beyond, was part of a much broader social movement, with wider political actions and claims. Over time, and particularly after the eviction from the first location, *Leoncavallo* became a national and international icon of the anarchist and squatter movement, scaling up beyond the confines of the neighbourhood in which it produces and delivers its services. It has also played a significant political role by formally participating in the Milan local politics.

But perhaps the most geographically spread and multi-scalar initiative is *City Mine(d)*. It acts as a network, rather than a close-knit organisation, which supports 'territorial sparks' across the city, giving them the necessary resources to create and sustain projects. Although it started in Brussels, it has now branched out to other European cities and its actions are now 'sparking off' to different contexts. *City Mine(d)* paradigmatically combines a sharp under-standing of the territory where it operates with a wider political and even academic awareness of the global scene. The knowledge, lessons and strategies that it learns from one city are reassessed in another place. *City Mine(d)* is able to materialise this 'glocal' scalar configuration because it fully apprehends the structural circumstances in which urban development takes place (global capitalism).

Is there a relationship between the territorial setting and spatial reach of initiatives and their relative 'success'? It seems that neighbourhood-centred initiatives have been partly successful at providing the local community with necessary services, at rebuilding community identity, at stimulating sensitivity about the precarious nature of the neighbourhood at higher scales of government, at raising funds, . . . However, the more inward-looking initiatives also seem to have struggled more to remain innovative, to sustain themselves financially or to reproduce their social capital. In contrast, the initiatives that have opened up more to other geographical perspectives and have pursued wider-scalar strategies seem to have managed better. By interacting with other groups, institutions and geographical scales, they have been more reflexive and self-critical. Initiatives that have developed a 'glocal' mentality and plan of action have become less dependent on the particular local institutional–political context or funding regimes, freer to experiment and move on when necessary. Moreover, they often had a more proliferating impact, as they were more visible to the 'outside world', thus serving as an example, a source of inspiration or a partner in a spatially wider learning environment.

Path-dependent dynamics of socially innovative experiences

If we consider the evolution of the case studies in their specific politico-institutional context, it is possible to assess the main factors that contributed to their success and failure. This, in turn, can help to work out how local initiatives may achieve a wider societal impact. We have organised this discussion in two parts: first, we briefly retrace the dynamics of social innovation (also referring to the ALMOLIN methodology of Chapter 3) and then we discuss the constraints and conditions for successful initiatives. Some of the elements considered are summarised in Tables 14.2, 14.3 and 14.4.

Dynamics of social innovation

The question 'In reaction to what?' has been largely covered in the first section of this chapter, more specifically under the title 'Satisfaction of human needs'. Among the ten cases analysed in this book, we can recognise at least three ideal types, based on the triggering factor ('In reaction to what?'), ensuing aims and prevailing innovative dimension. Obviously, as stressed earlier, the boundaries among these groups are loose and much overlapping exists.

In the first place, we have initiatives oriented first and foremost to the *provision of social services* to deprived neighbourhoods and/or marginalised groups (*AQS, Olinda, Alentour, Arts Factory*). In this regard, it is worth recalling that in the 'new' social movements of the 1990s and early 2000s (see Chapter 2) – of which the initiatives presented in this book are partial examples – 'material' exclusion has dramatically returned onto the agenda. The post-Fordist crisis and the deindustrialisation process, coupled with the intensification of the immigration flows and the generalised reduction of welfare provisions, have indeed brought back severe material needs (housing, jobs, education and training, social services). These are coupled with more immaterial and existential

Table 14.2 Spark-off motive and philosophical roots of socially innovative initiatives

Socially innovative initiatives *In reaction to what?* *Inspired by what?*	*Arts Factory, UK*	*Ouseburn Trust, UK*	*NDC Newcastle, UK*	*AQS, Italy*	*Leoncavallo, Italy*	*Olinda, Italy*	*BOM, Belgium*	*City Mine(d), Belgium*	*Alentour, France*	*Grätzelmanagement, Austria*
Responding to social needs										
Decline in morale and community spirit – refusal to be labelled 'a problem'	X		X						X	
Reaction to human, social and physical decay of neighbourhood				X					X	
Recognition of rights of self-determination for people with social and mental problems	X					X			X	
New urban governance										
Desire for community governance as an alternative to the breaking apart of community bonds	X									X
Reaction to property-led development and 'pull-down' renewal		X					X	X	X	
Integrated Area Development as an alternative neighbourhood development model			X	X			X			X
Self-organisation in response to political corporatism and crisis of social democracy	X				X			X	X	
Expressive motive										
Providing spaces for the production of alternative histories, identities and images					X			X		
Philosophical roots										
Social movements and philosophies of 1960 and 1970s (solidarity, democracy, personal emancipation)				X	X	X	X			
'Urban' movements of the 1960s and 1970s against authoritarian planning and/or for more participatory urban governance		X	X					X	X	X
Self-help/mutual aid/social economy tradition	X			X		X			X	
Social Christianism and/or community work tradition		X	X	X				X	X	
Niche, demonstrative, alternative experience (with roots in anarchist philosophy)						X			X	

Source: Authors

needs – albeit as 'basic' as the former – such as citizenship, self-expression, cultural identity – and both are, inevitably, related to issues of power.

Second, we have initiatives that started primarily in order to change *urban governance* processes, such as fighting authoritarian planning decisions or development pressures, aiming at empowering local communities in decision-making processes, and/or seeking to re-appropriate urban public spaces (*BOM, NDC, Grätzelmanagement, Ouseburn Trust*). Among these cases, *BOM* and *Ouseburn* were bottom-up initiated, whereas *NDC* and *Grätzelmanagement* were top-down engineered. In all cases, though, the initiatives – which often involved also the satisfaction of basic needs – were explicitly challenging the engrained hierarchical and authoritarian decision-making processes in the fields of urban planning and social policy, that were little attentive to real community needs.

Finally, we have *expressive, identity-seeking* initiatives – initiatives that, although pursuing either of the above aims, were especially centred on cultural and artistic ways to mobilise resources and pursue innovation (*City Mine(d)*, *Leoncavallo*).

Historical roots

As we showed in Chapter 2, there is a common European heritage in contentious action, although over the nineteenth century it diversified into national and regional trajectories. These traditions resurfaced in the twentieth century within the 'new' cycle of contention that arose in the 1960s and 1970s. In their actions, organisational forms, aims and visions, all the initiatives reviewed in this book do find inspiration in one or more of these antecedents. The majority finds its most immediate roots in the social movements of the 1970s, but a few also link to older traditions, such as social Christianism and mutualism (see Table 2.2. in Chapter 2, Table 3.1 in Chapter 3 and Table 14.2 in this chapter). There are obviously differences, partly related to the specific national and regional trajectories.

The Italian experiences – *Leoncavallo, Olinda* and *AQS* – as well as one of the Belgian cases – *BOM* – are direct offspring of the 'new progressive' social movements of the 1970s, which sought – in various forms, sometimes extreme and disruptive – personal emancipation, solidarity and greater democracy. In the *Leoncavallo* case the link is direct, since the centre was actually created during those years of extreme militancy and only later evolved into a more structured organisation. In this initiative, the libertarian and anarchist stance, oriented to disruptive, demonstrative and self-contained initiatives – outside both the state and the market – are much stronger than in the others. Their current repertoire of actions and the non-hierarchical style of management are, indeed, a clear expression of that heritage. *Olinda* shares the same anti-conventional and anti-authoritarian roots of social action, but its activities were strongly ingrained in the Italian movement for progressive mental health of the 1970s and the broader European movement for the 'deinstitutionalisation' of psychiatric services. The other two initiatives are instead more community- and neighbourhood-oriented. Both come from the 'New Left' social action movements of the 1970s as well, but *AQS* also found its inspiration in social Christianity, with a strong pedagogical focus, whereas *BOM* was, from the very beginning, a decidedly 'urban' project in focus and strongly committed to neighbourhood-based socio-economic development in response to earlier sector-oriented, often too fragmented policies and collective actions.

City Mine(d), *Ouseburn Trust* and *Arts Factory* are more directly related to the 'urban resistance' movements of the 1970s and 1980s, that is, against authoritarian planning choices involving gentrification and real estate-led redevelopment. *City Mine(d)*, however, shares with *Leoncavallo* a more libertarian, demonstrative and anti-hierarchical approach, whereas the *Ouseburn Trust* has strong links with the British tradition of 'community' social work and planning, with inputs from church militancy in community work. *Arts Factory* is an interesting case of community action, which has challenged the bureaucratisation of the workers' movement tradition and its disempowering governance system, trying to reconnect with the authentic roots of the UK community self-help activism (trade unionism and community chapels).

NDC, *Alentour* and *Grätzelmanagement* have weaker links with the 1970s' 'New Left' and 'urban' movements. *NDC* relates more to the British community development action from the 1970s, whereas *Alentour* is more in tune with both the French bourgeois philanthropism and the French social economy tradition of solidarity and self-help. *Grätzelmanagement* is based on the 'gentle urban renewal' policies of the 1970s, inspired by bottom-up approaches, and on the more recent attempt at modernising the Austrian public administration from above.

Political regimes and path dependency

No socially innovative initiative occurs in a void. The general political climate, the coalitions in power at the local level, the features of the national regulatory regime (neoliberal, conservative-liberal, progressive-technocrat, . . .) and their changes over time play a major role in explaining both the ignition of initiatives and their subsequent evolution. In many of our cases (e.g. *AQS*, *BOM*, *NDC*), the socially innovative initiatives started in a period characterised by favourable local/national political conditions in terms of available funding and/or attitude towards social exclusion and bottom-up action. Other initatives were born in reaction to increased external pressures (*Ouseburn*) or aggravated deprivation (*Alentour*), often in less favourable political contexts. In all cases, though, changes in the political regime significantly affected the further development of the innovative experience. But we will give a full account of the different aspects of the relations between state- and civil society-based innovative initiatives under different and evolving political conditions in Chapter 15. Suffice it to say here that some initiatives exhibit strong path-dependencies, whereas others feature ruptures in established dynamics (see Table 14.3).

The role of human resources and leadership

Among the resources mobilised in the initiatives (see Table 14.3), the existence of *charismatic figures* and/or *professional organisers* to initiate the mobilisation, rally support and structure actions proved critical in several cases: two former MENCAP (the UK association for people with learning disabilities) activists in the *Arts Factory* case; a professional community organiser in the *Alentour* case; a psychiatrist belonging to the progressive mental health movement in *Olinda*; a community leader – a vicar – and a council officer 'gone native' in the *Ouseburn* case. In the latter initiative, both leaders represented a key organisational asset for the construction of a collective vision and for mediating the dialogue between people and city council, also in terms of 'language'. In the *BOM* case, professional

Table 14.3 Resources mobilised for social innovation

Socially innovative initiatives

Resources mobilised	Arts Factory, UK	Ouseburn Trust, UK	NDC Newcastle, UK	AQS, Italy	Leoncavallo, Italy	Olinda, Italy	BOM, Belgium	City Mine(d), Belgium	Alentour, France	Grätzelmanagement, Austria
Human										
– Skilled professionals – hired	X	X[a]	X	X	X	X	X	X	X	X
– Other salaried labour force	X		X	X	X	X	X	X	X	X
– Volunteers	X	X	X	X	X	X	X	X	X	X
– Charismatic leader(s)	X	X		X		X			X	
Organisational										
– Networking with local partners	X	X	X	X	X	X	X	X	X	X
– Civil Society associations and networking				X	X	X	X	X	X	X
– Strong internal organisation		X						X	X	
– Collective learning	X	X	X	X	X	X		X	X	X
– Networking with national/international partners					X	X		X		
Financial										
– Local authorities	X	X	X	X		X	X	X	X	X
– Private thrusts/foundations	X				X		X			
– Private firms	X									
– National/regional public funds		X	X	X				X	X	X
– EU funds	X				X	X	X	X	X	X
– Membership contributions	X	X								
– Revenue from sales or renting of assets and services	X	X				X	X	X		

[a] Newcastle city officers

Source: Authors

planning, social work, urban sociology and other expertise from the urban movement tradition, with strong commitment to bottom–up community work, was critical. For *City Mine(d)*, professional intermediation between different actors, mobilising and producing common discursive frames and the nurturing of the role of 'broker' between often diverse if not competing interests were among the key features that defined the organisation's success.

But charismatic or professional leaders can also be a liability. In the *Alentour* case the eventual withdrawal of the initiator did jeopardise the initiative. In the *Ouseburn Trust*, and to a lesser extent in *Alentour*, the leaders themselves became caught in their own routines, losing their innovative drive. Similarly, in the *Arts Factory* experience the strong leadership may end up hampering effective democracy and participation in the long run.

Public funding: opportunity or constraining commitment?

The majority of the social innovation initiatives in our research combined financial resources of diverse provenance but, for all, public finance constituted the biggest contribution. Some sort of government programme or fund, whether municipal, regional, national or European, secured the financial sustainability of most initiatives. *AQS*, for example, pooled municipal, national and eventually EU funding, which permitted a leap in visibility and effectiveness. Also *BOM* was very successful in pooling resources, not only municipal, regional and national, but foremost European, acting as a veritable – professional – resources broker.

The prevailingly public source of funding, however, also brings specific types of problems. First, since public programmes and funds are generally of a limited duration, the sustainability of initiatives over time is constrained, or else requires a constant search for new funding. Second, the public origin makes the availability of funding contingent upon political shifts, which strongly affect not only the extent, but most importantly the orientation of programmes. In particular, with the neoliberal turn and the New Public Management approach of the 1990s and 2000s, many programmes, even within the EU, have become 'performance-oriented', that is, are granted on the basis of economic criteria and quantitative results, and are less attuned to social aims and participatory approaches.

This was certainly the case for *Arts Factory*, which persistently faced erratic and problematic fund-raising, and also repeatedly found its self-help and solidarity concerns at odds with the increasingly market-driven orientation of mainstream programmes. *Alentour* is another excellent example of how the search for funding and the compliance with the requirements of mainstream top-down policies can undermine the socially innovative character of initiatives and their sustainability over time. In the latter case, the solidaristic dimension of the initiative was eventually lost, as external pressures coming from the national government and the EU to comply with quantitative and performance criteria (number of jobs created, economically self-sustaining activities) could not accommodate many social services. As a consequence, internal tensions also developed among conflicting aims: for example, job tenure vs solidarity.

The *NDC* case is, perhaps, the clearest example of how the national government economic – rather than social – focus, as well as the efficiency-oriented management criteria (New Labour's obsession with measurable targets), prevented the durable empowering of the community in the implementation of the programme. Tensions then developed with other programmes, such as *Going for Growth*, which engendered significant distrust in the community towards both the local and central governments, as fear of gentrification and displacement intensified. Moreover, the central government asphyxiating reporting requirements clashed with the experimenting approach and the residents' involvement, inherent to socially innovative initiatives. Finally, even the positive social innovations actually achieved in service delivery were contingent upon additional funding of the programme that may not be re-authorised in the next funding round, or because of changes in the funding scheme.

In general, the positive – enabling – role of EU programmes and funding (Anti-poverty, URBAN, etc.), especially in the 1990s, must be stressed (see more on this in Chapter 15). Indeed, in many cases (*BOM, AQS, Alentour, ...*) the availability of EU funds, *above and beyond* the established local, regional and national support and provisions, represented a crucial opportunity for empowering organisations and making them recognised actors in negotiations with local authorities (see Table 14.3).

Organisational opportunities and tensions

The organisational forms and dynamics of innovative initiatives – comparable to what is called 'corporate governance' in the entrepreneurial world – play a significant part in their evolution. Organisations experience a structural tension between creativity and routine, spontaneity and hierarchy, flexibility and structuration, which ultimately determine their capacity of organisational reproduction and innovation.

Among the most interesting cases of virtuous capitalisation on such 'change dialectics' is that of *Leoncavallo*. The social centre, after a peculiar evolution from urban movement to niche, marginalised and self-contained experiment, has now found a loose form of institutional legitimation, without abandoning its challenging character. Self-management, with horizontal (non-hierarchical), informal (not rigidly fixed roles) and democratic (assembly decision-making) relations, remains a central asset of the centre, but there is a constant tension between this flexible and creative structure and the pressures to formalise in order to gain acceptance and legitimacy in the eyes of the state. The author of the case study calls this unstable organisational form 'flexible institutionalisation'. Another example of this 'fluid' approach, is the use of 'multiple spaces' within the centre: a plurality of physical spaces coexists, in which different activities, social relations and governance codes develop side by side.

Table 14.4 Constraints and vulnerabilities experienced in socially innovative initiatives

Socially innovative initiatives Constraints and vulnerabilities identified	Arts Factory, UK	Ouseburn Trust, UK	NDC Newcastle, UK	AQS, Italy	Leoncavallo, Italy	Olinda, Italy	BOM, Belgium	City Mine(d), Belgium	Alentour, France	Grätzelmanagement, Austria
Strict criteria of EU funding	X			X						X
Short time-horizons of funding mechanisms/project-based funding	X	X	X	X		X	X		X	
Competitive fund-raising procedures – dependency relations for funding		X	X						X	
Economically poor constituency						X				
Lack of clearly defined leadership										
Crisis in existing leadership								X		
Fragility of flexible/creative organisation							X			
Lack of adequate skills			X							
Rigid planning system	X	X								
Rigidity and hierarchy of public bureaucracy										X
Neoliberal urban policy – threat of real estate development		X				X	X	X	X	
Tensions state/market/civil society		X			X	X				
Competition between third sector organisations over funding				X		X				

Source: Authors

A similar story is that of *Olinda*, which, according to the case study author, deployed 'reflexive' qualities that enabled the organisation to sustain its innovative drive. Tensions were perceived from the beginning as resources and the dialectics among different actors, within and without the organisation, was a founding element of its innovative dynamics. The organisation has in fact managed to positively exploit different types of contradictions, thereby succeeding in adapting to and coping with different issues and challenges: between the specific interests of the community (providing concrete care services to its inpatients) and broader social participation; between the organisation's innovative vision of social policy and the mainstream approaches of local institutions; between the social and the economic sustainability of actions.

Also in *City Mine(d)*, the tensions between spontaneity and institutionalisation are mastered in a virtuous way. The organisation manages to hold an ambivalent position between facilitator and broker. This is certainly made easier by the fact that *City Mine(d)* uses art and culture as the main medium for empowering self-determined projects and operates in a city where 'alternative' artistic expression has become part of the local glamour. The paradox lies in the fact that it is precisely this glamour that attracts the very gentrification *City Mine(d)* is trying to fight and the organisation finds itself in the peculiar, partly opportunistic, and paradoxical position of exploiting international power elites to sustain its local action.

Born against top-down planning decisions and redevelopment pressures from outside the community, the *Ouseburn Trust* successfully engineered a form of co-operation with the local government, but is now facing internal as well as external problems: involution from within and delegitimation from outside. With regard to the first, the trust has had problems in enlarging and diversifying its constituency. Despite the relationships established with outside groups in the past, the trust seems increasingly locked in an 'introverted' or 'introspective' orientation and its leaders are accused of being inflexible and closed to broader groups and interests. As to the second, although the trust has attempted to be an institutional interlocutor in planning negotiations, the private developers do not recognise this role and directly speak to the city council. This is reinforced by an overarching central government policy and strict rules for spending public resources, which affect negatively the independence of the local government. Which is another good illustration of how the organisation and networking space of socially innovative organisations are highly sensitive to political regimes and their public management styles.

Can socially innovative neighbourhoods save the city?

Are communities local? And is society inherently top-down? In the final section of this chapter we make a plea in favour of overruling both the Russian dolls approach to communities within society and the simplistic opposition between community and society and between local and national or global, through a properly applied place–space dialectics.

The traps of localism and self-help

All the local initiatives investigated, in one way or another, engage and challenge social relations, agencies and governance dynamics at higher spatial scales. Often the challenge is to affirm the rights of the communities they represent to be acknowledged, to speak and to have an impact on policy, business initiatives, social networking and planning decision-making at the level of the city and the region.

As we discussed in Chapter 3, however, focusing on the scale of the local community or neighbourhood comes with specific dangers. First, there is the danger of *socio-political localism*, that is, a blind faith in the power of local agency, organisations, movements and institutions to address and deal with local problems and potentials, thereby ignoring the multi-scalar spatiality of development processes. Second, there is the danger of *'existential' localism*, that is, the idea that all needs are best satisfied within the local *heimat*, by local institutions or – pushing the localist argument even further – by drawing mainly on local resources. Third, there is the danger of *'fake subsidiarity'*, that is, accepting the hegemonic discourse that decisions are best taken at the local level, ignoring the fact that the higher-scale governmental and corporate levels tend to shed their budgetary and policy responsibilities onto the local scale. Fourth, and partly linking the three previous dangers, we must consider that communities are not necessarily 'local', but also that many neighbourhoods are actually a mix of communities, or have very poor neighbourhood dynamics. Sometimes, in particularly fragmented neighbourhoods, specific groups have stronger ties outside the neighbourhood scale. These arguments, of course, are in no way meant to undercut the vitality and the socio-political significance of the local scale in our cases, but to put them in a more realistic framework. How so?

Initiatives at the neighbourhood level are first of all about 'doing something', usually rather practical in a variety of ways. This of course requires mobilising resources, setting up an organisation, doing management, planning delivery schemes, respecting calendar and delivery qualities, and the like. Such 'tactics' can lead to forms of depoliticisation, that is, to the pre-emption of broader political voicing and action to obtain egalitarian inclusion in more universal ways. In other words, the 'political' question of fighting for equality and inclusion may, through such initiatives, be transformed into a 'sociological' local question, that is, organising social mechanisms based on local resources to mitigate processes of social exclusion, without really addressing the broader and structural mechanisms that produced exclusion to begin with. However, the choice for such tactics at the local level is a consequence precisely of the sustained autism vis-à-vis local voices by the 'higher-up' social, economic and political decision-making centres.

The issue is not just socio-political. This tension between community action and broader societal mobilisation evokes the old debate in classical sociology, which contrasted *Gemeinschaft* with *Gesellschaft*[1] – community vs society organisations and the 'organic' vs 'contractual' types of social relations (see Chapter 1). In cultural terms, for instance, communitarian values may be at odds with cosmopolitanism and with universal citizenship rights. In fact, community-oriented social initiatives, while arguably more expressive of 'some' people's needs and desires, and more democratic in their decision-making processes *within the community*, are often *self-contained, inward-looking* and *exclusionary* vis-à-vis *other* communities, therefore potentially undemocratic beyond community boundaries. In contrast, society-oriented movements, while being more impersonal, on the one hand, and more prone to hierarchical or automatic decision-making mechanisms, on the other hand, may be more socially *inclusive*, that is, allow for diversity within universalism based on general citizenship rights for all (Chapter 1).

A false antagonism

In reality, the tensions between community and society, local and regional, national or global, bottom-up and top-down are generally portrayed in an oversimplified and often purely dualistic manner. *Local* action is romantically depicted as inevitably grass-roots, community-based, democratic, bottom-up, creative and, ultimately, good; conversely, action launched at a higher spatial or institutional scale, related to broad societal issues, aiming at undifferentiated inclusion, is pictured as top-down, authoritarian, bureaucratic, blind to differences and ultimately bad.[2] However, first, the mechanistic association between the various attributes and the scale levels is highly disputable; second, spatially 'higher up', top-down, societal approaches are not necessarily 'bad'. Let us briefly develop these observations.

The mechanistic associations between attributes and scales are a sign of a poor socio-political geographical analysis. Both community and society dynamics are inherently multi-scalar and constantly interact with each other. If communities are more tangible than society – because of being the locus of immediate human interaction and action – they are the 'builders' of society; reversely, societal logics give a strong significance to the interactivity of communities. Therefore, their geographies are intimately and inter-scalarly connected.

In the second place, despite the fact they are often discursively earmarked as such, scales are not ethically constructed, nor do they reflect an ethically constructed hierarchy (e.g. what the local does is more in tune with people's needs). As argued above, historically speaking, many social innovations occurred through top-down and centralised organisation and agency. Mass movements and trade union mobilisations, for instance, through party and other structured organisations, have had a very innovative societal impact, creating spaces 'beyond the local' for information sharing, discussion, diffusion of culture, identity building, education, formation of political cadres and socio-political activism.[3]

A dangerous corollary of the above-criticised simplifications is the idea that administrative devolution and decentralisation can bring, by itself, local empowerment. A distinction must be made between the *political* dimension of governance (participation in decision-making procedures) and the *public–managerial* dimension (access to, control over and management of resources, primarily financial). As to the latter, decentralised governance, without control of resources, actually contributes to disempowering even further marginalised communities. In fact, when political changes are not followed by delivery in deeds, the distrust in these communities vis-à-vis the elites in general and the political class in particular, is bound to grow. As we emphasised earlier, the issue of sustained financial resources represents a major threat to the continuity of the innovative initiatives we analysed. But the former, the political dimension of governance is not an outcome of devolution either. From the society–community dialectics we learn that local forces of change and development must be present or must be built up in order to make local political empowerment work. Otherwise, devolution is just empty and ends up reinforcing the distrust in the socio-political system – 'society?' – altogether.

From community to society

Perhaps the most important outcome of our research on the socially innovative impact of neighbourhood-based community initiatives is that local action involves the broader scales of government and dynamics of society (city, region, nation, Europe) in at least three ways:

a) Necessary *governance interaction*. In all cases, the local actions inevitably affected higher scales of government, either challenging them or changing the modes of governance. At the same time, the higher scales of government affected, conditioned or enabled the local scale. We will come back to this in Chapter 15.
b) *Demonstration* effect. In many instances the local initiative had a symbolic, demonstrative effect on the broader urban scene, showing that change *is* possible. This was often the beginning of an interactive social learning process, blurring institutional and scalar boundaries.
c) *Networking* echoes and fallouts. By their networking activity initiatives reverberate and exchange their repertoires, issues and achievements with other similar experiences at the regional, national and international scale. A case in point is the *City Mine(d)* experience. The social capital and knowledge built at the local level have become shared resources in the supra-local network. At the same time the wider-area networks of initiatives provide expertise and legitimacy to the local ones. This is facilitated by the fact that *City Mine(d)* operates in the realm of artistic expression, which resonates more easily at the national and international levels.

The inter-scalar reverberations of local initiatives, especially those related to supra-local networking, do point at new possibilities. The wealth of socially innovative capacity that is already shared through networking relations across individual nations, Europe and the world could be made more instrumental to reinforcing local change. Also, collective pressures could be further exerted to change policy approaches at different government levels. The European Union has had such a paramount role in sustaining socially innovative experiences during the 1990s in the direction of more integrated and empowering programmes. This *élan* should be resumed. Finally, policies should be broadened to include issues of redistribution as well as recognition, integrated socio-economic development, customised social services, democratically accessible

218 F. Martinelli, F. Moulaert, S. González

arts and culture, while more room should be given to bottom-up participation, without hindering it with strict reporting and hierarchically imposed bureaucratic protocols.

Social innovation as we have conceived, analysed and experienced it, is a slow process. As our case studies have shown, whatever the mobilising grievance, in order to unfold and leave a durable trace, social innovation needs reliable funding and supportive institutional space. This does not mean that these experiences must transform into permanent institutions. The tensions between bottom-up mobilisation and institutionalisation, between creativity and bureaucratisation, between specific community interests and broader welfare institutions must be considered an asset and the fuel for sustaining social innovation. But in order to avoid both the traps of localism and the lapse into self-reliance, a bottom-line financial and institutional 'space' of manoeuvre should be provided on a more universal basis. Local human and organisational value added can then be mobilised and grafted onto this foundation.

Overall, our case studies are all struggling to remain innovative and, equally important, to survive. The current policy shifts occurring, at all government scales, towards narrowly defined economic and efficiency criteria, a reliance on real estate development for urban regeneration, the privatisation or externalisation of service provision, a re-conquest of public spaces by either private businesses or technocratic local governments are increasingly pushing civil society 'change agents' out of the social scene or forcing them to transform into mainstream social service or project managers. Moreover, the dwindling and erratic nature of funding is increasingly undermining innovative organisations, whose efforts in accomplishing alternative ways of responding to basic needs, changing social relations and empowering the excluded are diverted towards the task of fund-hunting and complying with spending requirements. These and other aspects on the relationships between state and civil society in social innovation initiatives will be the particular focus of Chapter 15.

Notes

1   The first to introduce this antithesis was Ferdinand Tönnies in his work *Gemeinschaft und Gesellschaft*, published as early as 1887.
2   This antagonism evokes the debate in social policy, which mechanically opposes the 'postmodernist' defence of diversity to the traditional 'welfarist' universalism (see Chapter 2).
3   *Mass participation to politics* has been a major social innovation by itself.

15 Socially innovative projects, governance dynamics and urban change

Between state and self-organisation

Erik Swyngedouw and Frank Moulaert

Introduction

This book has been devoted largely to experiments with and initiatives for fermenting socially emancipatory practices in urban neighbourhoods, often characterised by multiple forms of exclusion and deprivation. Ironically, the still persisting socio-spatial inequalities that choreograph everyday life in the poorest areas of cities are often exacerbated exactly by the perverse logic of uneven social development and deepening uneven power relations. These inequalities are etched in and accompany the tactics to rejuvenate, reinvigorate or otherwise render more competitive urban and regional economies in a globalising (neo)liberal world (Swyngedouw *et al.*, 2002). The inevitable moment of reckoning of this competitiveness obsession arrived with the onslaught, in the fall of 2008 of the deepest economic crisis since at least the 1930s, which will make matters undoubtedly worse for these neighbourhoods. More than ever before, innovative thought and creative practices will be required to deal with the fallout of this spiralling urban crisis (Harvey, 2009a), which will further widen the already considerable gap between rich and poor, between empowerment and disempowerment, between those who cannot any longer think about what new needs to chase and those who do not have the means to satisfy even the most basic needs.

In this closing chapter we mainly discuss the relationships between public policy, governance and social innovation at the local level. As we stressed throughout the book, socially innovative neighbourhood initiatives aim at achieving three interrelated objectives and the discussion of governance and policy issues has to be understood and explored in connection to these aims. First, they contribute to the satisfaction of *human needs* that remain unconsidered or unsatisfied by either or both state- and market-based delivery schemes. Second, they increase or enable a variety of *access rights* (e.g. by facilitating political inclusiveness, choreographing redistributive policies, organising entitlements, etc.), enhancing *human capabilities* and thereby *empowering* particular social groups. Third, they contribute to *change social relations and power structures* within the community but also between local groups and external actors, especially to change the modalities of *governance* in the direction of more inclusive and democratic practices and the pursuit of multi-scalar political participation systems.

We examine these relationships in three steps. First, we summarise why we believe that social innovation initiatives at the neighbourhood level are important, both as socio-political emblems of what is possible, but also as drivers of social innovation at higher spatial scales. This summary is largely based on the transversal analysis presented in Chapter 14. Second, we consider the wider political economic context of the emergence of socially innovative initiatives, their ambiguous relationship with both state and market, and their institutional embedding. In a final step, we review pointers towards sustainable social innovation strategies, political changes and policy initiatives – at a variety of geographical scales, but especially the EU – that might enhance and strengthen the proliferation of such initiatives and their wider urban and societal impact.

(Dis)empowering socially innovative neighbourhoods

Scholarly and civil society concern for social innovation *in urban development* arose as an alternative to the growing attention paid by policy-makers to technological and organisational innovation, as a means to trigger competitive territorial development dynamics. Concern for social innovation *in urban development* draws on the rapid proliferation of all manner of bottom-up grass-roots initiatives in urban areas throughout the European Union. It is now generally recognised, and has been further substantiated in this book, that such socially innovative practices enhance social capital and network formation, and may play a pivotal role in revitalising and re-energising the socio-economic and physical fabric of urban areas that have been disenfranchised, marginalised or otherwise excluded.

The right to the socially innovative city

This book is, first of all, about *cherishing and nurturing creativity and innovation as vital and necessary ingredients for emancipatory practices*. This is not the creativity associated with Richard Florida's 'Creative Class', which focuses unilaterally on the boys and girls that mobilise the best of their considerable cultural, economic, affective, intellectual and other talents in the pursuit of monetary gain and economic profit, but rather about fermenting the creativity that galvanises everyday life, that makes living-in-common with others a pleasurable, enriching, equitable, and mutually rewarding exercise. It is the creative and associated innovative practices that revolve around formulating, claiming and exercising what Henri Lefebvre called 'the Right to the City' (1995; see also Harvey, 2008; Mayer, 2009).

The experiences reported in this book are situated in a long tradition of emancipatory and democratising local initiatives that have historically been the pivotal terrains from where often broader political projects were launched. As discussed in Chapter 2, local social innovation practices have a long varied, and rich historical tradition, going back at least to the nineteenth century. They have often functioned as springboards for imaginative social or political projects that would spiral out from the local environment to galvanise the political energies of all sorts of social groups and often effectuate great social change.

The transformative and universalising ambitions of local social innovation

The cases presented in this book, and the general argument of which they are part, are 'glocal' in their outlook, universalising in their ambition, and transformative in their desire. They offer strong evidence against the 'community–society' duality criticised in Chapters 1 and 14. Therefore, our analysis inscribes itself squarely in a progressive vision, one that seeks to transcend uneven power relations, that presumes that humans are equal qua political speaking beings, that believes in the possibility of emancipation and that lives in the conviction that individuals and communities can muster the passion and have the capacity to self-organise and self-manage in equitable and inclusive manners. The book attests to the capacity of everyone to act politically, to engage in common with others, to show practically that another world can be built through the construction of socially innovative communities as constitutive parts of a society pursuing universal rights for all its members (see Harvey, 2009b).

The analyses presented through this collection, and the transversal reading of cases in Chapter 14, show how the urban neighbourhood is indeed a creative site of political, social, economic and cultural activity and action. *The neighbourhood, for us, does not only offer to save the city, it embodies urbanity or, at least, it is the site where the right to the city is staged and practised.* And of course, the neighbourhoods that this book talks about, those that are put on pedestals as the sites of experimenting with the new, the unexpected, the creative, are exactly those urban areas that are so often stigmatised, counted as marginal, labelled as poor or disintegrated (Moulaert, 2000). We have shown that these neighbourhoods – in contrast to the elite and the 'integrated' exclusive areas of the city, where, as Henri Lefebvre famously insisted, 'nothing ever happens and nothing ever will' – are brewing with life in all its heterogeneous forms, are cradles of innovation, and are marked by a desire to make the impossible real, often against all odds, indeed often against the powers that be, whether they be the state or the market logic.

Challenging institutionalised power

It is exactly this unruly streak, this anarchist feel, the risky business, the mobilised languages and practices of disobedience, of contempt for and distrust of institutionalised power, of the desire for transformation, that make these neighbour'hoods' and their contentious politics often suspicious in the eyes of institutionalised power. Their stories and practices are those of people who do not accept the place and the functions allocated to them in the existing social and political configuration by the state or by the economic or cultural elites. Their very activities challenge or 'exploit' the order through which they have become excluded; and their very ideas, vision and practices, therefore, embody and express both a critique of what is, and contribute to, the formation of counter-hegemonic discourses and practices. That is exactly why so many of these initiatives often meet with suspicion from city hall, chambers of commerce, financial organisations, even bureaucratised social policy institutions. This is also why the relationship between state and local initiatives is often wrought with unease, tension, and occasionally overt conflict and hostility.

However, the tense relationship between state and the social innovation initiatives observed in this book has in many cases gone through a stage of co-operative fruition. In social formations and communities where civil society was active at different spatial scales (e.g. through networking among multi-place initiatives) and in a diversity of domains of collective action, changing urban socio-political regimes during the 1980s and 1990s allowed the formation of coalitions of local actors and gave space to social planning initiatives, community emancipation or even integrated neighbourhood development strategies (Mayer, 2009). Yet such regimes are sensitive to global forces as well as to national and international political cycles which positively or negatively catalyse the opportunity space of socio-political change movements (Moulaert *et al.*, 2007).

There are several reasons that account for the often tense relationship between socially innovative initiatives and the state and many of its agencies. *On the one hand*, these initiatives are a reflection of the deficiencies of mainstream schemes, usually a failure of the state and/or the market to ensure that everyone has a proper place in the social edifice, a place that is not marked by exclusion, deprivation and disempowerment. With an unevenly effectual state and in a context in which corporate interests systematically meander around such deprived areas, these neighbourhood initiatives appear as a stain, a blemish, an indictment of the failure of both state and capital to fulfil their bio-political promises for equitable inclusion of all in a democratic, that is egalitarian, manner. *On the other hand*, from the perspective of several local authorities, the unruliness of many of these initiatives has to be tamed, institutionalised; has to be brought within the order of things and policed by the state. This does not exclude that many neighbourhood initiatives thrive well in a process of state institutionalisation and part co-optation, but many others do so reluctantly, keep on rebelling, desperately clinging on to the principles and practices of self-governing and self-management. *The very existence of the latter is of course in itself a threat to the legitimacy of the state and state functionalities.* To the extent that local initiatives are self-organised and self-managed and express the capacity of each and every one to be and act politically, they are living proof of the deficient state, of the fact that the social and the political can function without the state or at least without some of the state functions.

Governance dynamics and socially innovative projects

The emergence of a wide range of socially innovative activities in local area development has to be considered in the context of political–economic transformations and, in particular, of changing relationships between state, market economy and civil society. From Chapter 2 we remember that the rise of civil society initiatives is intimately coupled with transformations in the social and political articulation of socio-economic forces, and, among others, with the changing structures of social service delivery. There is no doubt that many socially innovative projects are directly concerned with the delivery of 'goods' and 'services' that are neither provided by the state nor by the market or whose quality is unacceptably low and increasingly de-socialised. To the extent that a growing number of needs, particularly those of the poor, remain unmet, social actors emerge whose central activity is aimed at initiating new or improving existing service delivery systems or at democratising the political mechanisms and procedures through which social and economic policies are decided and implemented.

In Europe, most social service delivery systems have, since the Second World War, become the privileged terrain of the (national) state. This welfarist approach to social integration and inclusion came under severe pressure from the 1980s onwards, as a combination of economic problems, neoliberal ideological entrenchment, and intense fiscal stress, which forced the state to partly withdraw from, or seriously curtail, traditional welfare-type forms of service delivery. As the increasingly affluent middle classes sought more social protection (pensions, life insurance, extra legal rights), the private sector (or the market) stepped in. Throughout the 1990s, pension schemes, health insurance, specialised education, child and health care, and a range of other privately produced social services multiplied. A more individualised, market-driven system, oriented to those who could afford it, established itself, while the uniform and standardised system of social service delivery deteriorated and could not keep up with the needs of the economically poor. This contributed to the real or latent exclusion of social groups from key services in a context in which democratic political practices and procedures to voice discontent or to stage alternative demands progressively closed down. Moreover, policy procedures, public decision-making and systems for the satisfaction of needs were increasingly de-politicised, as managerial–technocratic approaches began to overrule and overtake politically negotiated ways of securing access or entitlement to essential services.

The void in welfare provision to new target groups (migrants, youths, unemployed, . . .) became increasingly filled outside the traditional state-based arrangements by self-help and third sector initiatives. Many grass-roots organisations that pioneered social innovation initiatives to meet basic needs in deprived urban neighbourhoods and communities were 'organically' suspicious of (or were indeed reacting to) top-down hierarchical state-based – often insufficient – collective arrangements. Socio-cultural identity and local socio-cultural capital were experienced as vital ingredients of an inclusive development strategy. Thus, post-materialist and other affective concepts of economic life became articulated with traditional economic repertoires (see Chapter 2) through newly emerging civil society-based activities and actions: emotional affect, mutuality, self-expression, ecological sensitivities, everyday life qualities and the like became increasingly valued pointers for inclusive social life and well-being, as well as being considered to be vital collective consumption resources. These deeply political terrains remained largely outside the aegis of traditional state forms of service delivery and welfare, while market forces had little or no interest in providing these central, yet uncommodified and arguably non-commodifiable, collective socio-cultural goods.

While state, market and civil society were for a long time pitched in an antagonistic relationship with clearly demarcated and relatively sharp boundaries, the reorganisational patterning of socially innovative initiatives today points at a gradual blurring, if not erasure, of the lines of demarcation between state, civil society and market. Collaborative partnerships, stakeholder networks, multipartite institutional arrangements and other new governance formations have signalled a move away from the traditional commanding heights of state-based delivery to a collage of fuzzily organised formal and informal, but often highly innovative practices. Although there are significant differences between countries and case studies, they all point towards a similar recognition that insists on the centrality of such newly emerging state–market–civil society constellations and the establishment of social economy markets. The theoretical and empirical mapping of these initiatives cannot yet be exhaustively undertaken, but our findings show the prevalence and relevance of such practices in processes of community development and urban revitalisation. *This suggests in itself the importance of tuning policy frameworks around these socially innovative practices, and transforming governance arrangements accordingly.*

In sum, the new modalities of governance that have arisen over the past two decades signal a transformation of state-based models of service delivery, combined with, on the one hand, the rise of market-based delivery and, on the other hand, the growing attention to unsatisfied material and immaterial needs from an increasingly more vocal and empowered civil society. The latter sprung to action in the gaps and interstices left by a refocused (more entrepreneurial and market geared) state that could not be filled by encroaching market forces. They took the opportunity to introduce, along with new modes of service delivery, forms of social economy and humanly enriched social relations, more democratic governance systems provoking a socio-political creative osmosis between community aspirations and universal societal justice.

In the next sections we examine more closely the dialectical positioning of our case-studies within the 'state–market–civil society' triangle. We then reflect on the 'scalar politics', the socio-political cycles of regime change and the particular instrumentality of the EU as significant dimensions of these dialectics.

Gravitating within the state–market–civil society triangle

All the initiatives studied in the SINGOCOM project arose out of a sense of 'failure of the state', on the one hand, and 'failure of the market', on the other, in satisfying a series of essential needs. Driven by activist energies and galvanised by a variety of motivational drivers, all initiatives sought to enhance organisational capacity and social capital, and empower the traditionally disempowered.

While all projects are clearly articulated within the state–market–civil society triangle, the most creative and innovative in terms of generating new forms of delivery, attending to new needs, and experimenting with innovative institutional or organisational arrangements, are those that originate from within civil society. Those initiated by the state – usually the local state – tend to be less successful and are generally perceived – often rightly so – as instruments to re-establishing fading governmental legitimacy. To the extent that civil society initiatives are 'captured' by the state, their innovative dynamics generally weaken, as they fall prey to the public-managerial logic in the bureaucratic apparatuses. This is particularly clear in situations of resilient top-down and authoritarian planning and policy implementation procedures.

In the case of *Alentour*, for example, the attempt to introduce more bottom-up decision-making in the management of social services and programmes, clashed with the entrenched paternalistic and top-down tradition of the French state. This was by no means a monolithic pattern, since local institutions and authorities expressed different attitudes, ranging from support or partnership to conflict or indifference. But they all exhibited a tendency to control and reintegrate projects within the established centralised implementation frameworks. In the case of both *NDC* and *Grätzelmanagement*, the effort to engineer greater community participation in planning procedures was instead prejudiced from the start by the inertia of established mechanisms and inter-scalar institutional relations. In the *Grätzelmanagement* experience, in particular, the case study authors talk of 'controlled' modernisation to stress how the efforts to introduce more participatory practices remained frozen in the authoritarian social-democratic political culture on the one hand, and clashed with the 'New Public Management' strategies on the other. The attempt to involve the immigrant population through the creation of Neighbourhood Advisory Councils directly representing the residents conflicted with the 'official' establishment of QUANGO organisations (e.g. the Vienna Business Agency) and the continued involvement of the municipal staff.

But governments do not only have a tendency to sustain top-down control-based hierarchies. They also 'cherry-pick' from civil society those initiatives that are seen to be successful, that correspond to their own view of governance and delivery management, and that are not considered a threat to the existing socio-spatial order. Their incorporation, however, often saps their innovative and creative energies, such as was the case for *BOM* in Antwerp, once some of its key activities were integrated into the regular city services and its role as a project developer was challenged by strategic agencies within the local authorities' bureaucracy. Some of the initiatives are fully aware of this dialectic between integration and autonomy and try to maintain a fine balance between co-operation (with both market and state), on the one hand, and oppositional tactics on the other. The latter pre-empt full incorporation, generating a continuous innovative dynamic allowing the relationships with state and market to be revisited continuously.

Social innovation as scalar socio-politics

As community-based social innovation projects are looking for their specific identity and space within the state–market–civil society triangle, they also inevitably get engaged in 'scalar' politics. This refers to the articulation of the local initiatives with processes, institutions and social capabilities that operate at other spatial scales. To the extent that projects are successful in doing so, they have more long-lasting effects; by transcending place-specificity they engender the potential for broader political–economic transformations. Of course, such scalar politics are decidedly Janus-faced as the new institutional arrangements that accompany such trans-scalar networks are not necessarily as inclusive or participatory in outcome as is often aspired or portrayed. The initiatives that have proactively sought 'scaling up' as a socio-political strategy usually pursued a combination of aims: (i) to diffuse their innovative practices and activities to 'elsewhere' in order to get recognition; (ii) to organise wider mobilisation around social, cultural and political issues; (iii) to seek synergies among economic, social and political resources; (iv) to move regional and national civil society organisations towards lobbying for more appropriate multilevel governance systems; (v) to exert pressure on state institutions to force political transformations or, more modestly, policy changes.

Among the initiatives that to a greater or lesser extent engaged in multi-scalar strategies, we can mention *Olinda, Leoncavallo, City Mine(d), AQS, Arts Factory* and *BOM*. Other initiatives were relatively successful in breaking through the stalemate of higher-level state institutional dynamics (*Ousebum Trust* and some of the cases not covered in this book but part of the SINGOCOM analysis). The political significance of these apparently more modest results should not be underestimated: successfully challenging the state in its top-down authoritarian and controlling governing modes can not only empower the local community that launched the challenge, but can also generate more respectful relations between state and civil society organisations within cities and urban regions.

A range of 'scalar' tactics and politics is possible and visible, with a variety of outcomes and with different scalar registers and repertoires. The first set of tactics or scalar processes centre on articulating between already existing levels or scales of governance. For example, the *AQS* of Naples and *Alentour* articulated strongly with the national and European scale, particularly with respect to initiating, securing and managing financial support. For these forms of scalar articulation, the main emphasis is on securing economic sustainability through tapping into funding flows managed at different scales of governance. This tactic brings of course a clear and visible danger for a scalar dependency on the continuation of established funding flows on the one hand and requires adjusting objectives and strategies in line with policies and targets formulated at a higher spatial scale on the other. These sorts of scalar tactics are generally initiated by the initiatives themselves in a bid to secure continuity of operation.

A second set of scalar tactics emerges from the municipal or national scale. Both in the cases of the *NDC* in Newcastle and Vienna's *Grätzelmanagement*, the national respectively municipal scales were instrumental in setting up, articulating with and securing the relative independence of the initiatives, albeit that they remained locked in a multi-scalar organisational settings whereby the framework and terms of reference were set by the higher scales. This restricted both the autonomy and the field of operation of these local initiatives and invariably circumscribed their innovative potential to serve priorities and objectives in articulation with the 'higher' scales.

A third scalar tactic revolves around constructing or inserting the initiative in a network of related or like-minded initiatives elsewhere. A relational and networked politics of scale is mobilised here. The cases of *City Mine(d)* and *Leoncavallo*, in particular, showed clear strategies of extending their reach while strengthening their own operations through the production of more or less spatially extensive networking tactics. By so doing, this networked approach to engaging a politics of scale simultaneously contributes to extending or universalising the principles that galvanise the activities, permits to operate at a certain distance from the 'traditional' state forms of governing and to maintain a relative autonomy both vis-à-vis the traditional territorial forms of governance and the other networked initiatives.

Urban regimes and political opportunities

In earlier chapters, we stressed the importance of (local) political regimes, coalitions and networking for the development of socially innovative initiatives. Stability in socio-political conditions which favour social innovation initiatives from the beginning is strategically vital to their longer-term continuity. And changes in autocratic regimes are needed to open opportunities for socially innovative community initiatives. But in any case, political regimes, coalitions and contexts change and affect opportunities for socially innovative neighbourhood development.

Several examples show how the development and evolution of an initiative can be strongly conditioned by the changing political regime. For *AQS*, for example, the progressive politics of the 1990s in Italy, both at the municipal and national levels, together with the launching of the URBAN programme at the EU level, were critical to the organisational leap forward. In fact, during the 1980s, the organisation of *AQS* was rather informal and its activities were essentially based on the work of volunteers. During the 1990s, it was institutionalised as a development agency, which pooled funds from and virtuously interacted with both city hall and the EU, becoming a recognised actor in policy implementation, while networking with other such initiatives in other countries. But in recent years, there has been a return to top-down policy approaches and the association now suffers competition from more aggressive third sector organisations, while the resurfacing of an 'emergency' discourse in Naples diverts attention and resources away from processes that operate at a slower pace and at a more fundamental level, to make place for more eye-catching initiatives.

Another very good example of how the political context can condition the evolution of innovative initiatives is the *BOM* case, which successfully exploited a favourable political conjuncture in the 1990s, but has been progressively dis-empowered in the 2000s. In fact, one cannot understand the social innovation impact of *BOM* and its integrated community development approach (IAD) without giving credit to the urban policy context and the institutions involved at the time. But when such enabling political conditions changed, *BOM* could no longer sustain its innovative role and its achievements faded away.

A very different case is that of *Arts Factory*, which started in reaction to a suffocating – disempowering – local political context and merged with the mental health movement, which claimed the diversity of needs, as opposed to standard welfare provisions. In this declining working-class neighbourhood, the local governance system, although traditionally run by the Labour Party, was characterised by a male, hierarchical, conservative culture which encour-aged passivity on the part of the population, was suspicious of any active citizen-ship and blind to real local needs. *Arts Factory* challenged this local political context, trying to 'demonstrate' alternative ways of dealing with exclusion, finding funding support from the regional (Welsh) and European government levels.

Two further cases that prove useful to look at the impact of the political context on the local dynamics are *NDC* in Newcastle and *Grätzelmanagement* in Vienna. Both were top-down-engineered attempts to introduce more participatory planning practices. The *NDC* scheme, in particular, was launched in 1997 and was meant to be highly innovative compared to previous regen-eration programmes because of its focus on empowering communities. But from the beginning, there was a clash between top-down approaches and practices established by the local political machine on the one hand, and the attempts by community groups to control – and innovate – the programme on the other hand.

Impact of EU policies

The interaction between socially innovative initiatives and socio-political conditions has been significantly affected by EU policy. The EU itself has gone through a cycle, swaying from direct support to integrated neighbourhood development (especially within the Urban programme, but also through other initiatives within the structural funds) to the recent increased subsidiarity for regional and local authorities. For many initiatives this meant a drop in financial resources or an inevitable refocusing of activities from integrated area development to sector-based activation projects (such as in training, cultural education, security, surgical physical renewal, etc.).

Indeed, as Table 15.1 suggests, most projects received direct and/or indirect support from the European level. Although generally seen as important in securing long-term survival and providing bargaining power and legitimacy to neighbourhoods, it was also felt that both the lengthy and overly complex administrative procedures militated against effective mobilisation of resources. Very often, unless working with particularly skilled staff, civil society initiatives were unable to secure EU-based funding. With few exceptions, access to EU funding proved limited or difficult. Moreover, obtaining EU resources generally depends crucially on good relationships with the local or national state and this made oppositional strategies more difficult to pursue. In addition, also with EU funding, innovative dynamics must face regulatory and bureaucratic conditions that prevent innovative experimentation and change.

Between state and autonomy: What to do?

Civil society initiatives emerge in the interstices of governance relations dominated by the political and professionalised networks surrounding state practice; or as part of a porous hegemonic project within a local socio-political regime that leaves sufficient room for diversity and institutional creativity. These initiatives, we saw, develop as much from conflict and resistance as from invitations to participate by state actors. When they succeed to break into the arenas of state actors, there is always the danger of 'capture' – co-optation and pre-emption – by mainstream institutions and their modes of intervention. This suggests that the really important issue for state and EU policy is to encourage more civil society engagement within urban policy initiatives. While of course the state remains centrally important in terms of access to resources and regulatory arrangements, the really vital social innovative development dynamics reside within the domain of engaged civil society activities. Effective innovative initiatives involve a certain 'distance from the state', although they may exploit or, better, find fruitful accommodation within state institutional 'folds' or protective 'umbrellas' and enter into respectful collaborative arrangements.

Pointers towards supporting socially innovative development initiatives

Notwithstanding these reservations, the analysis supports the view that 'higher scale' (EU, national, regional, . . .) policy and financial support often have a leverage effect on generating and maintaining socially innovative dynamics in urban development; but it also shows that the innovative spark from the communities often gets lost in the maelstrom of top-down politics and inflexible

Table 15.1 Impact of European Union funding and policies on programmes

	Direct funding	Indirect funding	Impact of EU regulations	Impact of EU policy initiatives
Newcastle *NDC*	No	No	Financial regulations embedded in national budget rules	Very indirect
Ouseburn, Newcastle	Small amounts for EU Objective 2 (now withdrawn)	No	Environmental regulations embedded in planning system	Very indirect
Olinda, Milan	YES	Yes, via national and local state		Direct projects (EQUAL and HORIZON) as means of leverage to national level
Leoncavallo, Milan	NO, considers EU out of its reach			
Grätzelmanagement, Vienna	Objective 2 funding	Funding from European regional policies	Yes, but seen as restricting	Yes, but limits space for experimentation
Quartieri Spagnoli, Naples	YES	YES, through urban and social policies	Bureaucratic regulation seen as problematic	Participation in several EU programmes (INTEGRA, POVERTA, HORIZON, *et al.*)
Arts Factory, Wales	ESF and ERDF funding	Yes	Yes	Yes, regional and social policy
City Min(e)d, Brussels	Yes, cultural capital initiatives	Yes, via Flemish government	Yes	Yes, URBAN
BOM, Antwerp	Yes, from URBAN	Yes, via Flemish Government	Yes	Yes, URBAN
Alentour	Yes, from URBAN	Yes, via local and national government	Yes	Yes, URBAN

Source: Authors

bureaucratic practice. To let the innovative initiative become socially effective requires sensitivity to local activist and civil society initiatives and their dynamics on the one hand and to the particular arrangement between state and market in which they operate on the other. We shall consider the policy framework from the perspective of both the socially innovative actors and agents on the one hand and the possibility for national and/or EU policy on the other.

Taken together, the case studies offer a valuable set of mutually re-enforcing policy recommendations that are based on recognising the transformative capacity of socially innovative projects in urban development. Some of the key frameworks are summarised in Table 15.2. On the side of the community, civil society activists generally embrace the following views:

1   Seek out the cracks and spaces in state governance relations, and be prepared to widen and shape them.
2   Build networks with others pursuing similar agendas, operating in the same or other cities, to enlarge the 'scalar reach' of activist initiatives.
3   Maintain a continuously critical perspective when asked to join up with state and civil society actors, but avoid staying in 'entrenched' positions, as situations are in continual flux and entrenchment can provoke activism sclerosis.
4   Demand resources from state agencies with as much spending autonomy as possible and demand the freedom to fail as well as to succeed. Failure is never a goal, but when it happens, it often provides a rich learning experience.
5   Emphasise the importance of respect from state actors for the capacities and values of citizens and their organisations, inside or outside the state and market nexuses.
6   Recognise that state actors can learn new attitudes and practices and are often trying to escape from contradictions they are trapped in, providing a space for combined learning and design of new modes of governance.

The above civil society and activist proactive views are often confronted with, if not blocked by, the managerial and top-down approaches of established and institutionalised policy-making. In order to permit networked partnership approaches that enable local civil society to enact the views expressed above, policy frameworks should be reoriented according to the pointers put forward in Table 15.2. *Politically speaking*, this especially means the recognition of political identity for different types of new actors in civil society and the social economy as well as their empowerment to negotiate new terms of interaction and co-operation within the state–market–civil society triangle. These can only be materialised through *policy initiatives* that produce new types of collective agreement and networking models involving different spatial scales. Collective agreements and policy measures should also include sustainable funding initiatives, allowing community actors and their networks to focus on the triple

Table 15.2 General policy framework: stimulating social innovation

Type of policy	Pointers
Political initiatives	a) Local empowerment and civil society insertion require (political) citizen rights. Effective state–civil society articulation necessitates the granting of European political citizenship rights to all local area residents. b) Recognising the role of the social economy as a vital and key ingredient for social revitalisation alongside traditional top-down initiatives. c) Recognising voluntary and civil society service delivery organisations as an integral part of innovative economic development systems.
Policy initiatives	a) The fostering of collective contracts between civil society organisations and local, national or EU policy framework. b) Focus on active socially innovative initiatives as pointers for support rather than traditional territorially focused policies. c) Establishing cross-scalar and inter-local networks of socially innovative initiatives across the European space. d) Providing points of direct access for civil society initiatives at the national and EU level.
Funding initiatives	a) The formation and direct funding of European networks of socially innovative initiatives. b) The streamlining of funding procedures with an eye towards maximising access, minimising bureaucratic rules and by-passing deeply entrenched national procedures. c) Securing long-term viability of successful social projects, particularly those that generate continuous institutional, participatory and social innovation. d) The creation of social innovation centres. e) The creation of logistical support centres for local civil society initiatives.

Source: Authors

core business of social innovation, instead of having to search continuously for new or additional funding. Table 15.2 provides some pointers for orienting these funding initiatives towards particular forms of organisation and initiative. The application of the above general principles to socially innovative initiatives, political transformations and policy measures would facilitate the proliferation of socially innovative practices. But successful 'application' also requires shared experience and a desire to learn from it for the reformulation of social, urban and economic redevelopment strategies. Paramount in this is the recognition that civil society actors generate considerable social capital, thereby enabling both self-development as well as socio-economic and cultural cohesiveness, but also facilitating the valorisation of the social ambitions of market agents (e.g. exploring the frontiers of the Corporate Social Responsibility agenda), as well as encouraging the creative power of civil servants and government agencies. Many civil servants indeed started their career in civil society organisations and kept their socially creative skills actively alive in their government jobs.

Conclusions

Mundial integration unfolds hand in glove with increasing local differentiations, inequalities and combined but uneven development. Within the tensions, inconsistencies and exclusions forged through these kaleidoscopic, yet incoherent urban transformations, all manner of frictions, cracks, fissures, gaps and 'vacant' spaces arise. These fissures, cracks and 'free' spaces form 'quilting' points, nodes for experimentation with new urban possibilities. It is indeed precisely in these 'marginal' spaces – the fragments left unoccupied by the global urban order that regulates, assigns and distributes – that all manner of new urban social and cultural practices emerge; where new forms of urbanity come to life. While transnational capital flows impose their totalising logic on the city and on urban policy-making, the contours of and possibilities for a new and more humane urban form germinate in these urban 'free' spaces, where alternative forms of living, working and expressing are experimented with, where new forms of social and political action are staged, where affective forms of economy are practised, and creative living is not measured by the rise of the stock market and pension fund indices. Ed Soja (1996) defined these spaces as *Thirdspace*, the living in-between space that emerges through perception and imagination; a space that is simultaneously real and imagined, material and metaphorical, an ordered and disordered space. Of course, for the elites, as we saw in the previous pages, such *Thirdspaces*, spaces of unchecked and unregulated experimentation, re-enforce the dystopian imaginary of cities as places of chaos, disintegration and moral decay, and especially as a threat to their life styles and upmarket modes of consumption (Baeten, 2001). But of course, it is exactly these spaces where hope, new promises, freedom and desires are actively lived. In these cracks, corners and fissures of the contemporary fragmented networked city, looms and ferments a new hybrid conglomerate of practices, often in the midst of deepening political exclusion and social disempowerment. These are the radical margins that are an essential part of twenty-first-century urbanity. This book has celebrated these practices and insisted that it is exactly these practices that urgently require attention, nurturing, recognition and valorisation. They demand their own space; they require the creation of their own material and cultural landscapes, their own emblematic geographies. These are the spaces were the post-political condition is questioned and practices of radical democratisation experimented with. Their realisation requires considerable social, ecological, cultural, economic and architectural imagination and creativity. Intelligent actors from state and market have set aside the dystopian view of these spaces and seek to integrate them in either a new stage in the commodification of social relations in experimental spaces, or as an opportunity to save society from a democratic collapse by becoming involved in new modes of co-operation and governance which could lead to a new social contract for society as a whole. There are sufficient signs that socially innovative governance is becoming mainstreamed as part of reformist attempts to find a new socially acceptable gravity point for the state–market–civil society triangle.

But despite these reformative attitudes within 'new' public governance and Corporate Social Responsibility circles, the hard lessons, the real working materials to find out about liveable social innovation initiatives in the (social) economy, bottom-linked governance and political capacity formation are those experienced in the free spaces of the urban neighbourhoods, where socially innovative initiatives flourish. It is ironic, therefore, despite their significantly higher innovative content, that these initiatives have not gained the academic and policy attention they deserve compared with the more spectacular, although not necessarily more significant, strategies of urban redevelopment through large-scale top-down renovation mega-projects (Moulaert *et al.*, 2003).

References

Baeten G. (2001) 'Clichés of urban doom: the dystopian politics of metaphors for the unequal city – a view from Brussels', *International Journal of Urban and Regional Research*, 25: 55–69.

Harvey, D. (2008) 'The right to the city', *New Left Review*, 53 (September/October): 23–40.

—— (2009a) 'The urban roots of the fiscal crisis', Lecture by David Harvey, The American University of Beirut, May 29. Online. Available: http://vodpod.com/watch/1865700-david-harvey-urban-roots-of-the-fiscal-crisis (Accessed 15 October 2009).

—— (2009b) *Cosmopolitanism and the Geographies of Freedom*, New York: Columbia University Press.

Lefebvre, H. (1995) 'The right to the city', in *Writings on Cities*, selected, translated and introduced by E. Kofman and E. Lebas, Oxford: Blackwell, pp. 63–181.

Mayer, M. (2009) 'The "Right to the City" in the context of shifting mottos of urban social movements', *City*, 13(2–3): 362–74.

Moulaert, F. (2000) *Globalization and Integrated Area Development in European Cities*, Oxford: Oxford University Press.

—— Swyngedouw, E. and Rodriguez, A. (eds) (2003) *The Globalized City: Economic Restructuring and Social Polarisation in the City*, Oxford: Oxford University Press.

—— Martinelli, F., González, S. and Swyngedouw, E. (2007) 'Introduction: Social innovation and governance in European cities – urban development between path dependency and radical innovation', *European Urban and Regional Studies*, 14(3): 195–209.

Soja, E. (1996) *Thirdspace*, Oxford: Basil Blackwell.

Swyngedouw E., Moulaert, F. and Rodriguez, A. (2002) 'Neoliberal urbanization in Europe: large-scale urban development projects and the New Urban Policy', *Antipode*, 34(3): 542–77.

Appendix

Historical roots of social movements

Compiled by Flavia Martinelli

Social philosophies, thinkers and activists in the eighteenth and nineteenth centuries

Utopian socialism

Under this loose heading are grouped very diverse thinkers whose philosophies – ranging from paternalistic utopian experiments to utopian communism from below, often coupled with a reformist aim and in a few instances heralding a revolutionary order – had a tremendous and 'transversal' political, as well as practical impact. Intellectually formed during the years of the French Revolution, utopian socialists deployed their 'visions' throughout the nineteenth century. Concerned with the social problems engendered by the Industrial Revolution, they proposed a new moral order, a partial alternative to the utilitarian and individualistic ethics of liberalism. But they did not directly challenge the established order and only envisioned – and practised – 'alternative' forms of social organisation, often reminiscent of an ideal pre-capitalist 'community', with a 'demonstrative' aim.

- *Claude de Saint Simon* (1760–1825) was a French aristocrat inspired by scientific and rational principles. In his work on *New Christianism* published in 1825, he argued for the necessity of solidarism between workers and employers, in order to strengthen the development of industrial production against the parasitic landed aristocracy, and to bypass the anarchy of competition and the exploitation of man by man. He did not condemn private property and was strongly influenced by Christian principles. He was also in favour of universal education. His utopian community was implemented, after his death, by Owen (see p. 236).
- *Charles Fourier* (1772–1837), also French, criticised the organisation of distribution by and the parasitic role of commerce. He envisaged a world of social harmony in which the natural attitudes of man could be valorised and production and consumption could be integrated, bypassing the intermediation of merchants. This could be achieved through the *Phalanstères* communities of life and work – veritable cities – based on solidaristic principles. Fourier's principles were later applied – on a minor scale – by *Jean*

    Baptiste Godin (1817–89), a French industrialist, in the *Familistère*, an experimental community of production created in one of his factories, which integrated work and residence, as well as a number of services.

–   *Francois-Noel Babeuf* (1760–97) was a Jacobin leader in the French Revolution, who envisioned a utopian 'communist' community of workers, based on principles of social equality, collective property and a distribution of production according to needs, regulated by the state. He is considered the father of utopian communism. His state-regulated 'distributive' communism was a forerunner of Marx's dictatorship of the proletariat.

–   *Robert Owen* (1771–1858), an affluent British textile entrepreneur, was a reformist and a utopian. He was in favour of a national education system and contributed to the 1919 legislation limiting working hours for women and children. He also supported workers' self-help organisations. With him, utopianism merged with the workers' movement. He initiated the New Lanark experiment of a model textile community in Scotland (1800–25). He also founded the community of New Harmony in the United States (1825), inspired by Saint Simon's utopia, but which eventually failed.

–   *Etienne Cabet* (1788–1856) was a member of the Franco-Italian Carbonarist movement, who migrated to England and was strongly influenced by Owen. In his book *Voyage en Icarie* (1839) he proposed an ideal national community – Icaria – and described in great detail the urban organisation of its capital city – Icara. The founding principles were borrowed from Babeuf: everybody worked according to his/her capabilities and participated to production according to his/her needs. He and his followers also attempted a few demonstrative experiments in the United States.

With the exception of Babeuf and Owen, utopian visions were the product of enlightened liberal thinking, with reformist rather than revolutionary aims and weak links with the workers' movement. Most experiments were of a paternalistic nature, carried out by enlightened industrialists. Despite their diversity, they all shared a belief in a possible alternative societal organisation that could be achieved by demonstration, via the proliferation of like-minded exemplary experiments. In other words, they all believed in the perfectibility of society through social engineering.

Social Christianism

The first germs of liberalism within the very conservative Christian doctrines appeared during the Restoration period, both in the Catholic Church and the Protestant world.

    Among the former, *Hugues-Félicité Robert de Lamennais* (1782–1854) refused the 'natural' alliance between monarchy and the Church and supported liberal régimes as more receptive to authentic faith. Among the latter, the German pietism movement within Lutheranism supported a humanitarian view of society, condemning slavery and torture.

But it was the development of the socialist movements in the second half of the nineteenth century that forced the Roman Catholic Church to tackle the social question. Among the first to address the issue was the Bishop of Mainz, *Whilelm Emmanuel von Ketteler* (1811–77), who supported social legislation to improve the conditions of workers and also a 'moral' notion of economic life, in opposition to both socialism and liberalism. He was followed by many other influential Catholics in Austria, Belgium and Italy. Several Catholic associations developed in these countries in order to organise and indoctrinate industrial and agricultural workers.

The new philosophy was made official by *Pope Leo XIII* in his Encyclical *Rerum Novarum* of 1891, which condemned socialism and class struggle, confirmed property rights, but also supported social legislation. In this organicist vision, capital and labour were to collaborate in harmonious co-operation: workers should not strike, but employers should pay the right salary. The encyclical marked the end of the identification of Church authority with the most conservative and repressive forces of society and the beginning of an intense involvement of Catholic structures and groups in social work. From then on, the Roman Catholic Church recognised the 'social' character of poverty and exploitation and supported a solidaristic view of society, also through Christian workers' associations.

Cooperation and mutualism were further endorsed by *Pope Pius XI* in the encyclical *Quadragesimo Anno* (1931) against totalitarian regimes.

Workers' mutual aid associations and the co-operative movement

Workers' associationism produced, among other things, the most structured and lasting form of alternative productive organisation – the co-operative – which is still active throughout the world and especially in the third sector.

–   *Robert Owen* (1771–1858), besides his utopian experiments (see p. 236), was especially influential in the trade union and co-operative movements of the UK. He contributed to the unification of both into national organisations. He also contributed to the organisation of consumer co-operatives. Within the latter he supported the creation of an 'exchange bank'.
–   *Pierre Joseph Proudhon* (1809–65), French, is often associated with utopian socialism, although he belonged to a subsequent generation and had a more radical and libertarian view of society. In fact he inspired the most populist and anarchist forms of worker solidarism. He was critical of the state and was against any form of centralisation of authority. Therefore he also strongly opposed collectivism (in 1840 he had published a pamphlet with the famous statement 'Property is theft') and the seizure of power. His economic reformism was based on mutualism and democratisation: credit for all, craft production, workers' associations. The main leverage of his vision was the 'exchange bank', a bank where all kinds of goods could be exchanged – thereby eliminating commercial profit – and loans without interest could

be granted to workers. Such a 'People's Bank' was founded in 1849, but Proudhon was arrested and the bank closed.

- In 1835, in the context of the first mutual-aid movement among the silk workers of Lyons, *Michel-Marie Derrion* published his principles of what he called *Le commerce véridique et solidal* and founded the first consumer co-operative, which would last three years.
- *Friedrich Wilhelm Raiffeisen* (1818–88) was a German mayor who became a major leader of co-operative self-help and pioneered rural credit unions. He was inspired by the suffering of German farmers strangled by usurers and founded the first co-operative lending bank, in fact the first rural credit union, in 1864. Several credit union systems and co-operative banks are still named after him in the whole of Northern Europe.
- *Franz Hermann Schulze-Delitzsch* (1808–83) was a German economist and member of parliament, who devoted his life to the development and institutionalisation of German co-operation. As president of the commission of inquiry into the condition of the labourers and artisans, he supported the strategy of co-operation to enable smaller tradespeople to hold their own against more powerful capitalists. In 1958 he founded the *Vorschussvereine* (Peoples' Banks), which spread quite rapidly. In 1859 he promoted the first national co-operative meeting in Weimar and founded a central bureau of co-operative societies. In 1861 he again entered the Prussian Chamber, and became a prominent member of the Progressive Party. In 1865 the *Deutsche Genossenschaftsbank* was created. He also supported the passing of German legislation on association and its homogenisation throughout the different states.
- *Ferdinand Lassalle* (1825–64) was a German socialist political activist and reformer (he was in favour of universal suffrage), who took part in the revolutions of 1848–49 and founded the *Allgemeiner Deutscher Arbeiterverein* (General German Workers' Brotherhood, ADAV) in 1863. Although he did not believe in co-operation as an effective way to free the workers from capitalist bondage, by organising workers' unions he actively supported workers' production associations as a means of social self-defence. In 1875, partly through his efforts, the ADAV merged with the SDAP (Social Democratic Workers' Party) forming the Social Democratic Party of Germany (SPD).

The workers' movements

From trade unions to socialist movements

Unions in the UK were traditionally organised by trade and on a local or factory basis. Between 1829 and 1834 *Robert Owen*, together with the textile worker leader *John Doherty* and a former textile worker then entrepreneur and eventually MP *John Fielden,* contributed to organise a national association of all unions (trades union). The association did not last, because of an employer's counterattack, but the increased strength of the unions allowed the UK working class to gain substantial improvements at factory level, as well as in terms of social legislation. The workers' unions later allied with the radicals in the Chartist movement (which asked for universal suffrage). Although the movement did not succeed, it represented the first national alliance of a workers' organisation with a political movement.

In the French workers' movement *Louis Auguste Blanqui* (1805–81), a republican political activist who belonged to the Carbonari society, was very influential; he participated in both the 1830 and the 1848 revolutions and was imprisoned several times. He supported the general strike tool and founded secret societies of workers. He proposed a truly revolutionary brand of socialism (insurrection, abolition of private property and collective ownership of the means of production, establishment of a dictatorship of the revolutionary forces). Secret associations of workers were also founded by *Etienne Cabet* in several provinces of France.

Similarly influential in France was *Louis Blanc* (1811–82), a more reformist political activist, who published in 1839 a study on the organisation of work, in which he attributed all the evils of society to the pressure of competition and argued for the equalisation of wages and the convergence of personal interests in the common good ('*à chacun selon ses besoins, de chacun selon ses facultés*'). This was to be implemented via the establishment of 'social workshops' (*Ateliers Sociaux*), a combination of co-operative society and trade union, regulated by the state. The experiment was actually implemented by the provisional government of Paris in 1848, but did not last.

In the French clandestine context, a relevant role in the maturing of socialist ideas was played by the *League of Justs*, a secret society created in Paris by a group of German refugees, which later changed its name into the *League of Communists*, whose Manifesto, by Karl Marx and Friedrich Engels, was published in 1848.

In Germany, besides *Lassalle*, initiator of the German workers' movement and major actor in the founding of the social democratic party, a relevant role in the trajectory of the socialist doctrine was played by the radical writings of *Wilhelm Weitling* (1808–71), who endorsed revolutionary action and contributed to the transformation of utopian socialism into political communism.

The international workers' association and the first socialist parties

The workers' associations that had formed within the different national trajectories were very diverse. In the second half of the nineteenth century Marx and Engels tried to unify differences around a common programme – the *First International* (1864–76) – based on the principle of class struggle, the refusal of conspiratorial methods, and the aim of power seizure.

A fierce opponent of Marx's position was the Russian anarchist *Michail Alexandrovic Bakunin* (1814–76). Bakunin's Social Anarchism rejected any organised struggle and aimed at dismantling the existing social order through the violent action of individuals and groups. The new society would be without a state and naturally organised around small production groups, free of authority and hierarchy. Such a vision was clearly more in tune with a rural society than with the highly organised social structures of industrial economies. The clash between Bakunin and Marx, which led to the exit of the anarchist movement in 1872, as well as the failure of the Paris *Commune* thereafter, eventually brought the First International to its end.

However, the basis for the formation of true socialist political parties had been laid. Between 1875 and the end of the nineteenth century formal socialist parties were established in most industrialised European countries: in 1875 the Lassallian socialists and the Marxist socialists joined to become the German Social Democratic Party;[1] in 1879 a French socialist party of Marxist inspiration was formed, soon followed by a Belgian socialist party and a Spanish socialist party. After 1880 three political groups were formed in the UK: the Social Democratic Federation, the Socialist League and the Fabian Society. In newly unified Italy an independent workers' party was formed in 1882, which evolved ten years later into the Italian Socialist Party. In 1898 the Russian Social Democratic Party was formed.

In 1889 the *Second International* (1889–1914) was founded, which would last until the First World War. It succeeded in providing effective steering of the international workers' movement; despite the repression, most of its constituent parties had to suffer from their respective governments. Central issues were: social legislation, political rights and democracy, the alliance between industrial workers and peasants.

After the First World War and the Russian Revolution of 1917, the socialist trajectory split into the 'Revolutionary' socialists, who would then call themselves communists and would continue pursuing revolutionary strategies, and the 'Revisionists' who adopted a reformist approach and would be loosely identified with socialist and social-democratic political parties.

Note

1   Until the Russian revolution of 1917 the term 'social democracy' generally included socialist parties of Marxist inspiration, therefore also with revolutionary agendas.

Index